PRAISE FOR *LOVE, LEARN, PLAY*

If everyone spent more time to learn, to play, and perhaps especially to love, we would find more flourishing in our world. Akhil Gupta's book provides an engaging account, and one that can be backed up with empirical research as well. Let us learn, play, and love!

—Tyler J. VanderWeele, PhD
John L. Loeb and Frances Lehman Loeb Professor of Epidemiology; Director of the Human Flourishing Program, Harvard University

This book includes many thought-provoking ideas that caused me considerable introspection. Fundamentally, it was an inspiring journey because it makes flourishing seem accessible to everyone.

—Hamilton E. James
Chairman, Costco; Former Executive Vice Chairman, The Blackstone Group

Akhil has a gift for revealing the profound within the seemingly obvious. With this book, he brings our attention to *love*, *learn*, and *play*, and shows us how these deeply ingrained aspects of our being can be cultivated for maximum flourishing.

—Adil Zainulbhai

Chairman, Capacity Building Commission of India (established by the PM of India in 2021); Former Director, McKinsey & Company

In a world often defined by distraction and disconnection, Akhil Gupta gives clarity on what truly matters. In *Love, Learn, Play*, he distills a lifetime of experience into a generous, wise offering for anyone ready to define success not by what we accumulate, but by how we live more fully and authentically.

—Jacqueline Novagratz

CEO, Acumen; Best-Selling Author of Blue Sweater

Sharing his personal journey to seek answers on how humans can flourish, Akhil offers a prescription for a happier life, supported by scientific research and the wisdom of others. This book provides a comprehensive survey and offers much wisdom and insights that have the potential to transform one's life!

—Lee Hau Hian

Managing Director, Batu Kawan Berhad, Malaysia

Akhil has uniquely distilled cherished wisdom, cultivated across centuries and continents, into a compelling understanding of what is ultimate for us as we live. His beautiful words are deeply personal, professional, and profound. Readers can savor provocative thoughts on every page that make us reflect on what it truly means to be human—and fully alive.

—Howard Koh
Former United States Assistant Secretary for Health, US Department of Health and Human Services (HHS); Associate Dean of Public Health Practice and Director of the Division of Public Health Practice, Harvard T. H. Chan School of Public Health

Akhil Gupta's *Love, Learn, Play* is a generous gift for us all, wisdom to live by. The cure for what ails us is simpler than we think: slow down, think with care and attention, give thanks, and then commit ourselves to a life of love for our neighbors near and far. Deep down, all is grace—happiness born in the gracious and humble love that overflows the narrow boundaries of our short time on earth. May this lovely book help many on the path to meaning and wholeness in our troubled age.

—Francis X. Clooney, SJ
Parkman Professor of Divinity, Harvard University

Love, Learn, Play is a timely and insightful guide to living a life of meaning and purpose. Drawing on data-driven research and global wisdom, Gupta presents a simple yet powerful framework for human flourishing. In a world marked by distraction and division, this book offers a refreshing vision grounded in self-awareness, compassion, and joy. Both practical and profound, it is a must read for anyone seeking to lead with purpose and live with intention.

—Tiffany Steinwert, Ph.D.
Dean for Religious and Spiritual Life, Stanford University

LOVE LEARN PLAY

AKHIL GUPTA

TO FLOURISH IS TO

LOVE LEARN PLAY

A SIMPLE FORMULA FOR A HAPPIER, MORE MEANINGFUL LIFE

Forbes | Books

Published by Forbes Books, Charleston, South Carolina.
An imprint of Advantage Media Group.

Printed in the United States of America.

10 9 8 7 6 5 4 3 2 1

ISBN: 979-8-88750-694-4 (Hardcover)
ISBN: 979-8-88750-695-1 (eBook)

Library of Congress Control Number: 2025913247

Cover design by Matthew Morse.
Layout design by Ruthie Wood.

07-29-2025 12:9

To Krishna and Kusum, my dad and mom: Thank you for instilling in me the values that sustained me throughout my life and for guiding me and my siblings to focus on love, learning, and play. Your profound message to your children now echoes through the pages of this book, reaching the world.

CONTENTS

INTRODUCTION

TO PURSUE OR NOT TO PURSUE HAPPINESS

Across cultures and centuries, happiness has loomed large in the human imagination as the ultimate desire tucked within our hearts. The pursuit of happiness has been the holy grail of humanity for time immemorial. History's great sages have said that the quest for happiness is the driving force behind all our actions. "Happiness is the meaning and purpose of life, the whole aim and end of human existence," Aristotle said. The *Brihadaranyaka Upanishad*[1], a prominent Hindu scripture of sutras written in 700–600 BCE, offers this prayer: "May all be happy, may all be free from disease, may all perceive good and not suffer from sorrow." Notice the emphasis on the happiness of *all*. Many centuries later, the pursuit of happiness was enshrined in the United States Declaration of Independence as an inalienable right of all citizens. Around the same time, utilitarian philosophy emphasized the "greatest happiness of the greatest number" as the guiding principle for morality and legislation.[2] Nowadays, the fourteenth Dalai Lama states the pursuit of happiness as a simple precept: "The purpose of our lives is to be happy."[3]

Although we often experience fleeting feelings of joy and pleasure, lasting happiness is elusive for so many of us. The world's predominant state of unhappiness is certainly not due to a lack of either scholarly attention or popular interest. A long procession of philosophers, psychologists, prophets, religious leaders, spiritual gurus, scientists, poets, artists, and others have probed the topic and attempted to crack the code on how to live a happy life. The scientific study of happiness has been increasing at an exponential pace. A peer-reviewed and highly respected academic journal called the *Journal of Happiness Studies* has been in operation for over two decades now. Try searching the term *happiness* on Google. It will yield a staggering two billion search results! The self-improvement market is a $45 billion global industry and is projected to double by 2033.[4]

Why is humanity suffering from what has mushroomed into a happiness crisis that cuts across all socioeconomic groups? By many key measures of material progress, life on earth has gotten objectively better. Billions have been lifted out of poverty. We have made remarkable strides in science, technology, and medicine, doubling global life expectancy in the past century, even in the planet's least developed regions. Our knowledge of the world around us has been increasing at an exponential pace. Today, more computing power is available on a smartphone than was required to land a man on the moon in 1969. Isaac Asimov had one explanation for why people are still unhappy when he said, "The saddest aspect of life right now is that science gathers knowledge faster than society gathers wisdom."[5]

Yet, when the annual *World Happiness Report* asks people in more than one hundred countries to rate their own happiness with their lives on a scale of 0 to 10, the results keep getting worse.[6] Several wealthy countries have dropped in their ranking but none more sharply than the United States, which dropped to its lowest ranking since that survey began—and that result was driven by the unhappiness of people under thirty in the country, as younger generations report the biggest declines in self-reported well-being and the greatest rises in depression.[7] In the US, suicide rates have increased to the point of being twice as common as homicides and are now the second leading cause of death among those under thirty-five.[8] "Compared with their grandparents," says psychologist David Myers, "today's young adults have grown up with much more affluence, slightly less happiness and in fact a much greater risk of depression and all kinds of social pathology." He observes that more than one-third of teens are facing a true mental health issue.[9]

Broadly speaking, study after study points to the same diagnosis: Unhappiness is spreading in epidemic proportions across entire populations. This paradox of human happiness is what drew me onto a path that has resulted in this book. My life was a perfect example of this phenomenon. As a young man from a humble background, I approached my life and responsibilities with a sense of duty and wanting to succeed to provide for my family. I had a dream academic and professional career and reached my professional pinnacle when I joined as a partner in the most prestigious private equity firm in the world and served as founding chairman of Blackstone India. Previously, I had worked at two of India's most iconic companies: Hindustan Unilever and Reliance Industries Limited. I had gone to Indian Institute of Technology (or IIT, the MIT equivalent in India) for my undergraduate degree and received an MBA from Stanford University. But all the things that came my way due to a successful professional career—success; fame; wealth; access to the rich, famous, and powerful; flying private; staying in presidential suites—had lost their charm with a nagging sense that something was missing, a feeling of lack. I wondered if life had something more to offer.

Novelist Aldous Huxley is widely attributed to have written, "There comes a time, when one asks even of Shakespeare, even of Beethoven, is this all?" While I cannot even dream of comparing myself to Beethoven, I have considered myself enormously lucky to have achieved so much, coming from a humble background and without having the ambition to achieve this kind of success. But then, something momentous occurred, which really shook up my approach to life.

A PERSONAL TURNING POINT

On November 26, 2008, I had reservations for dinner at half past eight in the evening at the posh Tiffin Restaurant at the famous Oberoi, a five-star seaside hotel in Mumbai. My plans were to celebrate with Rajiv Kaul, the newly appointed CEO of Blackstone's latest investment deal, CMS Computers.

I'd been traveling for weeks and felt the guilt of not having exercised enough to justify sitting on airplanes and in meetings while also consuming too much food. But when I went to the gym and started working out, my knee began to hurt. After thirty minutes, I stopped, about an hour earlier than expected. I called Rajiv to suggest we meet earlier, perhaps for drinks at the hotel bar instead of dinner in the restaurant. After raising glasses at the bar to toast to our new venture, we walked by the restaurant and glimpsed the tables full of people. Five minutes later, all those people were murdered.

During the time of our dinner reservation, two gunmen, later identified as terrorists from Pakistan, burst into the restaurant and started shooting. Everyone dining or working there was killed as part of a coordinated series of terrorist attacks across the city that left 166 dead and hundreds more injured.[10]

I would have been sitting at one of those tables if not for my last-minute decision.

When I arrived home to have dinner with my parents instead, we watched the news of the terrorist attacks on television. The once-vibrant restaurant was now a tableau of carnage. Tables lay overturned, chairs scattered like fallen soldiers—I could not believe how I had just escaped certain death. It shook me to my core. The fragility of life became so clear. That was the moment I began to ask myself new questions that I had never actively considered before that extraordinary stroke of luck—or fate—spared my life. In that pivotal moment, my life went from being taken for granted to feeling like a gift not to be squandered.

What if I had just died? What mattered most to me in life? What did I need to do on a priority basis that I had been postponing? And for what purpose or end? What more could I be doing with this gift? What more did I have to offer in the time I had remaining?

MY QUEST FOR THE KEYS TO HAPPINESS

I have been driven by a sense of duty all my life, and my immediate responsibility remained to establish Blackstone in India. By my sixtieth birthday, on July 20, 2012, the company had become the most respected private equity firm in India. I felt I'd done my duty. I told my boss, Tony James (president of the company), that I wanted to leave Blackstone soon to pursue the "lack" in my life. He requested that I stay until the end of 2014, which I could not refuse, as Blackstone had been an amazingly good firm to work for, and both Tony and Steve Schwarzman (chairman and CEO) had been especially good to me.

Finally, in 2014, after six years of questioning what matters most in life, I stepped down from my leadership role at Blackstone to embark on a quest for answers. I've always had a passion for learning; in my twenties, when my friends were busy chasing girls, I was reading psychology and philosophy books. Not surprisingly, I was a nervous wreck when I started dating girls in America, and I remain single even today! I soon enrolled in Harvard University's Advanced Leadership Initiative because it allowed me to audit classes all over the university. I took more than thirty courses from brilliant academics alongside undergraduates with curious minds, eventually taking all available courses on happiness and related topics at Harvard, MIT, and Yale.

When you audit these classes in your sixties, you can learn a lot more than the undergraduates who are more worried about grades, jobs, finances, and relationships. I had no such distractions. I devoured the works of ancient and modern philosophers, the findings of modern science and psychology, and the wisdom of thinkers and prophets from different cultures and traditions, past and present. I joined over a hundred seminars, tapping into Harvard's power to convene the brightest minds.

Amid my reading and studying, I came across a particularly inspiring quote from *The New York Times* columnist David Brooks: "People on the road to inner light do not find their vocations by asking, what do I want from life? They ask, what is life asking of me?"[11] I asked myself, "What do I have that can provide a unique contribution to humanity?" In the words of Frederick Buechner, "Your vocation in life is where your greatest joy meets the world's greatest need."[12] My greatest joy throughout much of my life was my insatiable desire for learning. I now felt a desire to share these learnings with the world.

Gradually, the dots started to connect, and I developed valuable insights into some big questions that I had been asking but never had any time to pursue till I got to Harvard. I narrowed my options down to two fields where I thought I could contribute, given my life's journey across diverse cultures and the education I had received: The first was human flourishing and happiness.

I asked myself, "Do I have anything to add beyond the current state of the happiness literature?" I bounced my original ideas off a few of my fellow classmates in my happiness class, most importantly, Sara Al Zubi, who was also a teaching fellow for 150 students in one of the most popular happiness classes, taught by Professor Susan Rinard at Harvard. The answer to whether I should write a book was a resounding "Yes!" Sara even said, "I wish I had your book now to share with the students."

PUTTING THE PIECES TOGETHER

This book is the result of my interdisciplinary and cross-cultural exploration of the topic of happiness. I have synthesized insights from a wide range of cultural, intellectual, philosophical, religious, and spiritual traditions, as well as the academic disciplines of anthropology, sociology, sociobiology, neuroscience, psychology, medicine, psychiatry, folklore, and literary and artistic works.

Most of you do not have the time to go through such diverse literature on happiness and meaning. (I only received this exposure due to my almost four years at Harvard.) This book summarizes relevant insights from a wide range of wonderful researchers but is itself not an academic exercise. Accordingly, it may lack academic rigor in some ways, but I hope I will make that up by exposing you to a wide range of perspectives of some of the greatest thinkers on happiness-related subjects and, more importantly, my own lived experience and the experiences of those whose lives I know fairly well. Chapter twelve, on love, learn, and play and public life, written by guest writer Richard Parker of Harvard Kennedy School, provides a contrast in academic brilliance. The chapter is a treat you will enjoy. I present this book to you in the spirit of sharing my learnings. My grade will be the enhanced flourishing you may experience after reading it!

As I was preparing material for my writing, I grew frustrated at times, wondering whether I had truly new insights to offer. After all, many of the grandest thinkers who ever lived have already written volumes on these subjects. Every time I get excited about an idea that I thought was original, I would learn later that some famous person had already thought of it.

When I needed encouragement most, my friend and colleague at the Graduate School of Business, Stanford University, and then dean of Nanyang Business School in Singapore, Dr. Jitendra Singh, told me the words of the great economist Joseph Schumpeter: "The mother-lode of all inventions is the recombination of existing ideas."[13] In that moment, I realized my calling: Since I have lived my life straddling a wide array of cultures and breaking down silos, my mission is to integrate knowledge, insights, and lived experiences across continents and centuries and to share these learnings with the masses to promote human flourishing.

FAITH AND HAPPINESS

The second thought I had was about the commonalities across world religions. To promote these ideas, I founded Universal Enlightenment & Flourishing, a foundation with the mission of enhancing religious literacy and human flourishing. Some of my favorite learnings came from taking twelve courses at Harvard Divinity School on the wisdom and traditions of all the world's religions. I was afforded the opportunity to study Christianity, Islam, Judaism, Hinduism, Buddhism, Taoism, and other faiths, and I was especially struck to find that there are more commonalities than differences among religions. Our lack of awareness of such commonalities is why these religions have so long been at odds with one another. Throughout history, the differences have sparked wars and conflicts that have led to the violent deaths of millions because the followers of these religions did not know the underlying commonalities. Enhancing religious literacy will also contribute to human flourishing at the societal level.

I ended up writing a book, *Bridges Across Humanity*, in which I explore the intersections between religions and where they agree on basic teachings of love, kindness, compassion, gratitude, and other positive virtues that can make the world a better place. When I spoke to the Harvard Divinity School professors, they all provided encouragement and thought I could find fifteen to twenty commonalities. My book contains fifty-four commonalities, and thanks to large language models such as ChatGPT, Gemini, and Claude, our website—www.uef.org—now has 108 common themes across religions. Over seventy of these wisdom insights require no belief or faith in any religion. I asked myself why we are not aware of these commonalities. The answer—because we have been asking the wrong question: "Tell me about other religions," with the subtext being, "Tell me how my religion is superior to the other religions." I was studying all religions with a different lens, asking, "What are the similarities?" Human nature and our deep yearnings are the same, irrespective of our religious affiliation. All prophets preached moral behavior. So we must find similarities among religions, and I found 108 to my and everyone's amazement. I believe religious illiteracy leads to an exclusivity mindset, which is a false narrative to societal flourishing and hence is an important piece of my mission to enhance human flourishing.

A LONG SEARCH FOR CLARITY

While I was at Harvard, I came across this famous quote from Harvard University's former president, Derek Bok: "People ... are essentially no happier today than they were 50 years ago, despite a doubling or quadrupling of average *per capita* income."[14] It was clear that we needed new ways to study the age-old "happiness paradox." We have new tools to map the brain and understand the mind with the help of advancements in neuroscience, sending the field aflutter and setting off an avalanche of articles and books on happiness. There are dozens of TED Talks by experts exploring aspects of happiness, and the videos are being viewed by millions—including me—on YouTube.

Yet, I began to ponder whether happiness was really the holy grail of life. When we ask the question, "How should we live?" we're tempted to immediately start thinking about happiness. But not everyone agrees that happiness is the end goal. Well-being, fulfillment, love, meaning, purpose, pleasure, joy, serenity, equanimity, contentment, virtue, and success are a few of the many ways to think about a well-lived life.

As Leo Rostin, a Polish-born American author, humorist, and social scientist, said, "I cannot believe that the purpose of life is to be happy. I think the purpose of life is to be useful, to be responsible, to be honorable, to be compassionate. It is, above all, to matter: to count, to stand for something, to have it make some difference that you lived at all."[15]

Others, such as Stanford behavioral scientist Jennifer Aaker, believe that finding meaning and purpose is the goal in life, rather than happiness.[16] Interestingly, the Nobel laureate Daniel Kahneman believes that humans are not even as interested in happiness as we believe: "Altogether, I don't think that people maximize happiness in that sense … this doesn't seem to be what people want to do. They actually want to maximize their satisfaction with themselves and with their lives. And that leads in completely different directions than the maximization of happiness."[17] And Sigmund Freud went even further, saying, "One is inclined to say that the intention that man should be 'happy' has no place in the plan of 'creation.'"[18]

"A better goal of life is to be content," argues Dr. Andrew Weil. "Contentment is an inner sense of satisfaction that is really not dependent on external factors."[19] Indian wisdom also emphasizes the value of contentment, as illustrated by one of the most famous couplets written by the influential poet Kabir Das centuries earlier, when wealth constituted owning cows, elephants, and horses:

> *गोधन, गजधन, बाजधिन और रतन धन खान।*
> *जब आवे संतोष धन सब धन धूरसिमान॥*
> *(WEALTH OF COWS, WEALTH OF ELEPHANTS, WEALTH OF HORSES, AND WEALTH OF JEWELS:*
> *WHEN CONTENTMENT COMES, ALL OTHER WEALTH IS LIKE DUST.)*

Could it be, then, that happiness, as an end unto itself, is a false idol? When we dive more deeply into Eastern wisdom on happiness throughout this book, one thing will become clear: Traditionally, there is much less focus on pursuing happiness in the East, which, somewhat paradoxically, has appeared to foster greater levels of happiness. Maybe, then, we in the West are barking up the wrong tree. As David Robertson said, "Happiness is like a cat. If you try to coax it or call it, it will avoid you; it will never come. But if you pay no attention to it and go about your business, you'll find it rubbing against your legs and jumping into your lap."[20]

Maybe, instead of focusing on how to best pursue happiness, we should be asking ourselves simply how to live. As Viktor Frankl once said, "For success, like happiness, cannot be pursued; it must ensue, and it only does so as the unintended side-effect of one's personal dedication to a cause greater than oneself or as the by-product of one's surrender to a person other than oneself. Happiness must happen, and the same holds for success: you have to let it happen by not caring about it."[21]

THE UNIFICATION OF EAST AND WEST

I noticed that the majority of the popular books and approaches to happiness encompass wisdom mostly from the Western world. "Oh, happiness! Our being's end and aim!" Alexander Pope lamented in his 1733 text "Essay on Man"—"So near us, yet beyond us."[22]

As the chief satirist of the Age of Enlightenment, Pope had surveyed the happiness and wisdom of the West and found something lacking. Even to this day, the Western canon of happiness literature tends to lean more toward external aims such as health, success, financial security, and fulfilling lifelong desires. The desire satisfaction theory of happiness posits that happiness is attained when one's desires are fulfilled. According to this view, the satisfaction of desires, whether they are related to material possessions, relationships, achievements, or personal goals, contributes to a sense of well-being and happiness. Indeed, in Western societies, happiness is often defined by the degree to which an individual's most important, individualistic desires are realized.

Buddhism, which originated in ancient India, argues that desires themselves are the source of suffering and dissatisfaction. It proposes that true happiness and liberation come from reducing our desires. The practice of meditation, mindfulness, and the cultivation of wisdom are essential in Buddhist teachings.[23] The goal is to attain enlightenment, or nirvana, by realizing the true nature of reality and the self. According to Hinduism, desires are not the problem, but the *attachment* to desires is. By freeing oneself from attachment to desires, one can achieve a state of contentment and inner peace.

The wisdom of Eastern tradition emphasizes looking inward and is less individualistic. Rather than something to attain or the act of satisfying insatiable desires, happiness in Eastern thought is something we already have by our very nature. The parable "Mrig-Trishna" (translated as "the craving of the deer") from Hindu texts such as the Upanishads and *Bhagavad Purana* beautifully captures this. A musk deer, known for carrying a prized fragrance sac near its navel, becomes captivated by its own unique scent. Unable to identify the source, it embarks on a frantic search through the forest, sniffing every nook and cranny. Ultimately, exhausted and frustrated, the deer falls to its death, still unaware that the sought-after aroma emanated from itself all along. Harvard psychologist Daniel Gilbert has the same message but comes from a different perspective when he says, "Our longings and our worries are both to some degree overblown, because we have within us the capacity to manufacture the very commodity [happiness] we are constantly chasing."[24]

This parable serves as a powerful metaphor for seeking happiness or fulfillment outside ourselves. It illustrates the dangers of unchecked cravings and the importance of looking within. The deer represents our tendency to search for external things, possessions, or experiences.

Just like the animal, we often neglect to look within, where true value and lasting contentment might reside.

Hinduism's rich tradition includes Vedanta philosophy, yoga, and meditation to cultivate physical, mental, and spiritual well-being. Hindu philosophy posits that our true nature is one of *Sat-Chit-Ananda*–existence, consciousness, and bliss. According to the Hindu scripture the *Taittiriya Upanishad*, "From joy springs all creation. By joy it is sustained. Toward joy it proceeds. And to joy it returns." Yet, we find ourselves immersed in a world rife with suffering. This apparent paradox has puzzled seekers for millennia. Can we reconcile this dissonance between our inherent nature and our lived experience?

Many spiritual traditions, including Hinduism, Buddhism, and Sufism, offer a common explanation: Our true nature is obscured by layers of ignorance or delusion. According to Hinduism, our inherent state of *Sat-Chit-Ananda* is hidden by Maya, which refers to the illusory nature of the perceived world. Maya creates a false sense of separation from *Brahman* (the ultimate reality) by focusing on fleeting physical and emotional experiences. We mistake our transient identities, desires, and fears for our essential selves. This misidentification leads to a constant pursuit of happiness through external objects and experiences. Our goal is to overcome this illusion and recognize our true self (*Atman*) as one with the ultimate reality.

The equivalent concept of Maya also exists among Western thinkers. Plato explored the idea of "forms" versus "appearances," suggesting that the physical world we perceive is merely a shadow of a deeper, more fundamental reality. Kant distinguished between phenomena (the world as we perceive it) and noumena (the world as it is in itself). He argued that our understanding is limited to phenomena, which aligns with the idea that our perceptions are a simplified version of a more complex reality. The Nobel laureate Ilya

Prigogine echoes this idea: "Whatever we call reality, it is revealed to us only through the active construction in which we participate."[25]

The modern psychological equivalent of Maya is a combination of cognitive limitations and cognitive biases. Due to the cognitive limitations of our minds, we do not see reality as it is, and our minds, with their incessant thoughts and emotions, create a distorted perception of it. In addition, we develop several cognitive biases in the process of growing up, which distorts our perception of reality. We'll cover this in more detail in chapter four.

This Eastern perspective stands in stark contrast to many Western conceptions of happiness, which often focus on external achievements, material possessions, or fleeting emotional states.

The quest for understanding happiness has, in our modern era, drawn the attention of neuroscientists and psychologists. From the pioneering work of Sigmund Freud to the rise of positive psychology, researchers have developed sophisticated theories and a wide array of methods for measuring and analyzing happiness, exploring its intricate relationship with mental health and overall well-being.

My belief that I could contribute to the human quest for happiness stemmed from the effort to forge a synthesis of Eastern and Western thought. As someone who was born and raised in India, Eastern traditions were what I had known best. Yet the bulk of my liberal arts studies and much of my adult life have taken place in the West. If I could create a synthesized approach between Eastern and Western notions of happiness, perhaps mine would be a valuable contribution to the field. As Sir John Templeton said on the wisdom of the East: "The greatest wisdom is often found in the most unlikely places. The East has much to teach us about the art of living, the pursuit of happiness, and the meaning of life."[26] Rudyard Kipling wrote a lyrical poem titled "The Ballad of East and West" that goes:

> *OH, EAST IS EAST, AND WEST IS WEST, AND NEVER THE TWAIN SHALL MEET,*
> *TILL EARTH AND SKY STAND PRESENTLY AT GOD'S GREAT JUDGMENT SEAT;*
> *BUT THERE IS NEITHER EAST NOR WEST, BORDER, NOR BREED, NOR BIRTH,*
> *WHEN TWO STRONG MEN STAND FACE TO FACE,*
> *THOUGH THEY COME FROM THE ENDS OF THE EARTH!*[27]

OUR THREE DEEPEST LONGINGS IN LIFE

Yet, the more I learned about happiness, the more I began to question whether it was even correct to place it in the prime position as the "meaning and purpose of life," as Aristotle said. Another insightful period came to me on the subject of happiness versus meaning when, during the COVID-19 pandemic, my mother developed a minor fracture in her knee. We were not allowed to bring any physiotherapists or nurses into the apartment building we were living in, so I became her nurse and physiotherapist for almost a month. Of course, I was not able to do any of the things that result in what we call pleasure or happiness, but I would not replace that time with her for anything else. It provided me with some of the most meaningful moments in my life, and I also realized that if you have more meaningful activities in your life, the desire for ordinary pleasures will become less.

At first, the thought that happiness should not be our highest aim truly shocked me. But the more I pondered this notion, the more it began to ring true. There is a much-discussed thought experiment devised in the 1970s, which philosopher Robert Nozick called the experience machine. He described it as:

> *SUPPOSE THERE WERE AN EXPERIENCE MACHINE THAT WOULD GIVE YOU ANY EXPERIENCE THAT YOU DESIRED. SUPER-DUPER NEUROPSYCHOLOGISTS COULD STIMULATE YOUR BRAIN SO THAT YOU WOULD THINK AND FEEL YOU WERE WRITING A GREAT NOVEL, MAKING A FRIEND, OR READING AN INTERESTING BOOK. ALL THE TIME YOU WOULD BE FLOATING IN A TANK, WITH ELECTRODES ATTACHED TO YOUR BRAIN. SHOULD YOU PLUG INTO THIS MACHINE FOR LIFE, PREPROGRAMMING YOUR LIFE'S EXPERIENCES? OR WOULD YOU LIVE IN CURRENT REALITY WITH ALL ITS PAIN?*[28]

While this machine might sound alluring at first, most people reject the idea when they find out how it would involve floating endlessly in a tank of water and only *feeling* those experiences. So, most people choose reality over unlimited pleasure.

Would you want an existence like the experience machine? Would you want your kids plugged into such a machine? There may be exceptions, such as those who are in constant physical pain or are in prison, but surveys have shown that about 95 percent of people wouldn't want a constant feeling of happiness, especially since they know it's not real.[29] This reluctance to use the machine suggests that people recognize that true happiness isn't just about a constant stream of positive feelings; it's also about deeper aspects of flourishing.

BEYOND THE PURSUIT OF HAPPINESS

Counterintuitive though it may sound, I concluded that happiness, often conflated with pleasure, should not be our life's quest. Happiness must arise as a *byproduct* of living a meaningful life. Both ancient philosophers and modern researchers have found that happiness is neither all pleasure nor all meaning. In practice, pleasure and meaning are complementary and contribute significantly to happiness. A meaningful life isn't always easy or joyful. It involves a range of emotions, including sadness, frustration, and even anger. Accepting these emotions as part of the human experience can lead to deeper meaning and, paradoxically, greater happiness in the long run. My own arrived-at stance is much simpler but, I believe, more powerful. Well-being—or "flourishing," as I prefer to call it—stems from what I call the three (and only three) deepest longings of life: loving, learning, and playing. When we engage with these three yearnings, we automatically arrive at the right balance between happiness and meaning.

Just as I was pondering over issues of happiness, meaning, well-being, and flourishing, I had a fortuitous visit with my nephew's family and a welcome break from my studies. I've never married nor had children of my own but have always thought of my nephews and nieces as my own kids. My nephew's daughter, Aashi, a cheerful nine-month-old, was wary of me at first but soon warmed up to me and, to my delight, wouldn't leave my side. All she wanted to do was play, explore her still-new world, soak up the new experiences and information around her like a sponge, and then just lie on my lap with loving looks in her eyes. Like all children her age, she exuded *Sat*, *Chit*, and *Ananda*—simple bliss—which she effortlessly gave and received.

Unlike me and every other socialized adult, Aashi had no concept of happiness as a goal and therefore had no reason to chase it. Innocently and innately, she already existed in a state that I will posit in this book is higher than happiness—what I describe as the state of flourishing. And she flourished by doing these three simple things: loving, learning, and playing. I had the epiphany of the love, learn, and play (LLP) framework after my time with Aashi.

Spending time with Aashi brought me back to my own happiest days, when I was a child growing up with my parents, four siblings, grandmother, and aunt, all living together under one roof on a hundred-dollar-a-month budget in Old Delhi. We were a close-knit family who loved and cared for each other. We played together, read together, and had an insatiable curiosity for learning. We took full advantage of a public library just outside our home in Old Delhi. That was my most frequented place till I went to college.

At its core, this book is about unearthing those essential longings for love, learning, and play that we all have within us—longings that, when activated, can help us achieve a state of flourishing. *The premise of this book is that you can find your own unique way to flourish in how you actualize the LLP mindset in your life, given your endowments and circumstances.*

Therefore, I approach this body of wisdom with utmost humility. My favorite parable that teaches the lesson of humility is the one about the blind men and the elephant. According to the story, nine blind men were asked to describe an elephant after each touched a different part of the animal's body. The first blind man touched the elephant's leg and said, "It feels like a tree trunk." The others described the elephant as a rope, a snake, a fan, a wall, a spear, a boulder, a pipe, or a plow, depending on the part they touched.

This story illustrates that our perceptions of reality are limited by our experiences and that we can gain a more complete understanding of the world around us only by being open to the perspectives of others. Just as if all nine blind men shared their partial perspectives with one another, they would all have a much better understanding of the elephant. Based on scholarly understanding of Jainism, the Jain principle of *Anekantavada* (many-sidedness) offers similar wisdom for interfaith understanding. According to Jain philosophy, every view is partial and incomplete and truth can be approached from multiple perspectives. This is my hope, too, that the understanding I have reached due to my interdisciplinary and intercultural studies will add a more comprehensive perspective on happiness.

When it comes to fully understanding a problem as grand and complex as happiness, it is only by pooling perspectives from centuries and continents, by standing on the shoulders of giants who have studied these subjects, that the full picture and nature of happiness come into focus and the path to flourishing becomes clear.

Flourishing, as I will define and expand on in the pages ahead, is universally attainable for people across the spectrums of age, culture, level of education, and income. The formula for flourishing is so simple, in fact, that young children master it effortlessly. And in that state of flourishing, our desires for happiness and meaning are naturally fulfilled. When we flourish in this way, it then radiates outward as we bring joy not only to ourselves but to those around us, with our circle of impact continuing to grow.

To me, the complete picture of flourishing is the perfect concept for a fulfilling, rewarding, satisfying, empowered life. Yet each one of you will manifest these three interconnected forces of love, learning, and play differently from anyone else. The benefits can be applied to your personal relationships and your professional self, to parenting at home, or to leadership at work. But whatever your roles, be aware that your aim is to become your authentic self, which wants to love, learn, and play. As Joseph Campbell said, "The privilege of a lifetime is being who you are."[30] Let your heart be the compass and your passion the wind in your sails.

Together, we shall pursue these three deep longings so that happiness can follow, even as happiness itself remains a conundrum. We may never have the answer to the paradox of human happiness. Not only has the answer changed, but so has the question. One of the lessons from the large language models of AI is that the answer we get depends on our prompt. But have we been asking the right questions? The right one to ask yourself now is, "How do I flourish, given my circumstances, my endowments, and my uniqueness?"

MODERN TECHNOLOGY SETTLES IN

The fallback position—that although I may not be entirely happy, I believe my kids will be—is not necessarily available anymore due to seemingly intractable problems such as climate change, political polarization, growing digital and economic divides, and war and genocide. That's why the stakes are so much higher now. And it's why I only have one request for you while you read this book. It involves something that goes back to 2008, to something even more consequential than the terrorist attacks in Mumbai, as that was the year that smartphones with social media apps began to reach the masses.

Over the next several years after 2008, most of us opted into this new realm. Yet study after study in more recent years has singled out social media, specifically the way it is currently being consumed, as harmful to well-being, especially among the young.[31] Clearly, the projection of the socialized self into abstract online spaces, in the pursuit of likes and clicks and online connections, has backfired on our authentic selves to the point that our true nature gets lost. It's like the tale of the talking fish, with one fish in the ocean turning to their friend from school and asking, "How do you like the water today?" Whereupon, the other fish replies, "What's water?"

Younger generations, the ones who grew up with social media, might not realize that the water in which they are swimming is full of false narratives. We can fall victim to these false narratives because our lives have become so compulsive under the onslaught of advertising and social media. While you read this book, please turn your social media off. And then dive in, to swim in the waters of your authentic self, so that you can love, learn, and play—all in your own way.

PART I

THE FLOURISHING MINDSET

CHAPTER ONE

WHY HAPPINESS ELUDES US

> *"PERFECTION OF MEANS AND CONFUSION OF GOALS SEEM—IN MY OPINION—TO CHARACTERIZE OUR AGE."*
> **—ALBERT EINSTEIN**

In 2007, Stephen Schwarzman (whom I'll refer to as Steve), CEO of the Blackstone Group—one of the most prestigious investment firms in the world—came to visit India for the first time. Being chairman of Blackstone India at the time, I went to the Mumbai airport to welcome Steve and personally escort him to our office. As we drove through one of the city's poorest neighborhoods, Steve fell silent as he took in the scenes of street life that flashed past, at one point asking if we might slow down to watch a group of children playing ball in the street.

When we arrived at the office, he remained lost in thought as we made our way to the meeting room where he addressed the Mumbai team. He said, "Before I tell you what's happening at Blackstone globally, let me share one experience with you that has affected me this morning. As we drove through the airport, I saw poor children in the slums playing, laughing, and exuding pure joy. Their clothes were torn and smudged, as if they haven't had a bath for a month, but they were happy with an amazing purity in their smiles. In sharp contrast, right before coming to India, I had taken a walk through the New York office to meet and greet employees. I saw that my twenty-four-year-old colleagues, who are earning a substantial income, often had expressions that weren't particularly joyful." Although Steve is hardly the first to note the low correlation between material wealth and happiness, as a quintessentially wealthy and highly successful executive once referred to as the "King of Capital," his words carried considerable weight in my mind.

Although I had the same intuition, I thought it was clouded by my own cultural bias. I had gotten to know several highly successful and wealthy people who were miserable in their personal lives. Steve's observation that day heightened my awareness of this curious paradox and brought up questions that have stuck with me ever since. How indeed can people with so little material wealth be so happy and those with so much be so unhappy? And what does this say about the very nature of happiness and why it eludes so many of us? A hint to this puzzle was provided by Robert Biswas-Diener (son of the happiness pioneer Ed Diener), who, after traveling the world and interviewing people about their lives and how satisfied they were, concluded that, "While the poor of Calcutta do not lead enviable lives, they do lead meaningful lives."[32]

Ed Diener was a highly influential psychologist renowned for his pioneering work in the field of subjective well-being. His research and subsequent work generally show a correlation between national wealth and average life satisfaction up to a certain point. However, beyond a certain threshold of national wealth (which various studies have tried to pinpoint), the correlation between increasing wealth and increasing happiness tends to weaken significantly or even disappear. Factors beyond just wealth play a crucial role in national well-being. These include social support, freedom, trust in government, long life expectancy, and perceived corruption.[33]

GOALS ARE NOT THE GOAL

The pursuit of happiness often mistakenly leads us to believe that certain achievements—a beautiful home, a luxury car, career success, and financial abundance—are the keys to a fulfilling life. Of course, it's a false dichotomy to go to the other extreme and claim that happiness has nothing at all to do with wealth. While I consider ends as being, by definition, the ultimate goals within a fulfilled life, means do possess intrinsic value. Without satisfying a minimum level of means, the quest for ends does not even make sense; what is the point of dwelling upon meaning when one is hungry or cold? Means include the usual materialistic goods, such as money, shelter, and food, but they also encompass more sophisticated and abstract means, such as getting a good education, earning a well-regarded job, starting a family, volunteering for a cause, or serving society.

We all have an innate need to be loved, respected, and accepted by others. We start learning by imitating others whom we hold in high regard. We conform to societal norms. During our cognitive development process, we start overlaying a social self on top of our authentic self. In the process, we assimilate many false metanarratives that focus on means and not our ends. We start to measure the means and start to define our goals to maximize the means. Gradually, the means crowd out our ends. As we start to feed this socialized self, we increasingly start to starve our authentic self, which inherently longs for love, learning, and play. We succumb to what is known as "means/ends inversion," (MEI), mistaking the *means* to a good life for the *ends*.

The means and ends debate is not new. In his landmark 1930 essay British philosopher and economist John Maynard Keynes predicted that larger and larger numbers of people would be free from problems of economic necessity. He advised "to value ends above means and prefer the good to the useful."[34] By "good," he meant that economic gains should be obtained morally and spread among the maximum number of people, rather than be concentrated in a few hands. Using the words of Jean Baudrillard, "We wish to restore the original contradiction between ends and means, between individuals and social forces, to foster a confident yet socially considerate approach towards life for every individual."[35]

HOW MEANS CROWD OUT ENDS

MEI happens at the level of individuals, organizations, and countries. More often, this phenomenon happens without us even being aware of it. Let's illustrate MEI with a few broad examples on the individual and societal levels.

As Albert Camus said, "A man wants to earn money in order to be happy, and his whole effort and the best of his life are devoted to earning money. Happiness is forgotten; the means are taken for the ends."[36] In obsessively pursuing wealth or fame or power, believing it will automatically bring happiness and security, we often neglect relationships, health, and personal growth in the process. The means of wealth accumulation and seeking power or fame have become the ends, while the actual ends (happiness and relationships) are lost in the pursuit of the means.

Many of us fixate on achieving an "ideal" body image, believing it will lead to acceptance and admiration by others. However, this pursuit can become an obsession and lead to body dysmorphia or eating disorders. The means (perfect appearance) has become the end, while the end (self-acceptance/love) remains elusive, even if the physical goal is reached.

A company might prioritize maximizing profits above all else, even if it means cutting corners on quality or exploiting its employees. The means (profit) has become the end, while the end (providing valuable products and/or services and creating a positive work environment) is secondary. This can lead to customer dissatisfaction, ethical breaches, environmental damage, and long-term damage to the company's reputation.

A media outlet might focus solely on increasing website traffic through clickbait headlines and sensationalized content, even if it means sacrificing journalistic integrity. The means (website traffic) has become the end, while the end (engaging and informing an audience) is compromised. The media outlet might have high traffic, but it also has a poorly informed and disengaged readership.

The economic and social policies of most countries focus on maximizing GDP. They prioritize economic growth as the primary measure of progress, even if it comes at the cost of environmental degradation, social inequality, or declining mental health. The means (economic growth) has become the end, while the end (national well-being/flourishing) is not adequately addressed.

Society might become overly focused on technological advancement, believing it will automatically solve all our problems. However, technology can also create new problems, such as job displacement, privacy concerns, and increased social isolation. The means (technological advancement) has become the end, while the end (solving societal problems/improving lives) is not carefully considered.

AI designed to optimize social media engagement might prioritize generating sensationalist content to maximize likes and shares, even if it undermines the platform's goal of fostering meaningful communication. This misalignment arises when the AI, lacking humanlike judgment and ethical considerations, relentlessly pursues its narrow objective without regard for broader consequences. AI remains a tool serving humanity's intended purposes, not the other way around.

In universities, publishing rather than impacting the world becomes the goal of an academic department as professors get judged on quantity and the academic impact of their publications. The relentless pursuit of high grades can create a system where the means (achieving top marks) overshadows the end (genuine learning and intellectual growth). When grades become the primary focus, students, educators, and even institutions can inadvertently compromise the very essence of education.

Multiple articles and surveys (such as Harvard's Healthy Minds Survey and reports from the university's Task Force on Managing Student Mental Health) consistently show significant percentages of Harvard undergraduates and graduate students reporting symptoms of depression and anxiety.[37] Laurie Santos, who teaches the most popular online course on happiness from Yale, says, "In Spring 2018, I taught 'Psychology and the Good Life' for the first time. I created this Yale course because I was worried about the levels of student depression, anxiety, and stress that I was seeing as a professor and head of college at Yale. There's this Yale pressure cooker of expectations, failures, deprecation, anxiety. This pressure cooker wreaks havoc on the mental lives of every single one of us so that at the end of the year, we leave mentally battered and exhausted semester after semester."[38] While grades can be a useful measure of progress, they should not be the ultimate goal. One of the things I liked during my days at Stanford's Graduate School of Business was that grades were not disclosed to potential employers and were not prioritized. Hence, I audited an extra class every quarter to maximize my learning.

The means crowds out the ends in medicine when doctors are incentivized to take on ever more patients and spend less time with each of them, all for the goal of maximizing profit instead of maximizing patient well-being. I have many doctor friends at prestigious hospitals in India and the US who confide in me that they are given annual budgets that result in overdiagnosis and unnecessary tests, raising healthcare costs everywhere.

At the societal level, we may follow the herd, without questioning whether what we value is contributing to our well-being. We may constantly strive for attention on social media, obsess over celebrity culture, or care more about net worth than character.

WHY LOVE, LEARNING, AND PLAY ARE THE TRUE ENDS

While studying at Harvard, I arrived at a profound speculative insight: Our ultimate human purpose is to evolve through love, learning, and play. Knowing that our physical evolution is constrained by our place in the solar system, I now believe that our journey unfolds through these three essential and interconnected facets of ourselves, reflecting the very nature of the universe. We connect through love, seek understanding through learning, and embrace life's richness through play.

Loving, learning, and playing are the three deepest yearnings that form our intentional core. We will refer to the love, learn, and play core with the initialism LLP in this book. The existential questions we seek answers to are our mind's way of bringing our attention to this core. Just like we have feelings of hunger so we may eat food, we have a sensation of loneliness to overcome separation so we may love. We feel curious so we keep learning all our lives. And we have imagination for play, to celebrate life as a child does, and to experience the wonders and explore the mysteries of our world.

The path to human flourishing is remarkably simple, yet profoundly transformative. We can love, learn, and play in anything we do, any profession, and at any stage of our lives to truly flourish. Think of LLP as a software app. To use it, we may need to clear some space on our hard drives by eliminating old programming, dispensing with socially constructed desires, and removing false identities. The good news is that there is an app that is compatible with all operating systems: People of all races, nationalities, religions, beliefs, and socioeconomic statuses, as well as those who are SBNRs (spiritual but not religious) or nones (individuals who identify as religiously unaffiliated) are invited to download the LLP mindset. Just as the double helix of DNA controls many of our biological functions, loving, learning, and playing form a triple helix of human flourishing.

Initially, I thought this may be too simple a framework, but then I read two quotes that convinced me I'm on the right track. The first is from Sir Isaac Newton: "Truth is ever to be found in simplicity, and not in the multiplicity and confusion of things." The second is from philosopher Ludwig Wittgenstein: "The aspects of things that are most important for us are hidden because of their simplicity and familiarity."

Loving, learning, and playing are our deepest longings and, hence, ends, not means. To understand ultimate ends, ask yourself why. "Why do I want well-being? Why do I want love? Why do I want to learn? Why do I want to play?" An ultimate end is not a means to anything else. Nothing is worth doing unless the goal is an end in and of itself. In addition, there is no limit to how much you can love, how much you can learn, and how much you can play, especially when we define these in their widest manifestations, as I will in subsequent chapters. That is another criterion by which to differentiate ends from means.

HOW INDIVIDUALS CAN OVERCOME MEI

> *"IF YOU THINK A LOT OF MONEY WILL MAKE YOU HAPPY, YOU'VE PROBABLY NEVER HAD A LOT OF MONEY."*

This bit of wisdom or something similar is noted by several figures who have made a lot of money, such as Warren Buffett, and is sometimes echoed by those who have both made a lot of money and managed to lose all of it, at least for a time, including Mike Tyson.

I teach two classes at Stanford's Graduate School of Business about finding spiritual meaning in business. One of the questions always asked is, "What is your view on money?" We should be surprised if students completing their MBA don't ask that question! My answer is always, "Do not let money be a constraint in your life to meet your needs, but *never* let it become such a value in your life that you judge yourself and others by how much money you or they have." Surprisingly, some of the students find this quite insightful and even transformational!

Indeed, the world today is particularly afflicted with wealthy people who have amassed wealth beyond anyone's dreams, yet they are in constant need of more: more money, bigger mansions, more possessions, more fame, more attention, more headlines, more power, and more influence, even in realms in which they have little to no experience. They want more and more of what fewer and fewer people can have. This is because money, wealth, fame, and power became goals tied to their self-worth. Such unenlightened individuals never seem satisfied precisely because their external wants are endless. They are constantly feeding themselves with the socially constructed selves they project in the media. They seem fundamentally unhappy, yet since their self-awareness seems so low—their authentic self so lost—they might never recognize that they are on a perpetual path of dissatisfaction for themselves and missing something essential in life.

Yet, there are also wonderful examples of the opposite—famous figures who have seen through the veil of the endless pursuit of external rewards. People who have embarked on new journeys of self-discovery to learn about their authentic selves and have come to key epiphanies.

Jim Carrey is a Canadian-American actor and comedian who is known for his energetic slapstick performances and rubbery facial expressions. He rose to fame in the 1990s with a series of hit comedies, including *Ace Ventura: Pet Detective*, *The Mask*, and *Dumb and Dumber*.

After reaching the pinnacle of fame and wealth, he realized that the pursuit of external rewards wasn't worth it, famously saying, "I think everybody should get rich and famous and do everything they ever dreamed of so they can see that it's not the answer."[39]

Growing up facing poverty, Carrey learned the importance of pursuing his passion. His early success, while exhilarating, led him to question his identity and the true source of happiness. He recognized that, even while he was at the top of a mountain, he hadn't freed himself. But through self-reflection, philosophy, meditation, and artistic expression, Carrey embarked on a journey of self-discovery. He learned to disarm his ego, which constantly whispered, "I'll never be enough," and to distinguish between real threats and imagined ones.[40]

Carrey's story exemplifies overcoming MEI, choosing hope over fear, and embracing life's true ends: love, learning, and play. He now lives authentically, sharing his wisdom and acknowledging that happiness isn't perpetual, but a journey guided by love and playfulness is.

EASTERN TRADITIONS AS AN ANTIDOTE TO MEI

Jim Carrey has publicly discussed his explorations of Eastern religions and philosophies, and there's evidence that these studies have significantly influenced his personal and professional life. He's spoken openly about his practice of meditation and his interest in Buddhist teachings. He has described how meditation helps him find inner peace and disconnect from the pressures of fame. In his commencement address at Maharishi International University, Carrey emphasized the importance of intention, love, and pursuing a life aligned with one's true self, ideas that resonate with Buddhist philosophy.[41]

Carrey's meeting with the Dalai Lama seems to have had a profound impact on him. He has spoken about the Dalai Lama's teachings on compassion and altruism and how they have influenced his own views on life and happiness. Carrey's artwork often reflects themes of spirituality and self-discovery. His paintings sometimes incorporate imagery and ideas from Eastern religions. He has been open about his struggles with mental health and his search for meaning and purpose.

There are so many Western people who were deeply influenced by Eastern philosophy, which helped transform their lives. J. D. Salinger, author of *The Catcher in the Rye*, was a devoted practitioner of Zen Buddhism. He found solace and inspiration in its teachings, which influenced his writing and reclusive lifestyle. The German-Swiss writer Hermann Hesse was deeply influenced by Eastern philosophy, particularly Buddhism and Taoism. His novels *Siddhartha* and *Journey to the East* explore themes of self-discovery and spiritual enlightenment through Eastern perspectives.

Actor Richard Gere is a dedicated Buddhist and a vocal advocate for Tibetan rights. He studied with the Dalai Lama and actively supports humanitarian causes aligned with Buddhist principles.

These celebrities shifted their focus from external achievements to internal well-being. They embraced spirituality, meditation, and self-reflection as tools for personal growth. They found a deeper sense of purpose beyond their careers in entertainment. Their journeys demonstrate that true fulfillment comes from aligning with one's authentic self and contributing to something larger than oneself. They are testaments to the power of self-discovery and the courage to live a life guided by love, learning, and play.

At the societal level, counterculture movements can be seen as efforts to restore proper balance to means and ends. They seek to reestablish values and priorities that have been distorted or subverted by the dominant culture. A famous example is how The Beatles embraced Eastern thought in a way that resonated with the counterculture movement, which was also seeking alternative ways of life and meaning.

The Fab Four's journey into Eastern spirituality began in the mid-1960s, coinciding with the band's growing fame and search for deeper meaning. George Harrison, in particular, became fascinated with Indian culture and Hinduism, taking sitar lessons and incorporating Indian musical elements into songs such as "Norwegian Wood" and "Love You To." Their interest deepened after their encounter with Maharishi Mahesh Yogi, the founder of Transcendental Meditation.

ON A PERSONAL NOTE, I MET MAHARISHI IN 1972 WHEN HE CAME TO VISIT THE INDIAN INSTITUTE OF TECHNOLOGY IN NEW DELHI. I WAS A FOURTH-YEAR STUDENT AND WAS FORTUNATE TO BE ON HIS RECEPTION COMMITTEE. HE WORE A WHITE SILKEN KURTA (A LOOSE SHIRT THAT GOES TO THE KNEES AND IS POPULAR IN INDIA) AND A LONG GARLAND OF PRAYER BEADS. HIS KEY MESSAGE WAS THAT THE PRACTICE OF TRANSCENDENTAL MEDITATION HELPS CUT THE MENTAL NOISE, AND WITH THE HELP OF A MANTRA, WE CAN DIP INTO THE DEEP OCEAN OF CONSCIOUSNESS AND RENEW OURSELVES. THE BENEFITS WERE SUPPOSED TO INCLUDE INCREASING THE CLARITY OF THOUGHT AND PEACE OF MIND. ALL THROUGH HIS TALK, HE WOULD SMILE AND LAUGH AFTER HE FINISHED ANSWERING A QUESTION. HIS LAUGH WAS THAT OF A CHILD, COMING DEEP FROM HIS BELLY.

WHILE WE WERE TAKING HIM TO HIS CAR, I ASKED HIM HOW I COULD LEARN TRANSCENDENTAL MEDITATION. HE INVITED ME TO VISIT HIM THE NEXT DAY. HE DID NOT TUTOR ME PERSONALLY BUT SENT HIS NUMBER TWO TO TEACH TRANSCENDENTAL MEDITATION TO ME. AFTER A FEW RITUAL CEREMONIES, THE INSTRUCTOR GAVE ME MY MANTRA AND EXPLAINED THE PRACTICE. I CLOSED MY EYES AND STARTED TO MEDITATE. WHEN I OPENED THEM AGAIN, THE INSTRUCTOR ASKED ME HOW MANY MINUTES I HAD MEDITATED. I SAID ABOUT TEN TO FIFTEEN MINUTES. IT WAS ACTUALLY ONE HOUR AND TWELVE MINUTES. I FELT AMAZING AND CONVINCED OF THE EFFICACY OF THE PRACTICE OF MEDITATING. I HAVE BEEN MEDITATING EVERY DAY FOR FIFTY-TWO YEARS NOW. I ATTRIBUTE A LOT OF WHO I AM TO MY DAILY MEDITATION PRACTICE.

In 1968, all four Beatles traveled to Rishikesh, India, to study meditation with the Maharishi. This period had a profound impact on their songwriting, with songs such as "Across the Universe," "Within You Without You," and "The Inner Light" reflecting their spiritual explorations. Most of the band's album *The Beatles* (which later became known as *The White Album*) was written at Rishikesh. The song "While My Guitar Gently Weeps" is about the lack of love, and "Dear Prudence" is about the lack of play. Their music became a vehicle for exploring themes of peace, love, and spiritual awakening, influencing a generation to look beyond materialism and embrace inner peace.

The Beatles' openness about their spiritual journey helped popularize Eastern philosophies in the West. They demonstrated that music could be more than just entertainment; it could be a vehicle for exploring deeper questions about life and spirituality. Their influence continues to inspire artists and seekers alike, proving the enduring power of Eastern wisdom to touch the hearts and minds of people across cultures and generations.

Counterculture movements are diverse and complex, and their motivations and goals can vary widely. However, the theme of reversing MEIs can be a common thread running through many of these movements, as they seek to reestablish values and priorities that have been distorted or subverted by the dominant culture.

HOW EASTERN WISDOM OFFERS AN ESSENTIAL SET OF TOOLS FOR LIFE

For many of us, there's a gap in our awareness of Eastern wisdom that can be particularly useful for understanding our priorities and serving as a safeguard against MEI. To put some of the tools of Eastern wisdom into play, let's take a chronological look at what Eastern traditions have provided, beginning with Hinduism. The religion arose in India and is considered the oldest religion, passed down orally before being crystallized in the sacred Vedic texts between the years 1500 and 1200 BCE. The texts, known as the Upanishads, emphasize discernment (*viveka*) between means and ends and warn against mistaking money and power for prosperity.

Hinduism outlines a framework for a meaningful life through the concepts of the four *Ashramas* (stages of life): *Brahmacharya* (student), *Grihastha* (householder), *Vanaprastha* (forest dweller/retiree), and *Sannyasa* (renunciate). Each Ashram has four *Purusharthas* (goals of life): *dharma* (righteousness/duty), the foundation of a moral life; *artha* (wealth/prosperity), necessary for fulfilling one's duties; *kama* (desire/pleasure), a natural human drive that should be pursued within the bounds of dharma; and *moksha* (liberation, or true flourishing in our context), the ultimate goal, achieved through self-realization and release from the cycle of rebirth (*samsara*).

Ideally, these stages and goals work in harmony, with dharma guiding the pursuit of artha and kama, ultimately leading to *moksha*. However, the relative importance of each *purushartha* can shift throughout the Ashramas, reflecting the evolving priorities of life. Artha, the pursuit of wealth and prosperity, is recognized as a necessary part of life, but it is deliberately confined to the *Grihastha* stage.

The Hinduism framework—with its emphasis on dharma, the limitation of artha to a specific life stage, and the goal of *moksha*—creates a system of checks and balances. It acknowledges the importance of material well-being and fulfilling desires, but it also provides strong guardrails to prevent these means from becoming ends in themselves. This framework encourages a balanced life where the pursuit of worldly goals is always tempered by ethical considerations, with the ultimate aim being spiritual liberation. By emphasizing duty and ethical conduct, dharma helps prevent the pursuits of artha or kama (desire) from becoming ends in themselves. Hinduism also lists among human sins the accumulation of "wealth without work" and the seeking of "pleasure without conscience" and warns against becoming overly attached to the fruits of one's labor.

It is interesting that hormones related to pleasure, happiness, intimacy, and comfort, as per science, can be easily mapped to the four goals of Hindu existence. Dharma releases serotonin, artha releases dopamine, kama releases oxytocin, and *moksha* releases endorphins.[42] The Ashramas system, with its distinct stages of life, reinforces the idea that different goals have varying importance at different times. As one progresses through the Ashramas, the emphasis shifts from artha and kama toward dharma and, ultimately, *moksha*. The goal of *moksha* (liberation) provides a clear and overarching end that keeps all other pursuits in perspective.

After I joined Harvard's Advanced Leadership Initiative program at the age of sixty-two, I realized that I am in the third stage of the Ashramas, the stage of *Vanaprastha*, as per the Hindu system. This was not done consciously. However, since I was internally driven, it happened naturally and serves as a validation of the Hindu stage of life framework. I've been at this stage for ten years now, and I'm seeing another transition where my acceptance of things as they are has gone up enormously. This is the last stage, *Sannyasa*, where you become the witness to what's happening around you, and the amplitudes of ups and downs become much smaller.

While it is a little bit of a stretch for me, I find the following quote by Paramahansa Yogananda very intriguing:

> *"THE MAGNIFICENT PAINTING OF CREATION STRETCHES ACROSS THE INFINITE CANVAS OF TIME AND SPACE. EVERY OBJECT AND EVENT IN NATURE IS A MASTERFUL STROKE OF THE GREAT PAINTER. BUT THE ORDINARY PERSON SEES ONLY CONFUSING BITS AND PIECES OF THESE DEPICTIONS. CONSIDER EVERYTHING THAT HAPPENS AS A NOTE IN THE SYMPHONY OF THE COSMIC CONDUCTOR. INDIVIDUAL NOTES SEEM MEANINGLESS UNTIL HEARD IN RELATION TO THE WHOLE COMPOSITION. IN THE CREATION'S COSMIC MAGNUM OPUS, WHICH HAS BEEN PLAYING THROUGHOUT ALL TIME, EVERYTHING—STORM, DEATH, LOVE, LIFE—HAS ITS PART IN THE MEDLEY. ALL UNITE IN A UNIVERSAL RHYTHM OF HARMONY, WHICH IS HEARD ONLY WHEN THE SOUL IS ATTUNED TO GOD."*[43]

Taoism, or Daoism, is next up on the Eastern tradition timeline, arising in China around the fifth century BCE through the teachings of Lao-tzu, a legendary wise man who may have been created as a composite of several ancient philosophers. The Taoist view emphasizes acting in accordance with the natural flow of the universe. Tao means "the way" and points to finding your path in life via effortless action and by avoiding unnecessary striving. According to Tao, MEI occurs when we force things, trying to achieve an end through excessive manipulation or control, which ultimately disrupts harmony and leads to undesirable outcomes. Instead, we should exalt balance and harmony between opposing forces known as yin and yang. When we prioritize material success at the expense of health, relationships, or inner peace, we create an imbalance and suffer the consequences. Taoism values simplicity and naturalness. It suggests that the pursuit of excessive material possessions and complex technologies can distract us from the true purpose of life, which is to live in harmony with the Tao.

Around the same time in China, Confucianism emerged as a refinement of "the way" taught by the Tao. It emphasizes the cultivation of virtue as the foundation of a good life and a harmonious society. It stresses that external achievements (means) should be pursued in accordance with ethical principles (ends). In the context of MEI, Confucianism demands clarity about one's true goals and ensuring that one's actions are consistent with them. Means should remain as means in the service of ends that are clearly defined.

Like other Eastern traditions, Confucianism prioritizes social harmony and emphasizes the importance of fulfilling one's social roles and responsibilities. When individuals prioritize individual means over society-level ends, it disrupts order and leads to conflict. This is why Eastern traditions generally value inner development, self-cultivation, and spiritual growth over material possessions and external achievements.

In many Eastern practices, meditation and mindfulness are prescribed to encourage a focus on the present moment rather than constantly striving for future goals. Mindfulness allows us to zoom out and study our life from a non-consumerist-centered perspective; it allows us to step back and assess our life away from our screens, away from the constant behavioral economical search where the world is attempting to predict our next and every want, trying to determine what we desire before it leaves our unconscious. Society today constantly breeds this mentality of "This is not enough," of "I need more," of "I don't have all that I need."

Buddhism advocates for avoiding extremes, including both self-indulgence and self-mortification, through methods such as fasting. This "middle way" principle directly relates to MEI. For example, if the means of acquiring wealth becomes the sole focus, it can lead to suffering through greed, attachment, and anxiety, ultimately undermining the ends of living a happy life.

Perhaps most famously, the Buddha put forth the concept of the eightfold path, which provides guideposts to the way to liberate oneself from suffering, emphasizing ethical conduct, mental discipline, and wisdom. It prioritizes inner development and right intention over material pursuits. By focusing on right effort, right mindfulness, and right concentration, one ensures that the means (actions and thoughts) align with the end (liberation).

According to Buddhism, what blocks liberation and causes suffering is attachment: a clinging to material possessions, wealth, status, or power. But even attachment to ideas can be a root cause of suffering. When these means mushroom into ends in themselves, they create a cycle of craving and dissatisfaction. As Jim Carrey's ego told him, "I'll never be enough." This feeling, of always needing more and being in a state of constant anxiety about money and wealth, may never go away. It's why many billionaires never feel satisfied.

How do you know that you or someone you know has been the victim of MEI? The symptoms include sacrificing relationships for wealth, feelings of emptiness no matter what you achieve, a constant sense of striving and competition for zero-sum gains, an ego-driven identity, spiritual poverty, and a loss of peace of mind. "Like a gold leaf wrapped around poison," said the Buddha, "the pursuit of perfection in means without wisdom leads to suffering."

LOVE, LEARN, AND PLAY AS THE ANTIDOTE TO MEI

I take it to be axiomatic that our proper ends are to love, to learn, and to play. While I can offer no definitive proof (just as with axioms in general), I think that over the next several chapters, my assertion that love, learning, and play are our proper ends will be so obvious to you, too, as to not need further verification.

If you live in accordance with your natural state, all the activities you do will be some specific realization of either one or a mixture of two or all three of these three basic longings. For example, work may be composed of learning and playing but may also include loving if the work is done for duty, honor, or service to others out of love. We need all three super forces to unfold for us. If we pursue only one of these ends at the cost of the others, we will achieve only a partial or suboptimal flourishing. There needs to be balance.

But to practice that balance as a way of overcoming MEI in your life, you need to be aware that the MEI phenomenon is happening, and that it is so pervasive that you need to know the proximate cause and prepare yourself to guard against it. This will include understanding how our minds work, what our true motivations and compulsions are, and what drives us away from our true journey of finding purpose and meaning via our intentional core, the set of human traits given to us at birth—the yearning to love, learn, and play. This is in contrast with our extensional core, which is the acquired desire for money, power, fame, and so on.

We will also need to explore and understand what robs us of our internal autonomy and true freedom and leads us astray from forming the right habits and doing the right actions. Only when you recognize that you have fallen prey to MEI can you start to correct your situation. If you don't realize it, you could be stuck in a vicious cycle, chasing after something that is necessarily not able to give you the satisfaction that you want. You will never have enough of what you chase. Your thirst will never be quenched.

My greatest wish is that what can be beneficial for individuals can also hold true for nations and the world at large. The Buddhist peace activist Thich Nhat Hanh often cites this as a simple precept: "Peace in oneself, peace in the world."[44] And as Válcav Havel, a revered Czech playwright, essayist, and the first president of the Czech Republic, said: "The salvation of this human world lies nowhere else than in the human heart, in the human power to reflect, in human modesty, in human responsibility. Without a global revolution in the sphere of human consciousness, nothing will change for the better."[45]

I see the LLP mindset as the mechanism to achieve Havel's dream, and I hope you will too.

CHAPTER TWO

OVERCOMING FALSE NARRATIVES

> *"LIKE IT OR NOT, THE UNITED STATES BEARS PROBABLY THE GREATEST RESPONSIBILITY FOR THE DIRECTION THE WORLD WILL TAKE."*
> **—VÁCLAV HAVEL**

By the end of World War II, the United States had risen to become an undisputed leader of the world. Since then, what has happened in the US has affected the whole planet, albeit with a time lag. Hence, much of the discussion in this chapter is based on observing overarching trends in US society.

Narratives are the stories we tell about ourselves, about others, and about the world around us. Throughout history, humanity has been led by many narratives. We make sense of our lives through our stories. Next to playing, children like to hear stories the most. We all play parts in our own story, generally without being aware of its plot or the other players.

Narratives are like the air that we breathe. The process of forming them and seeing patterns that may or may not exist is quintessentially human. The award-winning memoirist Joan Didion put it this way: "We interpret what we see, select the most workable of the multiple choices. We live entirely by the imposition of a narrative line upon disparate images, by the 'ideas' with which we have learned to freeze the shifting phantasmagoria—which is our actual experience."[46]

While many narratives, if based on truth, can empower and guide us, others can lead us astray like a broken compass. These false narratives, often deeply ingrained in our culture, can have a profound impact on our behavior and our ability to lead fulfilled lives.

If the main narrative presented here is that the key to flourishing is as simple as deeply engaging in love, learning, and play in all our daily activities and at every stage of our lives, then why don't we? Earlier, we articulated that the reason we do not continue to flourish is because of MEI. Here, we get deeper to go underneath MEI to expose some major false narratives that lead to this inversion.

Often, we live for years unaware that a narrative we are telling ourselves is false. Remember the point of the parable about the fish who asks, "What's water?" even when it swims in water? We may not be conscious of the most obvious, important realities, yet those are the hardest to see and talk about in our lives and in our culture. But pointing out and articulating these narratives is vital for understanding both our world and ourselves. In the maze of modern living, several dominant narratives have been deeply embedded into societal structures. Sometimes, they can be at odds with our intrinsic needs of love, learning, and play and act as barriers to true human flourishing.

IDENTIFYING DOMINANT FALSE NARRATIVES

When I attended Stanford's Graduate School of Business in 1979, Charles Horngren, the famed accounting professor, taught my very first class. In the initial lesson, he introduced the dual-entry system of accounting in which every transaction is recorded as an asset and a liability. I had a philosophical bent of mind, so I tried to apply these business concepts to real-life situations. I concluded that false choices and inferences arise when we look at them with only a single entry: either the asset side or the liability side of a phenomenon.

Yet all dominant narratives that we will discuss have two sides. Capitalism, individualism, consumerism, competition, pursuit of self-interest, individual freedom, just to name a few, become false narratives if confused as ends rather than means.

Let us examine the balance sheets of some of these social "transactions."

SEEING CAPITALISM FROM DIFFERENT PERSPECTIVES

Free-market capitalism may very well be the greatest set of tools ever invented for solving human problems. It was responsible for destroying feudalism in Europe. Capitalism, as a means, is a gigantic asset for humanity. But capitalism as an end can wreak havoc on most of the world's population. Unconstrained capitalism, even today, is on the verge of destroying the planet and destabilizing society.

The false narrative that underlies this MEI can be called "capitalism as a modern-day religion." The biggest illustration is comparing the US to China. By adopting select aspects of capitalism in a communist society, China has uplifted over eight hundred million people out of poverty since the late 1970s.[47] Yes, inequalities have increased, and in 2021, President Xi Jinping set a goal of "common prosperity" in response to the side effects of capitalism.[48] However, capitalism has not yet become a religion in China. While it is a driving force in Europe, it's often moderated by stronger regulations and social safety nets, especially in Scandinavian countries.

Contrast China with the US, the most capitalist country, over the same period of time. The poverty rate in the US has remained stuck in a narrow band of between 11 percent and 15 percent of the population,[49] despite a dramatic rise in GDP, GDP per capita, the stock market, and mostly prolonged periods of economic growth over these past decades. This stubborn percentage has become known as the "permanent underclass."

The ever-widening gap between rich and poor is startling. In 2019, the global anti-poverty organization Oxfam estimated that just twenty-six individuals owned more wealth than half of the world's population, some four *billion* people. By 2024, Oxfam reported that the top 1 percent owned more wealth than the bottom 95 percent of the world's people combined.[50] The rise in wealth for these super-fortunate few is self-perpetuating, extending this imbalance further, creating the same processes that have held back social, economic, and political progress for all in both the most developed and least developed nations. You just have to look at the escalation of CEO compensation in America. In 2023, CEOs were paid 290 times as much as a typical worker. This is a dramatic increase compared to 1965, when the ratio was twenty-one to one.[51]

In 1937, Franklin D. Roosevelt said, "I see one-third of a nation ill-housed, ill-clad, ill-nourished. The test of our progress is not whether we add more to the abundance of those who have much; it is whether we provide enough for those who have too little."[52] The US

GDP has multiplied about eighteen-fold since the FDR statement,[53] and the per capita GDP has risen about seven-fold.[54] Yet, the bottom half of the richest nation in the world is struggling economically. This is because the key tenets of capitalism as a religion are trickle-down theory, free markets, and self-financing tax cuts, which have not been effective in taking care of "those who have too little."

Look at the US healthcare system, which is unique in the world in that the government doesn't offer healthcare for all. The result is that most people live in fear of losing everything they have due to an expensive medical emergency or a climate catastrophe. In the US, about a third of working people have no savings whatsoever. Another third of workers have less than $1,000. Of the remaining third, less than half have more than $10,000 in savings, including retirement accounts. Living with a perpetual fear of falling into poverty is no way to live. All the while, the billionaires get richer and more powerful. There are more than seven hundred thousand people who are technically homeless in the US, the richest country in the world![55] This is nothing short of a spiritual crossroads.

The climate crisis is perhaps the most horrifying result of that system. We have been warned by scientists for decades now that the greenhouse gas emissions from fossil fuels are warming the planet and will inevitably lead to catastrophic consequences such as wildfires, superstorms, floods, and droughts that are now hitting us with grim regularity. We have ramped up renewable energy, such as solar and wind, and the production of electric cars. Yet we have thus far failed to phase out fossil fuels fast enough.

Capitalism's inherent drive for continuous economic expansion necessitates increased production and consumption. Happiness has been socially redefined to be a consumerist method of "What can I buy?" "How can I have this?" or "Boy, do I want this." It has become a huge aspect of behavioral economics, which has led to the exponential exploitation of natural resources, particularly fossil fuels, driving greenhouse gas emissions. Industries prioritize profit over sustainability, neglecting the long-term consequences of pollution and resource depletion. As of this writing, the current president of the US calls climate change a hoax. It's always about the price of gasoline.

The 2008 financial crisis was a severe global economic downturn that had its roots in the United States. It was primarily caused by a combination of factors, including lax lending standards, the proliferation of complex financial instruments such as mortgage-backed securities, and a housing bubble. These were all manifestations of imprudent greed, which is fueled by the tenets of capitalism. When the bubble burst, it triggered a cascade of events that led to bank failures, a credit crunch, and a sharp decline in economic activity. The crisis had far-reaching effects, including widespread job losses, home foreclosures, and a loss of confidence in the financial system. The markets could not solve the problem, so the government had to infuse money into the system. The crisis also led to increased government regulation of the financial industry and a reassessment of risk management practices.

This state of affairs shouldn't be surprising, as the great British economist John Maynard Keynes wrote the following in 1946: "Capitalism is the astounding belief that the wickedest of men will do the wickedest of things for the greater good of everyone."[56] To me, that is due to capitalism being embraced as an end in itself, rather than as a means of achieving the goal of maximizing prosperity for as many people as possible. This is why I am a capitalist when it comes to *means*, but more of a socialist when it comes to *ends*. As American entrepreneur Nick Hanauer said, "When Capitalism is an end, unconstrained by social norms or democratic regulation, markets inevitably create more problems than they solve."[57] Climate change and the great financial crisis of 2008 are two easy examples.

My first job in India was at Unilever, a company officially established in 1930 through a merger of a British soap company and a Dutch maker of margarine. It was always a capitalistic enterprise, but Unilever adopted the simple mission "to improve people's lives by providing products for their daily needs," and it has since added "in a sustainable way" to that statement. In India, where Unilever's products indeed improved people's lives, we at the company believed in that mission.

Our management team was known as the best of any company in the country. We were highly motivated and hardworking. Our remuneration never entered into our motivation. Although many of my colleagues were competing with one another for promotions, these people who were my competitors were also my best friends and remain so even today.

My experience with Unilever taught me that there's nothing wrong with capitalism if practiced this way, i.e., as a means to an end. No one calls Unilever a socialist enterprise, even though it continues to promote social responsibility. Working for its Indian subsidiary is one of the most desired jobs for an MBA from Indian management schools. Paul Polman, the former CEO of Unilever, became an iconic business leader championing corporate social responsibility and sustainable growth. This is an example of conscious capitalism.

THE FALSE NARRATIVE OF INDIVIDUALISM

One of the key cultural factors for the exceptional material success of the US is the culture of individualism. The American Dream, the idea that any individual, regardless of background, can achieve success through hard work, is deeply ingrained in the psyche. This narrative champions individual efforts over communal contributions, often prioritizing personal gain over community welfare. As the American author Robert Wright puts it in *The Evolution of God*:

> *OUR CULTURE IS DOMINATED BY AN ETHOS OF INDIVIDUALISM. IT IS OUR CORE CULTURAL VALUE: WE ARE PROBABLY THE MOST INDIVIDUALISTIC CULTURE IN HUMAN HISTORY. OF COURSE, THERE IS MUCH THAT IS GOOD ABOUT INDIVIDUALISM: THE VALUE IT GIVES TO INDIVIDUAL LIVES, THE IMPORTANCE OF INDIVIDUAL RIGHTS, INDIVIDUAL CHOICE, AND OPPORTUNITY. IT EMPHASIZES FREEDOM, AND FREEDOM IS ONE OF THE GIFTS OF GOD. BUT INDIVIDUALISM AS A CORE VALUE LEADS TO A WAY OF SEEING LIFE THAT OBSCURES THE ENORMOUS EFFECT OF SOCIAL SYSTEMS ON THE LIVES OF PEOPLE. OF COURSE, INDIVIDUAL RESPONSIBILITY MATTERS, BUT NONE OF US IS REALLY SELF-MADE. WE ARE ALSO THE PRODUCT OF MANY FACTORS BEYOND OUR CONTROL."*[58]

As the most individualistic country on this entire planet, the US scores a whopping 91 out of 100 on the Hofstede scale of individualism—as defined by placing a high value of autonomy, self-expression, and pursuit of personal goals—closely followed by Australia and the UK, with the rest of Western Europe closer to the 80–70 range and the remaining parts of the world closer to 60–30.[59] It seems that individualism permeated American culture and life to the point where communal values aren't just treated as secondary to personal freedom and benefit, they are completely overridden by them.

European countries, especially those in the north and west, also value individual rights and freedoms. However, there's a stronger emphasis on social welfare systems, reflecting a balance between individualism and collectivism. In China, the Confucian values emphasizing family and societal harmony often take precedence over individual aspirations. However, with modernization, individualism is surging, especially among the youth.

We are all susceptible to suffering from the illusion that we are the center of the world. On an average day, everything in our own immediate experience seems to support this conviction. It is the foundational false narrative getting in the way of true flourishing at the individual level and the societal level.

In her book *Eastern Body, Western Mind*, author Anodea Judith writes that extreme individualism is not just an American ideal but also goes across Western culture. Our prevailing relational myth is that of the broken home. On a mythological, archetypal level, we are children of divorce. The consequence for the children of this divine breakup—the children being all of us—is a culture with separation at its center. We experience ourselves as separate from nature, separate from each other, and separate from God. We pull apart each other by race, class, gender, and age. Rugged individualism is our culture's core value. Success is defined as "pulling yourself up by your bootstraps" and "rising above the crowd." Life is a competition, with us against the world.

And, as Rabbi Jonathan Sacks said, "North Americans are so used to the extreme individualism promoted by capitalist values that we rarely think of ourselves as having responsibility for each other. But that is precisely what is needed—an ethos of responsibility to care for each other and the earth, central to Judaism, but a challenge to the ethos of 'looking out for number one' and the Anglo-Saxon legal tradition which rejects any legal responsibility to protect or care for others."[60]

The impact of this individualism is also dissected by cultural commentator David Brooks:

> *"I DON'T WANT TO SPEND TOO MUCH TIME DESCRIBING THIS CULTURE OF INDIVIDUALISM, AUTHENTICITY, AUTONOMY, AND ISOLATION BECAUSE IT HAS BEEN DESCRIBED SO MASTERFULLY BY OTHERS: PHILIP RIEFF IN* THE TRIUMPH OF THE THERAPEUTIC, *CHRISTOPHER LASCH IN* THE CULTURE OF NARCISSISM, *GAIL SHEEHY IN* PASSAGES, *ALASDAIR MACINTYRE IN* AFTER VIRTUE, *TOM WOLFE IN* THE "ME" DECADE, *ERICA JONG IN* FEAR OF FLYING, *CHARLES TAYLOR IN* THE ETHICS OF AUTHENTICITY, *ROBERT BELLAH IN* HABITS OF THE HEART, *AND ROBERT PUTNAM IN* BOWLING ALONE.
>
> *"IN OTHER CULTURES, PEOPLE ARE FORMED BY AND FLOURISH WITHIN INSTITUTIONS THAT PRECEDE INDIVIDUAL CHOICE—FAMILY, ETHNIC HERITAGE, FAITH, NATION. BUT THESE ARE PRECISELY THE SORTS OF INSTITUTIONS THAT THE CULTURE OF INDIVIDUALISM EATS AWAY AT, BECAUSE THEY ARE UNCHOSEN AND THEREFORE SEEN AS NOT QUITE LEGITIMATE."*[61]

While fostering self-reliance and autonomy, hyper-individualism often undermines the fundamental human need for connection and community, and it can lead to isolation, reducing opportunities for shared love and collaborative play.

Robin Wall Kimmerer, a distinguished American botanist, offers a biological metaphor. "We are not here on earth to be alone, but to be a part of a living community, a web of life in which all is sacred.

Like the cells of our body, all of life is in constant communication, as science is just beginning to understand."[62]

In my view, the biggest illusion of all is the illusion of separateness. Our differences enrich us, our connections sustain us, and our shared humanity defines us. At the heart of this truth lies Ubuntu, a Southern African philosophy that translates to "I am because we are." As the Nobel Peace Prize–winning Anglican bishop, Desmond Tutu, put it, "My humanity is bound up in yours—for we can only be human together."[63]

Like a player in an orchestra, it is our role as human beings to live in harmony with the world. What this means is that we must each play our note in a way that is beautiful and orderly with everyone and everything else. What that feels like is very similar to what listening to a great song imparts—a sort of euphoria, an out-of-body experience, a feeling of deep meaning where the suffering that is life ceases to be relevant. As Thich Nhat Hanh said, "We are here to awaken from the illusion of our separateness."[64]

MISAPPLYING "SURVIVAL OF THE FITTEST" TO HUMAN ENDEAVORS

Many leaders of Western society have pointed out the false narrative of the zero-sum society, in which a person's success or a nation's prosperity must come at the expense of another person or another country. As Bill Clinton noted, "Someone else is winning; you're losing. You can only win if someone else loses. It's fun in sports but bad in an interdependent world."[65]

The concept of "survival of the fittest," initially coined by Herbert Spencer and later adopted by Charles Darwin, has been both transformational in our understanding of the natural world yet controversial when misapplied to humans. Darwin's theory of natural selection, the basis of the phrase *survival of the fittest*, emphasizes that organisms best adapted to their environment are more likely to survive and reproduce. However, Spencer and others applied this principle to human societies, leading to social Darwinism, a philosophy often used to justify inequality and exploitation. While Darwin himself recognized the importance of traits such as generosity and sympathy, the phrase *survival of the fittest* later became a slogan for ruthless competition.

This interpretation fueled the competitive spirit of industrial capitalism, with its associated benefits and harms. It also contributed to racist and xenophobic ideologies. The negative connotations of the phrase stem from this historical misuse, evoking images of cutthroat competition and social injustice. Einstein criticized this competitive spirit, noting its destructive impact on human fraternity and cooperation: "Everywhere, in economic as well as in political life, the guiding principle is one of ruthless striving for success at the expense of one's fellow men. This competitive spirit prevails even in school and, destroying all feelings of human fraternity and cooperation, conceives of achievement not as derived from the love for productive and thoughtful work, but as springing from personal ambition and fear of rejection."[66]

However, Darwin's theory was incomplete. Evolutionary biologists such as Elisabet Sahtouris argue that "survival of the fittest" is just one stage in a larger evolutionary cycle. Purely selfish and competitive species are likely to die out without cooperation. Forest ecologists such as Suzanne Simard have shown how trees cooperate by sharing resources through underground networks.

Martin Nowak further challenged the traditional view by proposing "natural cooperation" as a fundamental principle of evolution.[67] He argues that cooperation is not just a byproduct of competition but a driving force behind complexity and diversity. From genes to cells to human societies, cooperation allows for specialization and advancement. Nowak suggests that seemingly altruistic acts can be beneficial in the long run, building trust and strengthening social bonds.[68]

Harvard University professor and author of *The Secret of Our Success* Joseph Henrich highlights that our species' extraordinary success is deeply rooted in our unparalleled ability to cooperate. He argues that what truly sets us apart is our capacity to collaborate on a large scale—even with strangers.[69] His research delves into how cultural evolution has shaped these cooperative instincts, enabling us to build complex societies, develop advanced technologies, and thrive in diverse environments.

THE MYTH OF FREE MARKETS

Free markets, driven by supply and demand with minimal government intervention, is a dominant economic model. Prices determined by free markets result in a more efficient allocation of resources. Competition fosters innovation, leading to better products, lower prices, and greater consumer choice. The "invisible hand," as defined by Adam Smith around the time the United States achieved independence, guides resources to their most productive uses, promoting economic growth.[70] Free markets also incentivize entrepreneurship and can contribute to political freedom by dispersing economic power.

However, unfettered free markets pose significant risks. They exacerbate inequality, as those with more resources are better positioned to succeed, widening the gap between rich and poor. Market failures such as pollution occur when the market fails to allocate resources efficiently. And market failures such as monopolies and information asymmetry can distort competition and harm consumers. Additionally, essential goods and services, such as healthcare and education, may become inaccessible to vulnerable populations if left solely to market forces.

The medical system exemplifies this, with its focus on efficiency leading to a lack of spare capacity during crises. "One of the problems with markets is they don't deal with what we call externalities," says Joseph Stiglitz, a Nobel Prize–winning economist known for his work on inequality, market failures, and public policy. He defines externalities as situations in which "one person's action has effects on others that are not reflected in the prices they receive or pay."[71] Climate change is an example of an externality. Free markets can also fail to provide essential public goods such as infrastructure and education, as these may not be profitable.

Furthermore, free markets are prone to boom-and-bust cycles, as demonstrated by the 2008 financial crisis. The challenge lies in balancing the benefits and risks of free markets. Unregulated markets can lead to unacceptable levels of inequality, environmental damage, and economic instability. Excessive government intervention, however, can stifle innovation and create inefficiencies. A nuanced approach is needed, one that recognizes the strengths of free markets while mitigating their weaknesses. Above all, free markets should be viewed as a means, not as an end.

THE MYTH OF THE LONE GENIUS

The archetype of the lone genius single-handedly changing the world is a misleading narrative. While figures such as Newton, Einstein, and da Vinci stood out, even Newton admitted, "If I have seen further, it is by standing on the shoulders of giants."[72] Popular culture often glorifies solitary brilliance, ignoring the collaborative nature of progress. Yet, the vast majority of major breakthroughs build on the work of many. Scientific discoveries, technological innovations, and artistic movements are rarely the product of a single isolated mind.

For example, the Human Genome Project, a monumental achievement in mapping human DNA, involved a massive international collaboration of scientists, researchers, and institutions. Similarly, the development of the internet was not the work of one person, but a series of interconnected contributions from engineers, computer scientists, and government agencies over several decades.

Failing to recognize this collaborative foundation can have several negative consequences. It can discourage teamwork and leave "non-geniuses" feeling inadequate, fostering a sense of learned helplessness. If people believe that only solitary geniuses can make a difference, they will be less likely to contribute their own unique skills and perspectives to group efforts. Similarly, the media often perpetuates the idea of a single, perfect solution to complex problems, creating unrealistic expectations. Issues such as climate change and poverty require nuanced, collaborative approaches—not simplistic fixes. These challenges demand the integration of diverse expertise, perspectives, and solutions, highlighting the importance of collective action and systemic change, rather than relying on a single "savior" or a magic bullet.

THE NEGATIVE EFFECTS OF EXCESS CONSUMERISM

The insidious nature of excessive consumerism lies in its ability to conflate material acquisition with genuine happiness, a fallacy perpetuated by a relentless barrage of marketing and social messaging. Today, we are inclined to define ourselves by what we consume and not by who we are. As economist Juliet Schor notes, "The dominant culture encourages us to buy more and more things, and to define ourselves by what we consume."[73] This cultural narrative fosters a sense of identity rooted in possessions, leading to a relentless cycle of consumption, spiraling debt, and ultimately, profound dissatisfaction.

While consumerism pervades global societies, its manifestations vary. In Europe, a historical emphasis on tradition, longevity, and sustainability tempers the excesses of a disposable culture. Conversely, China's rapid urbanization and burgeoning middle class have fueled a voracious appetite for designer brands and luxury goods. However, a countervailing narrative, rooted in traditional Confucius values and a preference for simplicity, also persists. As the Chinese proverb goes, "Contentment brings happiness," highlighting a cultural tension between material aspirations and the pursuit of inner peace. This nuanced perspective highlights that consumerism is not a monolithic force but a complex phenomenon shaped by cultural context and historical legacy.

Capitalism improves lives but also creates unnecessary desires. I once taught my godson, Shiv Chadha, this lesson when he insisted on getting a new iPhone despite not needing it. Denying his request led him to distinguish between wants and needs—a crucial realization. As Dallin H. Oaks, a leader in The Church of Jesus Christ of Latter-day Saints, said, "You cannot have too much of what you do not need."[74] Arthur C. Brooks attributes unhappiness to what he calls "miswanting," which is wanting what you do not need.[75] *If you do not establish how much is enough, it will never be enough.*

WHY "SELFISH GENES" OFTEN LEAD TO COOPERATION

In much of Western society, the dominant narrative about human nature has been the idea that we are fundamentally self-interested. It's considered to be so axiomatic that we are not even aware of it. The writer Jeremy Lent debunks this false narrative as forcefully as I have ever seen when he says that our era "was constructed on a myth of the selfish individual as the foundational value."[76]

While Jeremy Lent and others rightly critique the exclusive focus on self-interest, a balanced perspective acknowledges that a degree of self-interest is not only natural but necessary for individual and societal flourishing. Lent's point about prosocial impulses is crucial. Fairness, altruism, and compassion are vital and deeply human.

However, these impulses don't negate the inherent need for self-preservation. A healthy society recognizes that individuals must have their basic needs met before they can effectively contribute to the greater good. Self-interest, when channeled constructively, can drive innovation, productivity, and personal growth, ultimately benefiting the community. For example, pursuing education or developing skills can be seen as self-interested acts, but they also create a more knowledgeable and capable workforce.

The key lies in finding a balance between individual needs and the needs of others, recognizing that true flourishing comes from a dynamic interplay between self-interest and prosocial behavior. A society that ignores either side of this equation risks either individual neglect or unsustainable demands on altruism.

The father of modern economics, Adam Smith, is often quoted in support of this egocentric orientation. But in his own words, Smith says the opposite: "How selfish soever man may be supposed, there are evidently some principles in his nature, which interest him in the fortunes of others, and render their happiness necessary to him, though he derives nothing from it, except the pleasure of seeing it."[77]

The idea of the "selfish gene" is often quoted to justify the selfishness of individuals. However, evolutionists are now touting the role of cooperation and altruism evolving *via* the selfish gene! Evolutionary biologists such as Elisabet Sahtouris have concluded that without intra- and interspecies cooperation, a purely selfish and competitive species is likely to die out.[78] When we look at the progress we have made in science and technology that has resulted from cooperation, it is clear that cooperation, and not selfishness, is the cause of these giant strides made by humanity.

Children can discover this culture of competitive individualism at their school and learn in many ways that rewards are based on individual achievement and that there will be winners and losers. Or, they can simply learn to be themselves and embrace their true nature. However, this binary choice overlooks the potential for schools to cultivate both individual excellence and collaborative spirit. A balanced approach could foster a sense of personal accomplishment while also emphasizing the value of teamwork, empathy, and diverse contributions. Ideally, education should equip children to navigate a complex world, recognizing that success is often achieved through a combination of individual effort and collective support.

THE FALSE MANTRA OF "GREED IS GOOD"

The iconic, yet corrosive, declaration, "Greed is good," uttered by Gordon Gekko in the movie *Wall Street* (1987), epitomizes a distorted narrative that mistakenly conflates unchecked self-interest with societal flourishing. This deeply ingrained belief, often unconsciously embraced, perpetuates a system where individual avarice, rather than collective well-being, dictates the trajectory of progress with potentially devastating consequences.

This idea found intellectual support in figures such as the Nobel laureate Milton Friedman, whose influential statement, "The social responsibility of business is to increase its profits,"[79] became a cornerstone of corporate philosophy for decades. Friedman's argument, delivered with intellectual stature despite his diminutive physical stature, posited that businesses best serve society by focusing solely on maximizing shareholder value. This philosophy has dominated US corporate thinking for the past fifty years.

However, this perspective neglects externalities, such as the crucial role of ethical considerations, stakeholder interests beyond shareholders, and the long-term consequences of prioritizing short-term profits over sustainable practices and social responsibility. Many corporations argue that, as long as they follow public policies, their job is only to maximize profits for shareholders. However, these corporations ignore the phenomenon of state capture; i.e., powerful corporations and industries exert significant influence on political decision-making, often lobbying against policies that are socially desirable.

A truly flourishing society requires a more nuanced understanding of the role of business, one that moves beyond the narrow focus on profit maximization to embrace a broader vision of value creation that benefits all stakeholders. On August 19, 2019, the Business Roundtable—a prominent association of CEOs from major US companies—issued a Statement on the Purpose of a Corporation. This declaration marked a significant shift from the traditional focus on shareholder primacy, emphasizing instead a commitment to all stakeholders, including customers, employees, suppliers, communities, and shareholders. The statement was endorsed by 181 CEOs, reflecting a collective move toward stakeholder capitalism.[80]

Milton Friedman's vision stands in stark contrast to another mission statement, that of Jamsetji Tata, who founded the Tata Group in India some 150 years back. "The community is not just another stakeholder in business," Tata proclaimed, "but is in fact a very purpose of its existence."[81] Today, Tata is India's largest business group, with a market value of over $400 billion, and is the most trusted and most respected as a leader in its fields of operation. It has a diverse business portfolio, strong ethical reputation, global presence, and community focus. In the Global 500 2025, which ranks brands based on value and strength, Tata sat at number sixty with a brand value of over $30 billion.[82] It's the only Indian brand in the top one hundred.

IF IT'S GOOD, IT'S MEASURABLE

This mantra echoes through business schools, reinforcing the dangerous notion that if something can't be quantified, it doesn't exist or isn't worth pursuing. But, as Robert F. Kennedy, a 1948 Harvard graduate, eloquently stated, "GNP [gross national product] measures neither our wit nor our courage, neither our wisdom nor our learning, nor our compassion nor our devotion to our country. It measures everything in short, except that which makes life worthwhile."[83]

Yet the obsession with quantifiable, dollar-based metrics perpetuates a distorted view of value, feeding the false narratives we tell ourselves about money and wealth. Markets, money, crony capitalism, and competition, in their crudest forms, become the sole focus of life, obscuring the deeper values in intangibles—such as community well-being, ethical conduct, and genuine human connection—that should guide our economic and social interactions. We risk prioritizing efficiency and profit maximization at the expense of these crucial yet often immeasurable qualities. Kennedy's words remind us that this pursuit can be tragically misguided, leaving us materially rich but spiritually impoverished. By clinging only to narrow metrics, we risk creating a world where we know "the price of everything, but the value of nothing," as Lord Darlington says in Oscar Wilde's play *Lady Windermere's Fan* (1892).

A truly thriving society must look beyond mere metrics and embrace a more holistic vision of progress, one that values the immeasurable aspects of human experience. After all, there are no measures of how much you can love, how much you can learn, and how much you can play in their broadest definitions.

THE ARRIVAL FALLACY AND THE HEDONIC TREADMILL

The "arrival fallacy" is a deceptive belief that reaching a specific goal will guarantee lasting happiness. This illusion is illustrated by the "hedonic treadmill" concept introduced by Philip Brickman and Donald Campbell in 1971.[84] It postulates that any initial surge of joy from achieving that goal quickly fades as we adapt and crave ever-increasing stimuli. This is another version of the diminishing marginal utility concept that Economics 101 is based on. Daniel Gilbert, Harvard University professor and renowned social psychologist known for his research on affective forecasting, says that we don't realize we have this ally of hedonic adaptation that acts as the psychological immune system. Gilbert uses this powerful metaphor to describe the unconscious cognitive processes that help us cope with negative events and mitigate their emotional impact. Just like our biological immune system fights off physical threats, our psychological immune system employs strategies such as rationalizing, finding positive meaning, comparing ourselves to those worse off, and downplaying the significance of a specific event to protect our emotional well-being.[85]

But the problem runs even deeper, fueled by mimetic desire. We don't simply desire things in isolation; our desires are often shaped by what others desire. This amplifies the arrival fallacy, as we chase goals that aren't inherently fulfilling but are merely reflections of societal or peer-driven aspirations.

Consequently, the hedonic treadmill spins faster, as we are not only adapting to our own achievements but also constantly chasing the moving target of what others want. This creates a relentless cycle: We strive for an imagined "arrival" dictated by mimetic desire, experience a fleeting sense of accomplishment, and then find ourselves immediately chasing the next goal, perpetually trapped on the treadmill of adaptation and driven by the ever-shifting desires of others. The perceived destination of lasting happiness constantly shifts, leaving us feeling unfulfilled forever, as the fleeting joy of arrival is swallowed by the insatiable appetite of both the hedonic treadmill and the mimetic desires that drive it.

Let me illustrate this with an example from my own life. In 1997, I bought a beautiful apartment on the Upper West Side of Manhattan overlooking the famous Central Park. For someone like me, born in Old Delhi, this was more than I had ever dreamed of.

Later, a very dear friend who was previously my neighbor and inspired me to move to that part of New York suddenly relocated to Fifth Avenue on the Upper East Side and invited me to his new apartment. It was twice the size of his previous home and very beautifully decorated. When I came back home, I was very unhappy, as I did not like my place anymore. It felt so small—so inferior compared to my friend's new apartment. I was possessed by my wants.

But then I had a dialogue with myself, reflecting on how foolish this reaction was. After all, most people would probably be thrilled to be in my place. Why was I trapping myself in an apartment I now saw as insufficient compared to my desires? Why did I allow myself to compare what I had to what my friend had? After all, my apartment satisfied all my needs for an abundant life. I realized that my bout of envy offered me little personal fulfillment. Now, more than two decades later, I still enjoy living in that same apartment, despite a multifold increase in my wealth.

A deeper insight into our desires is provided by the brilliant philosopher at Harvard University, Roberto Unger. He says, "Our desires are insatiable. We seek from the limited the unlimited. We must fail. Human desires are indeterminate. They fail to exhibit the targeted and scripted quality of desire among other animals. The root of insatiability is the social construction of desire."[86]

One key that will help you help unlock more value from this book is knowing the difference between "ultimate longings" and "proximate desires." Our ultimate longings come from the heart—our authentic self. By contrast, proximate desires are constructs of the mind; these are the specific, culturally, and individually shaped ways we try to fulfill our ultimate longings. They are influenced by external factors and are the desires of the mind because they involve conscious thought, planning, and strategies.

The key is to see the connection between the two. As an example, for some, their ultimate longing is loving (connection, belonging), whereas their proximate desires are getting married, having children, and joining a community group. As another example, you might choose to pick up a particular skill because it's required for a job, even though your ultimate desire is simply to learn and grow. The job is the incidental reason, while the underlying longing for learning is the ultimate one. Similarly, playing video games, joining a recreational sports league, and performing with a musical instrument are all proximate expressions of our ultimate longing for play.

Our proximate desires are the means to the end of fulfilling our ultimate longings. Sometimes, we can lose sight of this connection, pursuing proximate desires that don't actually steer us to greater love, learning, or play. This can lead to dissatisfaction and a sense of meaninglessness and impede our flourishing. Einstein echoed a similar thought: "Feeling and longing are the motive force behind all human endeavor and human creation, in however exalted a guise later may present themselves to us."[87]

VIOLENCE IS NOT NORMAL

The pervasive narrative that violence is an inherent human trait is a dangerous falsehood. Our screens, saturated with stylized brutality, reinforce this myth, portraying violence as a natural— even effective— problem-solving tool. From choreographed fight sequences in video games to explosive action films, we are relentlessly bombarded with the message that ferocity is normal.

However, anthropological research paints a different picture. As Steven Pinker argues in *The Better Angels of Our Nature*, "Despite the impression you might get from 24/7 news, or from history books focused on wars and atrocities, violence has been in decline over long stretches of history, and today we may be living in the most peaceable era of our species' existence."[88] This challenges the notion that violence is an immutable part of our nature, and the consequences of this false narrative are profound. Desensitization to violence through media erodes our empathy, normalizing its presence in real life. It limits our understanding of conflict resolution, fostering a belief that force is the only viable option. This is particularly damaging for young minds who are highly susceptible to media influence, potentially shaping their perceptions of acceptable behavior and conflict resolution. The high prevalence of gun violence in the US contributes to a situation where acts of violence, particularly those involving firearms, become increasingly perceived as a normal part of the social landscape; thus, any solutions to gun violence are escaped.

Moreover, history offers powerful counternarratives. Figures such as Mahatma Gandhi demonstrated the transformative power of non-violent resistance, proving that profound social change can be achieved through peaceful means. Under his guidance, India defeated the mighty British Empire by nonviolent means to earn its independence from British colonial rule. His philosophy, rooted in the concept of ahimsa (nonviolence), stands as a testament to the potential for human beings to resolve conflict without resorting to force.

OTHER FALSE NARRATIVES THAT IMPEDE FLOURISHING

False narratives are not limited to money. Arthur C. Brooks, a current guru on happiness, debunks some of the current narratives plaguing modern life: "The first untruth is that you must know your destination; the second is that a good life is one that minimizes suffering; and the third is that you must know and live your own truth. The Dominican sages and the modern scientists together show that these are all fake news and serious impediments to a happy life."[89]

False narratives abound in the realm of religion and other belief systems as well. The manipulation of religious narratives can manifest in various ways, such as selectively interpreting scripture to justify prejudice or fabricating stories that paint other groups as inherently evil or dangerous. Such actions not only distort the true message of compassion and understanding that lies at the heart of most religions but also foster division, hatred, and even violence.

Some narratives urge us to exclude or minimize diversity and even do away with certain groups of people. Others tell us that each population is so uniquely and wholly different that there should be no interaction between them. We have false narratives that aim to divide us and make us fear *the other*. Those in control—or who wish to be in control—put out propaganda meant to tear us apart.

Leaders have historically exploited the masses through such false narratives. Hitler used the idea of *the other* in Nazi Germany. There is a narrative currently being pushed by some in the United States that immigrants are *the other*. Meanwhile, China has recently implemented a social credit system[90] that tracks individuals and assigns each of them a social score based on how well they live up to the state's expectations. Instead of using new technology to increase individual autonomy, these leaders are using it to control their citizens and decrease their chances of flourishing.

Other false narratives advance political goals. An example is the attribution of gun violence in the US to mental illness rather than the prevalence of guns, despite data showing that people actually suffering from mental illness are more likely to be victims of gun violence rather than the perpetrators. And, of course, massive numbers of marketing campaigns are generated to produce false narratives to compel us to buy things. One of the classic examples is tobacco companies. Scientists working for these organizations concluded early on that their products caused cancer and heart disease, yet these companies spun convincing narratives that smoking was glamorous, exciting, or a sign of rugged masculinity.

HOW WE CAN GUARD AGAINST FALSE NARRATIVES

False narratives arise from ignoring counterevidence, misattributing intentions and/or emotions, and identifying patterns where none exist. Societies also have shared narratives, or intersubjective realities, which are believed to be true just because we agree that they are. The concept of money itself is an intersubjective reality. Pieces of paper or digital entries have value only because we collectively agree that they do. This shared belief enables complex economic systems to function. The value of the stock market is based on the collective belief of the people who engage with it. National identity is a shared narrative that binds people together. Concepts such as "patriotism," "national pride," and "shared history" are constructed through collective agreement and reinforced through rituals, symbols, and stories.

Accepting false narratives is often easier, especially dominant ones. The folktale "The Emperor's New Clothes" illustrates this. People conformed to avoid appearing unfit or stupid, even when they knew something was wrong. Only a child, not yet fully socialized, pointed out the truth. Similarly, we gravitate toward narratives that align with our biases, especially with the decline of traditional media and the rise of social media echo chambers. To guard against false narratives, we must ask critical questions: "What are my biases? Is the narrative supported by evidence? Is the source credible? Are there other perspectives? Is this story true for me? Am I being manipulated?" Remember what Mark Twain said: "It's easier to fool people than to convince them that they have been fooled."

Storytelling is powerful, but social media algorithms can create echo chambers. Education is crucial in developing critical thinking to challenge false narratives. Even institutions such as the Catholic Church have revised their own dominant stories. The Church no longer teaches that the earth was created six thousand years ago or that the sun revolves around the earth. The Church no longer says that salvation is only through Christ. But these narratives were dominant for over a millennium, and some believers still adhere to the old word.

Religions and other institutions that wish to foster flourishing must continue to reevaluate their narratives, remove falsehoods, and align themselves with common human values and modern sensibilities.

Having navigated the murky waters of false narratives—a relentless stream of materialistic promises and digital demands, often orchestrated by those vying for our attention, wallets, or allegiance—a crucial question emerges: How do we chart a course toward genuine flourishing amidst this constant barrage? It necessitates a fundamental shift in how we engage with the world. To effectively navigate this landscape and distinguish between the deceptive narratives and genuinely valuable insights, we must cultivate a more conscious way of being. In the following chapter, we will explore the benefits of cultivating a heightened state of awareness, a conscious presence that allows us to discern truth from illusion and reclaim our attentional landscape.

CHAPTER THREE

THE SHIFT TO LIVING CONSCIOUSLY

> *"TO BE CONSCIOUS IS THE FIRST STEP TOWARDS TRANSFORMATION. LIFE EVOLVES THROUGH CONSCIOUSNESS."*
> **—SRI AUROBINDO, INDIAN YOGI**

My favorite story of the Buddha involves a man on the road who was struck by the radiance and peacefulness of the Buddha's presence. The man stopped and asked, "My friend, what are you? Are you a celestial being or a God?"

"No," said the Buddha.

"Well, then, are you a magician or wizard?"

Again, the Buddha answered, "No."

"Are you a saint?"

"No."

"Well, my friend, what are you then?"

The Buddha simply replied, "I am awake."

That's how Siddhartha Gautama, born in Nepal, son of King Śuddhodana, got his name Buddha, which means "the awakened one" from the Sanskrit word *budh*. For nearly half a century, he taught others how to awaken. To be awake is to be aware of ourselves and mindful of all life around us or live consciously. This simple yet powerful teaching has inspired billions of people around the world for 2,500 years and led to art, books, and films, including famous ones such as *The Matrix*.

GETTING OUT OF THE MATRIX

The phrase "escaping the matrix" is often used metaphorically as well as being a reference to the 1999 science fiction film directed by the Wachowskis. In essence, getting out of the matrix is a metaphorical concept often used to describe a process of awakening or enlightenment. Does art imitate life, or does life imitate art? The answer, of course, is both, and there is no better example of it happening at scale than *The Matrix*.

In the movie, the Matrix is a simulated reality created by intelligent machines to control and manipulate humans who are kept in a state of artificial consciousness while their bodies are used as energy sources. The movie's protagonist, Neo, played by Keanu Reeves, is offered a choice between a red pill, which will awaken him to the harsh truth of the Matrix, and a blue pill, which will allow him to remain in blissful ignorance of those harsh realities. Choosing the red pill is often seen as a symbol of seeking truth and knowledge over comfortable illusions. Sometimes, it is seen as breaking free from conformity. "Escaping the matrix" can also refer to flouting societal norms and expectations. It's about questioning the status quo and pursuing a more authentic and meaningful life.

The character Neo eventually learns to transcend the Matrix, to exist in the liminal space between this false choice of the red pill or the blue pill. The whole point of the movie is often lost as we reenter real life. In our polarized politics, it often seems as if people have taken the red pill or the blue pill, enabling us to cling to an ideology or a belief that the color we chose is superior to the other. "Take the red pill," declared Elon Musk in a 2020 tweet that drew wide attention. "Taken!" replied Ivanka Trump immediately.[91] Is it an eerie coincidence that US politics in particular bears a close resemblance to this red pill/blue pill divide? Or did the writers of the movie recognize something deeper—that we are all susceptible to living compulsively, self-deluded, trapped in an illusory world programmed by higher powers with vested interests?

When people talk about "escaping the matrix," they are usually referring to the idea of waking up from a false or illusory reality and gaining a deeper understanding of the world or their own existence, seeking truth, and/or breaking free from self-imposed limitations.

Keanu Reeves seems to understand this quite deeply, as if he's taken the real lesson of *The Matrix* to heart. He is often called "the nicest guy in Hollywood," and there are numerous stories of him popping up to help homeless people, or buying a round of drinks for everyone in a restaurant, or taking a pay cut on a movie in order to give higher pay to the crew, or waiting in line in the rain with everyone else to get inside an event for his own movie.[92]

When asked to explain the meaning of *The Matrix* and his takeaway lessons, he speaks about living consciously. Ever since he first read the script, Reeves has said that he has seen it as "a film about questioning, awakening, consciousness, love, support, faith, evolution, and man's relationship to machines."[93]

This is remarkable because it seems that so many fans of the film fail to see this and instead debate whether they would rather choose the red pill or the blue pill. They seem ready to accept that one of these two realities is better, without calling into question that, either way, you are being programmed by a high-tech pharmaceutical. But according to Reeves, Neo is "using his mind and his imagination searching for an answer to a question, to help him define his world and reconcile himself. He is feeling that there's something wrong with the world, and it's driving him mad."

At its core, Reeves says, the film is about personally investigating the nature of reality. "In the film," he says, "it's like a crossroads ... it's about being asleep or awake. It is also a morality play, 'should I take the high road or the low road?' And that occurs in the lives of everyone I know, I am faced with that choice every day."[94]

Ultimately, says Reeves, "It is not a dark film, it's a very hopeful film." At the end, Neo gets to experience love with Trinity, the character played by Carrie-Anne Moss. "What love has opened up for him is that he has taken on responsibility and he can fly, which is a metaphor." Reeves's essential lesson is this: Do not accept "any system of thought, just on the basis of its existence or the power it represents. You don't have to live your life that way, you can choose your own life. ... You're going to get into some battles, but you'll live a richer, better life."[95]

The spirituality of this science fiction trilogy is essential for Reeves. "It's a film that utilizes a lot of mythic and religious themes," he says. "There might be an aspect of the rebirth, of dying and being reborn from Christianity or of freeing one's mind in the context of Buddhism and Siddhartha's journey," Reeves concludes. "It's like the birth of compassion through experience, he understands everyone's right to life. It's almost like this classical phrase, the struggle for compassionate consciousness."[96]

WHAT IT MEANS TO LIVE CONSCIOUSLY

To live consciously, we must first recognize that we are plugged into a matrix of our own making before we can transcend the illusions of life. In reality, we live compulsively under the influence of marketers of all sorts. The powerful advertising and entertainment industries in the US play a pivotal role in shaping desires. From Hollywood's portrayal of success to Silicon Valley's tech allure, there's a continuous narrative about aspiration.

Marketing professionals have become increasingly powerful in hacking the human mind with advances in communications and internet technology. In a sense, "they know us more than we know ourselves," says Yuval Harari, an Israeli historian, philosopher, and bestselling author known for exploring macro-historical trends and the future of humanity, and we let it happen unconsciously.[97] In Vance Packard's 1957 book *The Hidden Persuaders*, he demonstrates how advertisers use techniques such as subliminal messaging and depth psychology to tap into our unconscious desires, effectively manipulating our thoughts and feelings to persuade us to buy their products.[98]

Now incorporating AI, these techniques aren't limited to selling just products. They are employed in political campaigns, social movements, and even everyday interactions. While Packard was among the first to shed light on the insidious ways in which our minds are influenced by business, media, and politicians, in the sixty years since, the power of manipulation has gone up multifold.

As Vance Packard later observed, "The crucial change is data. The ability to get inside our heads and therefore the ability to manipulate us is so much more invasive and intense than it was in the 1950s. It's now personalized and deeply exploitative of anxiety. We're with these technologies all the time. You might have turned off your TV, but your phone is always by your side."

To make matters worse, we are in a state of constant distraction, always feeling too busy, and do not have time to see through these manipulations. The former tech executive Linda Stone identified this as "continuous partial attention," where we are never focused on the task at hand because we are always monitoring our texts, emails, and social media feeds.[99] We exercise too little free will, make few conscious decisions, and live as if on autopilot. We scroll to see a stream of messages programmed by algorithms aided by artificial intelligence that are only getting more and more clever at infiltrating our humanity.

No matter who you are or what level of consciousness you think you are in, two things always apply. The first is that you use your awareness every day in all kinds of scenarios. You think, feel, wish, perceive, and observe. The second thing is that you constrict your attention through a process that the English writer Aldous Huxley called the "reducing valve."[100] Instead of finding yourself in a state of expanded, receptive awareness, your mind edits, censors, ignores, and denies attention to many aspects of reality. The reducing valve squeezes your "whole mind," another term favored by Huxley, to a small flow of permissible thoughts, perceptions, and feelings.

All this starts to happen naturally when you are born into this world, just so your young mind is not overwhelmed. This way, you can fall asleep peacefully. The process of using your awareness and constricting it also enables you to conform to conventions of society. We all create value and meanings. At our best, we do so by engaging authentically, in a process of becoming ourselves.

While the reducing valve is a necessary function for navigating childhood and conforming to societal norms, its continued constriction in adulthood can severely limit our potential for growth and authentic self-expression. By habitually filtering our experiences, we become trapped in a narrow band of perception, missing out on the richness and complexity of the world around us and the vast landscape of our own inner lives. To transcend these limitations, we must consciously work to expand the valve, to widen the channels of awareness and allow a fuller spectrum of experience to flow through. This involves challenging our ingrained assumptions, questioning the narratives we've internalized, and cultivating a willingness to embrace the unfamiliar. We must dare to ask ourselves the basic questions of who, what, when, where, and why. Answering those questions usually provides us with a level of awareness that enlightens us.

When we live consciously, we will also become aware of our beliefs. No matter what worldview we adopt, we will end up adopting some set of values that are, on some level, subjective. What is important is how we came to adopt these sets of beliefs and how we respond to others who decided to adopt a different set. It's also often the case that people are unaware of where their deeply held feelings come from. Often, people get their beliefs like they catch colds—by being around other people! And since ideas are everywhere—on television, in books and magazines, at the movies, and in conversation with friends and family—it's easy to pick these ideas up without considering whether they're worth believing.

ELEVEN TRANSFORMATIONS RESULTING FROM LIVING CONSCIOUSLY

At the risk of appearing that I'm trying to one-up the Ten Commandments, I'd like to offer a sequence of transformations that living consciously offers to anyone. Each is an aspect of the shift to mindfulness in our lives. I aim to offer these as eleven guideposts to conscious living, starting with the one transformation from which all others flow.

I. FROM EVERYDAY BANALITY TO THE MAGICAL

> *"DON'T LOOK FOR MIRACLES. YOU YOURSELF ARE THE MIRACLE."*
>
> ***—HENRY MILLER***
>
> *YOU ARE THE UNIVERSE, EXPRESSING ITSELF AS A HUMAN FOR A LITTLE WHILE."*
>
> ***—ALAN WATTS***

What if we lived our lives noticing the beauty in ordinary things? "If we could see the miracle of a single flower clearly, our whole life would change," says Jack Kornfield, a prominent Buddhist teacher.[101]

Our human body is a masterpiece of biological engineering, and it stands as a testament to the awe-inspiring complexity of life. Far from a mere assemblage of organs, the body is a symphony of coordinated systems, a self-repairing machine that manufactures over four hundred distinct chemicals. It operates as a real-time analysis system, maintaining precise homeostatic balance, constantly and instantly adapting to environmental changes. All its internal systems are automatic and do not require conscious control. Our heart beats one hundred thousand times daily. Our lungs process eleven thousand liters of air daily. Our kidneys filter 1.5 liters of blood per minute. Our liver performs five hundred-plus functions. It has over thirty-seven trillion cells working in harmony, involving billions of chemical reactions per second.

Our body is also nature's supercomputer system. Our neural network surpasses any artificial structure. It has eighty-six billion neurons processing simultaneously, each connected to ten thousand others. It processes at a speed of 268 miles per hour, with a storage capacity estimated at 2.5 petabytes, and operates on a mere 20 watts of power. From the beating heart to the vast neural network, ponder the seamless symphony of biological processes; are you not convinced that your body is nothing short of a miracle?

Furthermore, the human body is inextricably linked to the wider ecosystem and deeply integrated with universal rhythms. The air we breathe, the water we drink, and the food we consume are all products of intricate ecological cycles that sustain life on earth. We are children of the sun; our very existence dependent on the energy it provides. The spectrum of visible light is precisely what we see in the sun's emissions. Our circadian rhythms are totally aligned with the earth's rotation.

We are not merely passive recipients of nature's gifts; we actively shape and are shaped by our surroundings. Our bodies contribute to the carbon cycle, not only through respiration but also through decomposition after death, returning vital nutrients to the soil. We are agents of seed dispersal, carrying plant life to new locations, sometimes intentionally through agriculture, sometimes inadvertently as we move through the world. Our activities, from building shelters to cultivating land, alter landscapes and influence the habitats of other species. Even our waste products, when managed responsibly, can become resources for other organisms. We are part of a complex web of interactions, constantly influencing and being influenced by the environment.

As Thich Nhat Hanh beautifully says, "Around us, life bursts forth with miracles—a glass of water, a ray of sunshine, a leaf, a caterpillar, a flower, laughter, raindrops. If you live in awareness, it is easy to see miracles everywhere."[102]

How much of this is in your awareness? The previous magical description by Thich Nhat Hanh is only about a few species! Did you know that we are only one of the nearly nine million species in this world?[103]

Understanding the miraculous nature of the human body and its world should inspire profound wonder, foster genuine humility, encourage responsible stewardship, and awaken spiritual awareness. The human body represents the universe's greatest miracle, demanding our gratitude, reverence, care, and humble appreciation.

2. FROM ILLUSIONS TO ENLIGHTENMENT

> *"AUTHENTIC FREEDOM IS LIBERATION FROM LIFE'S ILLUSIONS."*
>
> ***—THOMAS MERTON***
>
> *"ENLIGHTENMENT IS REALIZING THAT THERE IS NOTHING TO CHANGE, BUT EVERYTHING TO PERCEIVE DIFFERENTLY."*
>
> ***—ZEN***

The first step to becoming enlightened is simply to live consciously and heighten our awareness. It all begins with knowing thyself, the precept that underlies all philosophy. "An unexamined life is not worth living," said Socrates. Something like this has been echoed by Buddha, Confucius, and in the Hindu Upanishads. Yuval Harari makes the point that "know thyself" is so fundamental a precept that it has propelled the evolution of humanity.[104]

When we live consciously, we realize that we have limited cognitive abilities relative to the infinite nature of reality. As the famous Harvard biologist E. O. Wilson writes in his book *Consilience,* "Visible light, we have learned, is not the sole illuminating energy of the universe, as prescientific common sense decreed. It is instead an infinitesimal sliver of electromagnetic radiation, comprising wavelengths of 400 to 700 nanometers (billionths of a meter), within a spectrum that ranges from gamma waves trillions of times shorter to radio waves trillions of times longer."[105]

Going further in his book *The Meaning of Human Existence*, Wilson notes that "our species is programmed to detect only twenty to twenty thousand hertz (cycles of air compression per second). Above that range, flying bats broadcast ultrasonic pulses into the night air and listen for the echoes to dodge obstacles and snatch moths and other insects on the wing. Below the human range, elephants rumble complex messages in exchanges back and forth with other members of their herd."[106]

To further compound the problem of limited cognitive abilities, we will also likely realize that we have unconscious biases that we have developed over the course of our lives. Part of the reason for the existence of these biases is that our brains have evolved from very different circumstances than we are currently in, when we had very few decisions to make—unlike today, when there is a decision to be made at every moment.

Our bias toward short-termism is an instinct evolved from our roots as hunter-gatherers spotting danger. Our brain is marvelously adapted to the past, yet not fast enough for the modern world, which is getting more complicated by the day. We are wired for efficiency, not necessarily accuracy. We take shortcuts and rely on past subjective experiences. Cognitive biases get the best of us.

Confirmation bias, for example, makes us look for patterns that confirm what we already believe, ignore anything that contradicts it, and prevent us from learning new viewpoints. As Warren Buffett said, "What the human being is best at doing is interpreting all new information so that their prior conclusions remain intact."[107] You will immediately recognize another deception, the frequency illusion, also called the Baader–Meinhof phenomenon, which is a cognitive bias in which you notice a word, idea, or thing more frequently shortly after becoming aware of it. It's not that the thing is appearing more often, but your awareness of it has increased. We seek patterns when randomness is the truth. We suffer from knowledge illusion because of the limitations of our own perception. We often mistake correlation for causation because we attribute some sort of meaning to a circumstance.

Self-awareness helps us overcome our illusions. One of my favorite quotes comes from Swami Vivekananda, the nineteenth-century Hindu monk. "Hold to the idea, 'I am not the mind, I see that I am thinking, I am watching my mind act,' and each day the identification of yourself with your thoughts and feelings will grow less, until at last you can entirely separate yourself from the mind and actually know it to be apart from yourself." In other words, you'll know you are truly self-aware when you are able to realize when your mind is playing tricks on you, and you can put your mind in its place.

You are not your mind or your thoughts. You are much bigger than those pesky things. This realization is the goal of the Vipassana Meditation retreat[108], where, for ten days, you observe your mind while remaining totally silent. As a conscious person, you are independent of the character that you play in real life. Consciousness is not an object that we experience; rather, consciousness *is* us. This is the most important realization of an enlightened mind. "All human unhappiness comes from not facing reality squarely, exactly as it is." This is a common saying attributed to the Buddha, reflecting his teachings on the origin of suffering.

3. EGOCENTRICITY TRANSFORMED INTO INTERCONNECTEDNESS

> *"WE ARE LIKE ISLANDS IN THE SEA, SEPARATE ON THE SURFACE BUT CONNECTED IN THE DEEP."*
>
> ***—WILLIAM JAMES***
>
> *"EVERY INDIVIDUAL IS AN EXPRESSION OF THE WHOLE REALM OF NATURE, A UNIQUE ACTION OF THE TOTAL UNIVERSE."*
>
> ***—ALAN WATTS***

How many people do you think have lived and died since the dawn of humankind? The number will surprise most of you: It is over a hundred billion people. Most have suffered from the illusion of thinking they are the center of the universe. Copernicus postulated that even the planet Earth itself—forget about individuals—is not the center. Earth, after all, revolves around the sun. Darwin postulated that we are all related to each other, that every individual is part of a larger humanity, and that humanity itself is part of a larger natural world.

Carl Sagan said, "The cosmos is within us. We are made of star-stuff. We are a way for the universe to know itself."[109] And Nikola Tesla said, "We are all one. Only egos, beliefs, and fears separate us."[110] In Buddhist philosophy, the concept of interbeing emphasizes the interconnectedness and interdependence of all phenomena. It suggests that everything exists in relation to everything else, and individual well-being is intimately tied to the well-being of others and the environment. One of the most powerful sentences from the Hindu book *Mahōpaniṣad*, (VI.71) says, "अयं बन्धुरयं नेतिगणना लघुचेतसाम् | उदारचरितानां तु वसुधैव कुटुम्बकम् ||" ("Discrimination saying 'this one is a relative; this other one is a stranger' is for the mean-minded. For those who're known as magnanimous, the entire world constitutes but a family."[111])

"Some amount of ego or self is very important," says Mark Epstein, the Harvard-trained psychotherapist and author. "But we also need the ability to observe our own mind, thoughts, and feelings."[112] Therapy is built on a therapeutic split in the ego that promotes a kind of watchfulness of our inner lives. Meditation does that by training the mind to observe itself. Both therapy and meditation can help us get past the ego's need to control everything, transforming egocentricity into interconnectedness. Those who can transcend egocentricity report the same things: a feeling of oneness with all living things, a feeling of connectedness, a feeling of being rooted in our essential nature. As Neil deGrasse Tyson said, "When I look up in the universe, I know I'm small, but I'm also big. I'm big because I'm connected to the universe and the universe is connected to me."[113]

Anthropologist Gregory Bateson believed that the first thing children should learn is how the various life systems are interconnected: What is the relationship between the food we eat, the garbage we produce, and the survival of fish in the sea? "When the individual soul realizes the unity of all beings and sees only the One God dwelling in all, then one reaches the highest state of Brahman," says the Bhagavad Gita (6:29).[114]

Yet, I see how most people view the world as a place of zero-sum competition, a place of striving to accumulate more money and possessions, and where each individual person sees themselves as the center of the universe, rather than a part of a community or of a single species—humanity—that can flourish together. The result is an epidemic of loneliness.

The alarm bells are finally starting to ring. In 2018, the United Kingdom published the world's first government strategy dedicated to tackling loneliness.[115] Japan followed suit in 2021, appointing a Minister of Loneliness[116] to help tackle the issue. Since then, the US has joined the ranks of countries making loneliness an official talking point for policy. Previous US Surgeon General Vivek Murthy has said that loneliness is an epidemic in the United States and a major public health concern. And finally, toward the tail end of 2023, the World Health Organization launched a commission to combat global social isolation due to the paucity of social connections and increase in loneliness—the subjective experience of lacking meaningful relationships.

The German humanistic philosopher and psychologist Erich Fromm further diagnosed the central malady of materialism in his pioneering treatise on the tradeoffs between having and being: "The full humanization of man requires the breakthrough from the possession-centered to the activity-centered orientation, from selfishness and egotism to solidarity and altruism."[117]

4. PRIDE TRANSFORMED INTO HUMILITY

> *"WITH PRIDE, THERE ARE MANY CURSES. WITH HUMILITY, THERE COME MANY BLESSINGS."*
>
> ***—EZRA TAFT BENSON***
>
> *"HUMILITY IS THE SOLID FOUNDATION OF ALL VIRTUES."*
>
> ***—CONFUCIUS***

This transformation follows naturally from the prior ones. As miraculous as our bodies are, we are nonentities in the cosmic sense. We had no role in creating this miracle of the universe. In addition, when we focus on the universe's vastness, it raises an existential question about our place in the cosmos, resulting in a humble acknowledgment of our limited importance in the cosmic sense or even as one person among a collective human species, currently eight billion strong.

Nature is the first teacher of humility. We stand dwarfed by ancient redwoods, humbled by their timeless presence. We witness the destructive force of a hurricane or the unstoppable flow of a glacier, acknowledging our own fragility in the face of these powerful forces. The universe itself, stretching back billions of years and encompassing countless galaxies, dwarfs our human experience and reminds us of the impermanence of our existence.

There is no scope left for our egos after such awareness. Humility is not an option; it's a basic truth of our existence. Cultivating humility is not a sign of weakness but rather a testament to one's strength of character and commitment to continuous growth and collective well-being. In today's fast-paced, competitive world, where self-promotion and individualism often take precedence, humility is often overshadowed by the drive for success, recognition, and personal achievement.

Humility is the antidote to arrogance. It paves the way for learning and growth. By acknowledging that we don't possess all the answers, we open ourselves to valuable lessons from others. In essence, humility strengthens our connection to others and fuels our lifelong journey of learning. This quote from C. S. Lewis is a good guide for remaining a humble person: "True humility is not thinking less of yourself, but thinking of yourself less."[118]

Many philosophical and religious traditions emphasize humility as a key virtue. In Christianity, humility is seen as a pathway to grace and spiritual growth. In Buddhism, it is associated with the abandonment of ego and the pursuit of enlightenment.

5. JUDGMENT TRANSFORMED INTO COMPASSION

> *"LOVE IS THE ABSENCE OF JUDGEMENT."*
>
> ***—DALAI LAMA***
>
> *"JUDGE NOT, THAT YE BE NOT JUDGED."*
>
> ***—JESUS CHRIST, MATTHEW 7:1***

We judge situations, people, and even ourselves, often without fully understanding the underlying factors that shape actions and behaviors. Often, this judgment stems from fear—fear of the unknown, fear of difference, fear of our own perceived inadequacies. By understanding these underlying emotions through conscious effort, we can begin to dismantle their power and create space for more compassionate responses. This self-reflection is not a one-time event but a continuous process, a gentle and honest exploration of our inner landscape.

Some of the world's greatest minds valued compassion above almost all else. "Compassion is the keen awareness of the interdependence of all things," said Thomas Merton.[119] "Compassion is the basis of morality," said Arthur Schopenhauer.[120] "And in Einstein's words, "Our task must be to free ourselves from this prison by widening our circle of compassion to embrace all living creatures and the whole of nature in its beauty."[121]

Furthermore, conscious living encourages us to extend our awareness beyond ourselves and to cultivate empathy for others. It requires actively listening, not just to the words spoken but also to the unspoken emotions and experiences that lie beneath. This involves challenging our assumptions and recognizing that everyone is on their own unique journey, brought up in their unique narratives, facing their own unique set of challenges. By consciously choosing to see the world through the eyes of another, we begin to break down the barriers of separation and cultivate genuine connection. As Einstein said,

> *"A HUMAN BEING IS A PART OF THE WHOLE CALLED BY US UNIVERSE, A PART LIMITED IN TIME AND SPACE. HE EXPERIENCES HIMSELF, HIS THOUGHTS AND FEELINGS AS SOMETHING SEPARATED FROM THE REST, A KIND OF OPTICAL DELUSION OF HIS CONSCIOUSNESS. THIS DELUSION IS A KIND OF PRISON FOR US, RESTRICTING US TO OUR PERSONAL DESIRES AND TO AFFECTION FOR A FEW PERSONS NEAREST TO US. OUR TASK MUST BE TO FREE OURSELVES FROM THIS PRISON BY WIDENING OUR CIRCLE OF COMPASSION TO EMBRACE ALL LIVING CREATURES AND THE WHOLE OF NATURE IN ITS BEAUTY."*[122]

The transformation from judgment to compassion is not always easy. It requires consistent effort; however, the rewards are immeasurable. A more compassionate world is a more just and peaceful world. Ultimately, the journey from judgment to compassion is a journey toward greater understanding, connection, kindness, and love, both for ourselves and for all beings. As Mother Teresa said, "If you judge people, you have no time to love them."[123]

"But compassion also asks us to go where it hurts, enter into the places of pain, and share in brokenness, fear, confusion, and anguish," said the writer and theologian Henri Nouwen.[124] Compassion requires us to be weak with the weak, vulnerable with the vulnerable, and feel powerless with the powerless. "Compassion means complete immersion in the condition of being human."[125]

Neuroscience provides valuable insights into the neural basis of empathy and compassion. By understanding how our brains are wired for these prosocial emotions, we can gain a deeper appreciation for their importance in human connection and well-being. Neuroplasticity research suggests that cultivating empathy and compassion through practices such as mindfulness can strengthen these neural pathways, fostering greater interconnectedness and resilience. This neuroscientific perspective moves us beyond abstract concepts, demonstrating that empathy and compassion are not merely desirable traits but fundamental aspects of our biological makeup, essential for both individual and collective flourishing.

The Dalai Lama has been engaging with the community of neuroscientists to find the commonalities between Buddhism and neuroscience. "Love and compassion are necessities, not luxuries," he says. "Without them, humanity cannot survive. The purpose of our lives is to be happy. For this, we need inner peace. Such peace requires concern for others—in other words, compassion."[126]

6. SELF-DOUBT TRANSFORMED INTO SELF-LOVE

> *"YOU ARE WORTHY OF YOUR OWN AFFECTION."*
>
> ***—THE BUDDHA***
>
> *"YOU ARE IMPERFECT, PERMANENTLY AND INEVITABLY FLAWED. AND YOU ARE BEAUTIFUL."*
>
> ***—AMY BLOOM***

The journey from judging others to understanding them inevitably turns inward, fostering self-compassion and overcoming self-judgment. As we extend empathy and kindness to those around us, we begin to recognize that we, too, are deserving of the same understanding. We realize that we are not perfect, that we make mistakes, and that these imperfections are a part of the human experience. Just as we offer compassion to others struggling with challenges, we learn to offer it to ourselves when faced with our own shortcomings. This shift from self-judgment to self-compassion is not about excusing our mistakes but rather about acknowledging them with honesty and understanding, allowing us to learn and grow without the added burden of self-hatred.

Self-compassion acts as a buffer against stress, anxiety, and depression. When we treat ourselves with kindness, we are more resilient in the face of adversity. By nurturing self-compassion, we create a foundation of inner strength and stability, enabling us to navigate the challenges of life with greater ease and grace.

Lao-tzu reinforces Buddha's wisdom: "Because one believes in oneself, one doesn't try to convince others. Because one is content with oneself, one doesn't need others' approval. Because one accepts oneself, the whole world accepts him or her."

One person who symbolizes a journey to self-compassion is Jane Chen, an MBA graduate from Stanford's Graduate School of Business. As a fellow Stanford alum, I've had the privilege of knowing Jane, witnessing her navigate both professional triumphs and personal challenges. Her path has been anything but linear—a true roller coaster of highs and lows. She is the cofounder of Embrace, a remarkable social enterprise that developed a low-cost infant warmer designed to save the lives of premature and low-birth-weight babies in developing countries. The impact of Embrace has been staggering, with its infant warmers having saved over two hundred thousand babies in twenty-five countries.[127]

However, this incredible achievement didn't come without its share of struggles. Jane's story, as featured in the Stanford Graduate

School of Business magazine, *Stanford Business*, is a testament to resilience, innovation, and the power of self-compassion in the face of adversity. She openly shared her experiences, the setbacks, the doubts, and the moments of near despair, revealing the human side of building something so impactful. It's a reminder that even those who achieve extraordinary things often grapple with self-doubt and that cultivating kindness toward oneself is an essential part of the journey. Jane's vulnerability in sharing her story offers a powerful example of how self-compassion can fuel perseverance and ultimately lead to making a profound difference in the world.

"I began to learn self-compassion for the first time when I learned the true resilience comes from finding an inner sense of self-worth. I realize I'm enough, regardless of my achievements or failures," Jane said.[128] She started her journey to embrace babies, and she ended up on a path of self-discovery and healing so that she could also learn to embrace herself. The key sentence here is, "I am enough."

For some people, these forms of self-judgment are crippling to their self-esteem, but no one is completely free of them. If you are honestly asked to make a list of all the times you've failed, fallen short, let other people down, and felt disappointed in yourself, the exercise would be very depressing. Accepting yourself the way you are can be accomplished by this next transformation.

Quite often, we suffer because we compare reality to our wishes and expectations. Many times, the gap between what we expect and what we get is a circumstance that we could not anticipate or control. There are so many forces that determine the outcomes in our lives. We can't control most of them, starting from who we are born to. One of the most insightful quotes on the topic is from Protestant theologian Reinhold Niebuhr, who also served as a visiting professor at both Harvard and Princeton and is often cited as being the creator of the

Serenity Prayer. The quote comes from the Serenity Prayer: "God, grant me the serenity to accept the things I cannot change, the courage to change the things I can, and the wisdom to know the difference."[129]

7. FEELING OF LACK TRANSFORMED INTO GRATITUDE

> *"GRATITUDE TURNS WHAT WE HAVE INTO ENOUGH."*
>
> ***—AESOP***
>
> *"THE ROOT OF GOODNESS IS GRATITUDE."*
>
> ***—THE BUDDHA***

Self-acceptance leads to gratitude in many ways. I think anyone who's ever been seriously ill says, "Why me? Why now? Why this?" But there are no answers, are there? We learn, with difficulty, with grace, that our suffering is itself the answer. It shapes and molds us into full, whole things. Our scars, too, are our gifts—we should respect them. Then we gain what we cannot otherwise have: empathy, courage, wisdom, gratitude for who we are, liberation from the impossibly heavy burdens of perfection. As Thich Nhat Hanh said, "The art of happiness is also the art of suffering well. When we learn to acknowledge, embrace and understand our suffering, we suffer much less. Not only that, but we can also go further and transform our suffering into understanding, compassion, and joy for ourselves and others."[130]

It's more than just saying thank you. It's a deep appreciation for the good in our lives, both big and small. Cultivating gratitude shifts our focus from what we lack to what we have, fostering contentment; reducing feelings of envy or dissatisfaction holds the key to unlocking a more fulfilling and joyful life. It's about recognizing the kindness of others, the beauty of nature, and even the lessons learned from challenges.

Practicing gratitude can be transformative. It can improve our mental and physical well-being by reducing stress, boosting mood, and even strengthening our immune system. "Feeling grateful activates regions of the brain associated with emotional regulation and reward, such as the prefrontal cortex and ventral striatum."[131] Gratitude also strengthens our relationships. Expressing appreciation to others reinforces bonds and creates a positive cycle of giving and receiving. It reminds us of the interconnectedness of human experience and the value of connection. Additionally, gratitude toward others increases activity in social dopamine circuits, which makes social interactions more enjoyable.

Cultivating gratitude isn't about ignoring the difficulties we face. Instead, it's about finding balance, acknowledging the challenges while simultaneously recognizing the strength, resilience, and support that help us navigate them. Even in difficult times, there are often glimmers of light—a supportive friend, a moment of beauty, a lesson learned. During the Friday the 13th mini-crash in 1989, I lost almost all my wealth. I got a call from two of my friends offering to wire me funds. I knew they were my close friends, but I was so deeply touched by those gestures. The joy of knowing the depth of my friendship completely negated the sadness of losing my wealth. By focusing on these glimmers, we can find hope and resilience even amid adversity. Whether through journaling, expressing thanks to others, or simply taking a moment to appreciate the present moment, making gratitude a daily practice can profoundly impact our lives, leading to greater happiness, resilience, and connection.

The German sociologist Georg Simmel said, "Gratitude is the moral memory of mankind."[132] It is also the result of us acknowledging that we are a combination of trillions of protons and electrons that have become this magical entity that enjoys the most basic things in life. Think of new things as much as possible. You'll soon see that even on your worst day, there are an infinite number of things already happening that are positive.

8. ROBOTICISM TRANSFORMED INTO AUTHENTICITY

> *"TO BE YOURSELF IN A WORLD THAT IS CONSTANTLY TRYING TO MAKE YOU SOMETHING ELSE IS THE GREATEST ACCOMPLISHMENT."*
> ***—RALPH WALDO EMERSON***
> *"THE GOAL OF LIFE IS TO MAKE YOUR HEARTBEAT MATCH THE BEAT OF THE UNIVERSE, TO MATCH YOUR NATURE WITH NATURE."*
> ***—JOSEPH CAMPBELL***

Modern life, with our hyper-connected and consumer-driven world, its relentless pace, and technological enticements, often resembles a robotic existence. Most of us are programmed by algorithms, driven by deadlines, and compelled by societal expectations, leaving little room for our sense of authenticity.

The automation of our daily routines is a prime example of this robotic existence. We wake to the insistent buzz of a programmed alarm, navigate traffic with the aid of GPS, and spend our days responding to a barrage of digital notifications. Our social interactions are often mediated by screens, leading to a superficial connection that lacks the depth of genuine human interaction.

Furthermore, the influence of social media has fostered a culture of comparison and validation-seeking. We curate our online personas, striving to project an image of perfection that often bears little resemblance to our true selves. This constant performance of an idealized self creates a sense of detachment from our own inner reality, leading to a profound sense of inauthenticity. We become enslaved by the approval of others, sacrificing our own values and desires in the process. Laurie Santos observes, "Yale students reported that they 'put on a happy persona to hold things in until they crack and break' and that 'it takes a real crisis for us to actually admit something is wrong.'"[133]

However, we can reclaim our authenticity by living consciously and observing our compulsive behaviors. Carl Jung wrote, "The psychological rule says that when an inner situation is not made conscious, it happens outside, as fate. That is to say, when the individual remains undivided and does not become conscious of his inner opposite, the world must perforce act out the conflict and be torn into opposing halves."[134]

This involves questioning the narratives we have internalized and the societal expectations that dictate our choices, cultivating mindfulness, paying attention to the present moment, and becoming aware of our thoughts, emotions, and actions.

The economy has become our human-made ecosystem. Propelled by technological innovations, it has evolved much more quickly than our brains have developed the capacity to recognize the threats it poses to us. Disconnected from nature, we've become unmoored from the primal relationship that, since the beginning of time, has been a trustworthy source of cues for our survival.

In his prescient 1985 book, *Amusing Ourselves to Death*, media critic Neil Postman stated, "Americans no longer talk to each other, they entertain each other. They do not exchange ideas, they exchange images. They do not argue with propositions; they argue with good looks, celebrities, and commercials."[135] The best antidote is to turn off the TV or your phone and focus on being your authentic self.

Oprah Winfrey said, "There is a sacred calling in your life, and the question is: Will you spend your life fluttering and fluttering about, or take the time and really heed that call and create your own path to your highest good? You cannot let other people define your life for you. You are the author of your own life … Real power is when you are doing exactly what you are supposed to be doing, the best it can be done. Authentic power."[136]

As we have seen, these false narratives can come to govern our lives and all our decisions. The real test of intelligence is the degree to which you are willing to nonconform in order to do the right thing. "I wish I'd had the courage to live a life true to myself, not the life others expected of me."[137] This was the biggest regret in Bronnie Ware's 2011 book, *The Top Five Regrets of the Dying*. We are deeply and widely interconnected, and yet we are unique. The purpose of life is to play on that uniqueness in harmony with the world.

9. EXTERNALLY DRIVEN TRANSFORMED INTO INTERNALLY DRIVEN

> *"LET ONE CULTIVATE A BOUNDLESS HEART TOWARD ALL BEINGS. LET ONE RADIATE BOUNDLESS LOVE ABOVE, BELOW, AND ACROSS—UNHINDERED, WITHOUT ILL WILL, WITHOUT ENMITY."*
>
> ***—BUDDHISM***
>
> *"NOTHING CAN BRING YOU PEACE BUT YOURSELF."*
>
> ***—RALPH WALDO EMERSON***

You are internally driven if you are aware of the forces trying to make you what you are not, telling you how you are inadequate, and creating FOMO (fear of missing out). When we turn inward to seek answers to the mystery of life, we eventually discover ourselves to be the blissful consciousness that is all and everything. We are no longer limited by the illusion of separation. We live in the fulfillment of the primary intention in consciousness—to be fully itself.

This concept of going inside to find the big answers is universal. Luke 17:21 quotes Jesus as saying, "The kingdom of God is within you." Well, you don't enter that kingdom by listening to the cacophony of chatter spewed out by your conceptualizing mind. You get there by focusing within, as you do with the Tao, by entering the state of no-thought, or still presence, as Eckhart Tolle calls it.[138] In other words, you sense the Tao/God/consciousness. The Tao Te Ching asks, "Can you step back from your own mind and thus understand all things?"[139] So, how does one come to understand the Tao? By sensing, by feeling.

So many of us often live in a sort of waking dream, never quite understanding ourselves, why we are here, and how we are all connected. Like leaves in the wind, we get blown around by whatever comes at us, instead of questioning why things are the way they are. "Your visions will become clear only when you can look into your own heart," said Carl Jung. "Who looks outside, dreams; who looks inside, awakes."[140]

In moments of solitude, we can peel back the layers of societal expectations, external influences, and the roles we play in various relationships. Introspection can lead to a deeper understanding of our values, beliefs, strengths, weaknesses, and aspirations. Through introspection and contemplation, we gain a clearer perspective on our motivations, desires, and the paths we wish to pursue. Just as a caterpillar undergoes a metamorphosis to become a butterfly through internal change, we, too, must undergo a transformation to reach our highest potential. "Within you, there is a stillness and a sanctuary to which you can retreat at any time and be yourself."[141] With this simple reminder, the German poet Hermann Hesse argues that the existential answers to life and our happiness can be found within us.

I was discussing with Sara Al-Zubi, the teaching fellow for Professor Susan Rinard's happiness class at Harvard, about her experiences teaching happiness to Harvard undergraduates. She described a conversation she was happiest with: "One of my students once stayed after class to ask, 'How do you find inner peace?' I wish I had an answer. But, for a first-semester college student, I couldn't be more proud of them for thinking of this question. This is exactly the beginning of a longer life journey."

10. DISTRACTION TRANSFORMED INTO FOCUS

> *"THE QUIETER YOU BECOME, THE MORE YOU ARE ABLE TO HEAR."*
>
> ***—RAM DASS***
>
> *"TO STILL THE MIND IS TO ARRIVE AT THE DOOR OF THE UNIVERSE."*
>
> ***—LAO-TZU***

The human mind has always grappled with the challenge of focus. Even before the advent of the internet and smartphones, one's inner world was a landscape of competing thoughts, desires, and anxieties. Distractions weren't always external; they often arose from within, from the constant chatter of the ego and the pull of unresolved emotions. The industrial revolution, urbanization, and the rise of mass communication all exacerbated this problem.

Diminished attention leads to diminished caring, say many wisdom traditions. When we do not care or feel cared for, we suffer. How do we filter out the noise and distraction, overcome inertia, and tackle other obstacles to design the lives we want? How can we regain some control and switch on our innate ability to focus on what matters most while still living amid the cacophony of modern life?

One of the coping responses in America has been the penetration of yoga, which has become popular in the country over the last twenty-five years. I remember when I moved to New York City in 1997 and joined Equinox gym, I used to take yoga classes. When I shared with my American friends what I was doing, they accepted that I was an Indian doing weird things. Today, yoga classes have flooded all workout centers, and you can't get a spot in any of the New York City gym yoga classes if you are late.

The practice of yoga goes back five thousand years, to northern India, where the word yoga was first mentioned in ancient sacred texts called the *Rig Veda*.[142] The Vedas are a set of four ancient sacred texts written in Sanskrit. In the US, yoga has been adapted and popularized with a focus on the physical aspects to make it accessible to a wider audience. This emphasis on physical fitness has led to the proliferation of various yoga styles, such as Vinyasa yoga and Power Yoga, which prioritize strength, flexibility, and cardiovascular health. While in the US it's often perceived as a form of exercise for physical well-being, its essence goes beyond the postures and stretches. Yoga is a holistic practice that integrates physical, mental, and spiritual elements.

There is a growing movement within the US yoga community to integrate these deeper dimensions into the practice. Many studios and teachers now offer classes that incorporate meditation, breathwork, and yoga philosophy, encouraging students to explore its holistic nature. This integration can lead to a more profound and meaningful experience, allowing individuals to tap into the full potential of yoga for overall well-being.

"Attention is the most powerful tool of the human spirit," argues Linda Stone. "We can enhance or augment our attention with practices like meditation, breathwork, and exercise, diffuse it with technologies like email, texting, and social media, or alter it with pharmaceuticals. In the end, though, we are fully responsible for how we choose to use this extraordinary resource."[143]

"The most precious gift we can offer anyone is our attention," agrees Thich Nhat Hanh.[144] When a mindful person embraces someone they love, they will both bloom like flowers. Shunryu Suzuki, the Zen Buddhist monk, explains how focus can be cultivated through meditation: "The state of mind that exists when you sit in the right posture is, itself, enlightenment. If you cannot be satisfied with the state of mind you have in *zazen*, it means your mind is still wandering about. Our body and mind should not be wobbling or wandering about. In this posture, there is no need to talk about the right state of mind. You already have it. This is the essence of Buddhism."[145]

Says Erich Fromm: "The most important step in learning concentration is to learn to be alone with oneself without reading, or listening to the radio, or smoking or drinking. Indeed, to be able to concentrate means to be able to be alone with oneself—and this ability is precisely a condition for the ability to love."[146]

The lack of focus among the distracted lifestyle of so many people is epidemic nowadays. But it is not a new problem: Back in the seventeenth century, French philosopher and mathematician Blaise Pascal wrote: "All of humanity's problems stem from man's inability to sit quietly in a room alone."[147]

Author Michael Singer recommends not only letting go of all distractions but also clearing your mind of all assumptions and thoughts: "Let go of who you think you are to discover a deeper you. Rediscover the miraculous nature of every unfolding moment. End the struggle with a noisy mind once and for all. Release inner blockages and old emotions. Keep the heart open. Go beyond yourself to live from a place of surrender to the flow of life. Live in harmony with that flow."[148]

II. FEAR TRANSFORMED INTO CURIOSITY

> *"CURIOSITY WILL CONQUER FEAR EVEN MORE THAN BRAVERY WILL."*
>
> ***—JAMES STEPHENS***
>
> *"THE ONLY WAY TO MAKE SENSE OUT OF CHANGE IS TO PLUNGE INTO IT, MOVE WITH IT, AND JOIN THE DANCE."*
>
> ***—ALAN WATTS***

Fear is one of the predominant human emotions, and I do not mean to trifle with it. After all, it serves an evolutionary purpose. Early humans and their earlier ancestors survived because they knew to fear giant animals that could kill them in an instant. It is the natural and appropriate response to a saber-toothed tiger coming at you, but there's a difference between a real tiger and the one in your head. In the modern world, the chances are pretty low that a saber-toothed tiger is waiting outside the entrance to your home to eat you. Yet, if that occurrence were suggested enough by marketers or politicians, they could easily implant that very fear into your mind.

These manufactured fears are everywhere. Manufacturing fear works, and it does almost every time, no matter how absurd it seems. During the US presidential campaign in 2024, many people laughed when they heard that immigrants were coming to eat people's pets, because it was absurd. Others became instantly fearful that their pets were going to be eaten by immigrants.

How can you negotiate both rational and irrational fear? How do you get rid of the monsters in your head? After being tormented by his fear of failure and never being enough, Jim Carrey did it by painting, putting the monsters on the canvas. He created some dark images, some of which he shared with others, but at that point, they were fantastical and imaginative. In other words, they became art. That's a transformation right there, and the power of the human mind: to take your thoughts and channel them into new conclusions.

The transformative power of the human mind is wondrous—so much so that fear itself can be transformed into curiosity and even wonder. "The cave you fear to enter holds the treasure you seek," said Joseph Campbell.[149]

Indeed, the visionary mind is capable of reaching new epiphanies about almost anything. William Blake, the English poet and printmaker, had them on a regular basis. There's his famous poem, "Auguries of Innocence," that opens with, "To see a World in a Grain of Sand / And a Heaven in a Wild Flower / Hold Infinity in the palm of your hand / And Eternity in an hour."[150]

Fear can transform into a state of curiosity and wonder, like that of a child. "The important thing is not to stop questioning. Curiosity has its own reason for existing," said Albert Einstein.[151] "In the modern world, however, the spirit of wonder and awe has been succeeded by one of sophistication. Today, man worships his own accomplishments, and either relegates the immensities of time and space to the background of his consciousness or disregards them entirely," writes Manly P. Hall in his book *The Secret Teachings of All Ages.*[152]

Perhaps the best way to encounter wonder and awe is by being out in nature. Trailblazing marine biologist Rachel Carson encouraged her readers to consciously cultivate habits of awe, to pay careful attention to the often-overlooked beauties and mysterious rhythms of the natural world. "We look too hastily," she lamented. "People everywhere are desperately eager for whatever will lift them out of themselves and allow them to believe in the future."[153]

Awe is also the wonder we feel when we contemplate the mystery of ourselves and nature. This can help people to cut through self-critical, ruminative thinking and to look beyond their daily concerns so that those concerns no longer make such a dent in their well-being. Wonder and awe are the starting point of transformation.

We started our transformation toolset with wonder and awe, and, appropriately, we're now ending with it. Having explored the reasons why happiness often eludes us and the deceptive narratives that shape our understanding of it, we've established the groundwork for a more conscious and intentional approach to living. It's clear that genuine fulfillment requires a shift in perspective, a move away from passively accepting societal definitions of happiness and toward actively cultivating a mindset that prioritizes our authentic selves.

PART II

DECONSTRUCTING HAPPINESS

CHAPTER FOUR

THE FOUR DIMENSIONS OF SELF AND HAPPINESS

> *"ALL THE GREAT THINKERS OF HUMANITY HAVE LEFT HAPPINESS IN THE VAGUENESS SO THAT EACH OF THEM COULD DEFINE THEIR OWN TERMS."*
> **—HENRI BERGSON, FRENCH PHILOSOPHER**

Not only has the concept of "happiness" changed throughout history, but it can also mean different things to different people at different stages in their lives. From fleeting moments of pleasure to a state of contentment to a sense of meaning and purpose and even spiritual enlightenment. Many one-size-fits-all approaches have been proposed, and they all have more than their fair share of limitations and pitfalls. To steer clear of them, we'll take a closer look at some of the sources of differences that influence how we experience and define happiness.

Who we are and how we derive meaning are fundamental components of happiness that are essential for understanding all the other points of contrast. Cultural differences, meanwhile, are the result of different permutations of collective meaning-making. Worldviews, metanarratives, vocations, and temperaments all influence how meaning-making manifests itself as we move through life. This, in turn, determines how our stances on happiness change over time.

Let's draw connections across time, culture, religion, philosophy, and science to understand our concepts of happiness better.

DIMENSIONS OF SELF AND LEVELS OF HAPPINESS

Some of the most profound insights into understanding happiness come from building a strong foundation of self-exploration. We can better understand who we are by deconstructing the human into a few key parts of selfhood. Different wisdom traditions and philosophical and belief systems offer very different takes on the age-old question, "Who am I?" This is a crucial question when it comes to understanding happiness because, as author Roy T. Bennett points out, "If you don't know who you truly are, you'll never know what you really want."[154] So if we want to understand the differences in conceptions of happiness, we must understand differences in how we conceive of who we are in the first place.

On one end of the spectrum, we have essentialism, which tells us that our purpose is defined by God as explained to us in different scriptures or by different prophets and as interpreted by their respective disciples and priests. On the other end is nihilism, which postulates that life has no meaning. Modern science tells us that we are just dust from the big bang dating back thirteen billion years. Therefore, we are all subject to the laws of physics, sparking debates over whether we could have any free will or purpose, or indeed whether these are relevant questions at all. The twenty-first-century seeker finds themself disillusioned with both ancient dogmas and modern materialist nihilism. As Jiddu Krishnamurti said, "It is no measure of health to be well adjusted to a profoundly sick society."[155] Increasingly, people are seeking spiritual autonomy and experiential wisdom, not inherited beliefs.

Hinduism, at the other extreme, says, "You are That," meaning you are the manifestation of the ultimate reality and potentially divine. I am sure you are confused now as to what you should believe.

Let us try to understand this complex matter from first principles. In 2023, I attended a deep dive on education at Harvard's Advanced Leadership Initiative program. Michael Ferguson, instructor of neurology at Harvard Medical School, was giving a talk titled "Education and the Self." He started by asking, "What do you think of when you think of self?" I opened my notes on this subject, and he projected the slide. I was amazed because it looked as if I had projected my Apple notebook page onto the screen.

The self encompasses the body, the mind, the social self, and the transcendent self. These four dimensions correspond to at least four different levels at which happiness is experienced. To find fulfillment in life, we need to cater to all parts of ourselves. The relative importance of each level varies across different stages of our lives. Many happiness prescriptions fail, as they do not address all four dimensions.

THE BODY/PHYSICAL WELL-BEING

The body, as the physical manifestation of the self, is the immediate and tangible vessel through which we experience the world. It is the sensory gateway, the instrument of action, and the biological foundation of our existence and emotions. As David Abram said in his book *The Spell of the Sensuous*, "Humans are tuned for relationships. The eyes, the skin, the tongue, ears, and nostrils—all are gates where our body receives the nourishment of otherness."[156]

Beyond its mere physicality, the body is deeply intertwined with our emotional and mental states. It is an active participant in our interactions with the world. It is the site of pleasure and pain, of strength and vulnerability, of growth and decay. It is a repository of memories and experiences, both conscious and unconscious.

Physical health and well-being directly influence our cognitive function, emotional stability, and overall sense of vitality. Indeed, our bodies, with their unique features and capabilities, shape our experiences and provide a basis for self-expression. By caring for and nourishing them through healthy practices, we can enhance our overall well-being.

Happiness is certainly influenced by the extent to which we take care of our bodies. Proper care, a balanced diet, regular exercise, and avoiding harmful substances are crucial for supporting our health and functionality. Sensual pleasures, culinary delights, and relaxation methods all lead to physical well-being and bodily happiness.

THE MIND/MENTAL WELL-BEING

It is through the mind that we make sense of the world around us. It is the processing center that interprets sensory input, generates thoughts and feelings, and directs our actions. It is not a passive receiver of information; it actively constructs our subjective reality, filtering and interpreting data through the lens of our past experiences, our cultural conditioning, and our individual biases. It is the source of our beliefs, values, and aspirations, and the site of self-reflection, self-awareness, and self-regulation. As John Milton said, "The mind is its own place, and in itself can make a heaven of hell, a hell of heaven."[157]

Previously, I talked about the cognitive limitations of our minds compared to the infinite reality and several cognitive biases we develop in the process of growing up that distort our perception of reality. An equally important feature of the mind that affects its performance is the internal conflict within its various constituents due to the way it is structured. In the epic of Bhagavad Gita, the physical war Arjuna faces actually symbolizes the internal battleground within each of us—the struggle to overcome our mind's negativity, doubts, and conflicting desires. This is the human struggle for clarity and inner peace.

As per the Vedic philosophy, the mind has multiple layers: There's *Mana*, the sensory mind, which processes immediate perceptions. There's *Ahamkara*, the ego or sense of "I." There's *Citta*, the memory and subconscious mind. There's *Buddhi*, the intellect and reasoning faculty. And, finally, we may reach *Atman*, the higher, authentic self, or soul, considered the observer of the mind.[158] We can observe all these layers ourselves, as each performs the mind's varied functions. I am sure you have experienced these conflicts yourself.

In "The Lonely Man of Faith," Rabbi Joseph B. Soloveitchik explores the tension between two aspects of human nature that he identifies in the biblical Adam: the creative, majestic side (Adam I) that seeks to master the world and the spiritual, covenantal side (Adam II) that seeks communion with God. The work draws on both Jewish religious thought and existentialist philosophy to examine the religious person's experience in the modern world.[159]

Scientific research from diverse fields such as cognitive psychology, neuroscience, and evolutionary biology also posits that the mind is composed of modules, each dedicated to specific functions, and that these domains operate with a degree of independence. They all have their own agendas that often come into conflict with one another; just as our smartphone apps vie for attention through notifications, different modules of our mind compete for our awareness. As Sam Harris says, "You are not in control of your mind—because you, as a conscious agent, are only part of your mind, living at the mercy of other parts."[160] In Eastern philosophy, mind and consciousness are two different entities, however.

While the smartphone analogy illuminates many aspects of the mind's functioning, it also reveals its limitations. Unlike a device, even one equipped with advanced AI, the mind has the capacity to transcend its programming, achieve states of pure awareness beyond all apps, experience consciousness without content, transform its own operating system, and connect directly with universal consciousness. The mind, even amid the cacophony of modern life, possesses a remarkable capacity for self-regulation and growth. Neuroplasticity, the brain's ability to rewire itself, allows for the formation of new neural pathways, effectively rewriting old, negative patterns. In Dr. Joe Dispenza's book, which combines findings from neuroscience, quantum physics, and genetics, he explores how people can change their habits, behaviors, and, ultimately, their lives by understanding and reshaping their thought patterns. Dr. Dispenza is known for his work on the connection between mind and matter and how mental processes can affect physical health and personal transformation.[161]

A chariot allegory from ancient India's Hindu *Katha Upanishad* emphasizes the importance of self-control through our mind, discipline, and wisdom in navigating life's challenges. The chariot symbolizes the physical body. The five horses represent the five senses: sight, sound, smell, taste, and touch. They symbolize the desires and impulses that can pull us in different directions, like the different apps on a smartphone. The reins represent the mind and symbolize the control and direction of thoughts and emotions. The charioteer represents the intellect or the higher self, symbolizing wisdom, reason, and the power of discernment. The charioteer uses the reins to guide the horses, signifying the intellect's control over the mind. The passenger represents the true self that is experiencing the journey of life.

This metaphor highlights the need for the mind to rein in our senses and desires, rather than being controlled by them. Every external stimulus, relevant or irrelevant in our life, creates a series of mental processes, often confusing the individual, underscoring the role of the intellect in guiding our actions and decisions. Every thought has an agenda created by different wants, urges, fears, desires, wishes, aspirations, intentions, and emotions. Our happiness depends on the harmonious functioning of our mind, which depends on how the various parts function as well as the management process (our mental habits). As James Allen said, "Man's mind may be likened to a garden, which may be intelligently cultivated or allowed to run wild."[162] So, to fully flourish, we should appoint our authentic self, rather than our socialized self, as the charioteer. The search for meaning and purpose is not external but rather an internal journey of the mind.

We can break down mental happiness into the affective (emotional) aspect and the cognitive aspect. The affective aspect refers to the emotional experience and subjective feelings associated with it, such as joy, contentment, pleasure, excitement, and satisfaction. The cognitive aspect involves the evaluations and judgments individuals make about their lives and well-being, which includes comparing one's current life circumstances and achievements to internalized standards and aspirations. Happiness is our subjective judgment of our objective reality. We normally return to our baseline level of happiness after big ups or downs. The base level varies from person to person, and many believe it is determined by genetics. However, Deepak Chopra emphasizes the role of epigenetics, the study of how environmental and behavioral factors can influence gene expression without altering the underlying DNA sequence. He argues that our thoughts, emotions, and experiences, including those cultivated through meditation, can directly impact which genes are turned on or off.[163]

Another dimension on which happiness can be understood is that proposed by Daniel Kahneman, who argues that we have two selves: the "experiencing self" and the "remembering self."[164] These two selves often have conflicting interests, which can lead to confusion about what truly makes us happy. The remembering self often dominates our decisions, leading us to prioritize experiences that will create good memories, even if they don't maximize our moment-to-moment happiness. This can lead to situations where we pursue experiences for the sake of the story we'll tell, rather than the enjoyment we'll have in the moment.

Essentially, the remembering self is the one that makes decisions, but the experiencing self is the one that lives through those decisions. Therefore, to obtain a more complete sense of happiness, it is important to try to balance the needs of both selves—to enjoy the moments of life, and to also have good memories of those moments.

We can also help keep our minds healthy through physical exercise, mental exercise (such as reading or doing puzzles), a balanced diet, adequate sleep, limiting substance use, limiting screen time, engaging in hobbies and other things that bring us joy, and maintaining healthy social relationships. Cultivating mindfulness, practicing meditation, and engaging in cognitive exercises can enhance our mental clarity, emotional resilience, and overall well-being.

The interplay between the body and the mind is a dynamic and reciprocal process. Physical sensations can trigger emotional responses, and mental states can influence physiological functions. Recognizing the interconnectedness of these two dimensions is crucial for cultivating a holistic understanding of the self.

Social scientists have also found that emotions can be reeducated through conscious decisions and actions. Put simply, if you want to feel differently, act as if you do. This principle, often referred to as the "as-if effect,"[165] suggests that acting "as if" you possess a desired quality or are in a desired state, you can actually bring about that feeling or outcome. As Laurie Santos of Yale says, "We think that happiness is about our circumstances ... but, really, happiness stems from our behaviors."[166] And a related idea is echoed by Michael Singer: "Eventually you will see that the real cause of problems is not life itself. It's the commotion the mind makes about life that really causes problems."[167] Still, as Eckhart Tolle said, "Unhappiness is to the mind as sickness is to the body. It is a state of disharmony and imbalance. It is a signal that something is amiss and requires attention."[168]

From an Eastern perspective, the mind is thought to be merely an instrument of consciousness rather than its source. Our individual minds are the way consciousness is manifested in living creatures, but consciousness itself is a unifying force that makes us all interconnected. When viewed this way, individual cognitive happiness is inseparable from collective or social happiness.

THE SOCIAL SELF

The important insight we gain when reflecting upon the social self is that we cannot survive alone—we need others. This is true on the most basic level. Our physical survival in infancy and childhood depends largely on our parents. We also need others not just to survive but also to grow and develop. Experiments and observations in developmental psychology have shown how devastating the consequences of social isolation can be for a child's development.[169] And the COVID-19 pandemic reminded us how difficult it can be to maintain well-being and happiness under circumstances of social isolation in adulthood as well.

The social self, in its essence, is the persona we present to the world, the identity constructed through our interactions with others and our roles within society. It's the sum of our relationships, our professional identities, our cultural affiliations, and the expectations placed upon us by our communities. It's how we are perceived by others, and how we, in turn, perceive ourselves within the social fabric.

This social self is not static; it is constantly evolving, shaped by our experiences and the feedback we receive from our environment. It's the student in the classroom, the parent at the playground, and the employee in the boardroom. It's the part of us that seeks belonging, recognition, and validation within our social groups. It is also the part that can be influenced by mimetic desires and external pressures. However, an overreliance on the social self can lead to a sense of superficiality, a feeling of being defined solely by external factors, and a loss of connection with our inner selves.

THE TRANSCENDENTAL SELF

Beyond the physical and interpersonal dimensions lies the realm of self that transcends all others. Philosopher Immanuel Kant posited a fundamental "transcendental self," a unifying "I" beyond empirical experience.[170] Advaita Vedanta, a school of Hindu philosophy, identifies this as *Atman*, the true self, which is identical to *Brahman*, the ultimate reality.[171] As Antoine de Saint-Exupéry wrote, "Behind all seen things lies something vaster: everything is but a path, a portal or a window opening on something other than itself."[172] The fundamental human need to see further and further beyond these various windows is tied to the transcendent self.

This concept can be explored through various spiritual practices, including yoga, prayer, meditation, contemplation, Taoist *wu wei* and *zazen*, and Buddhist *Vipassana*. According to Patanjali, achieving *chitta-vritti-nirodha* (the stilling of the fluctuations of the mind) is one of the main goals of yoga. By stilling the mind and reducing the mental chatter, one can attain a state of inner calmness, clarity, and heightened awareness. This state is often referred to as "yoga" itself, which means union or integration of the individual consciousness with the universal consciousness.[173]

Sufism adds the dimension of *fana*, the annihilation of the ego through love, leading to *baqa*, abiding in the Divine. Aboriginal spirituality shows us connection to the land, and to the ancestors, as a way to connect to the transcendental self. Conversely, it is common to see people suffer from deep existential unhappiness because they neglect or struggle to connect to this aspect.

In many traditions, the transcendental self is considered eternal, unchanging, and limitless. It is associated with concepts such as "pure awareness," cultivated through Vipassana; "cosmic consciousness," realized through Sufi union; and the "Tao," experienced through effortless alignment. According to French priest Pierre Teilhard de Chardin, "We are not physical beings with a spiritual dimension, but spiritual beings with a physical dimension."[174]

The transcendental self rises above the artificial cultural dressings and social narratives we are born into and socialized into believing. It refers to the self that is at the core of all human beings, possibly even extending beyond the physical realm to be a fundamental core of reality. The transcendental self is the part of us that seeks connection with something greater than ourselves, whether it be a spiritual or philosophical understanding of the cosmos, a sense of universal consciousness, or a profound connection to our inner reality. It is the part of us that can find peace and contentment, independent of external circumstances.

It is the search for truth and a sense of unity. As such, to the extent that there could be a one-size-fits-all solution to happiness, it would have to focus a great deal on understanding the transcendental self.

INTEGRATION AND HOLISTIC SELFHOOD

As George Vaillant said, "Putting it all together, everything I see tells me that far from being a disease, happiness is an all-too-rare condition, of short or long duration, with wonderful symptoms and not one but many causes."[175]

The many dimensions of self are all causes that impact happiness in individuals. Embracing our physicality, cultivating a mindful and self-aware mindset, fostering meaningful relationships, and exploring the transcendent realm all contribute to a more holistic and fulfilling experience of the self. Through this integration, we can unlock our true potential, finding meaning, purpose, and a deep connection to the world around us, all of which contribute to happiness. I refer to this successful integration as flourishing.

We are selling ourselves short in terms of who we are, what we can accomplish, and how much we can flourish if we do not recognize the transcendent self. Denying it may also cause us to go down a path of pursuing the wrong things in a misguided quest for happiness. For instance, when we forget our interconnectedness with the world at large, we get corrupted by selfishness, greed, jealousy, and xenophobia, which arise out of extreme forms of individualism. I believe that the three yearnings of loving, learning, and playing arise in our transcendental self to be fulfilled by the three other selves.

THE LADDER OF HAPPINESS: ASCENDING STAGES OF JOY IN VEDANTIC THOUGHT

A respected senior nun of the Ramakrishna Sarada Mission, Pravrajika Divyanandaprana offers a compelling framework for understanding happiness, not as a singular state but as a progressive journey through various levels of experience and awareness. This "ladder of happiness,"[176] as she calls it, masterfully blends ancient wisdom from the Upanishads and Vedanta with contemporary psychological insights, providing a practical road map for those seeking deeper and more lasting fulfillment. Her framework also deepens our understanding of the integration of the four components of the self, discussed above.

The first rung of this ladder is "sensory happiness" (*indriya sukha*). This is the most basic level, derived from the gratification of our senses. While these experiences are enjoyable, they are also fleeting and dependent on external stimuli. Divyanandaprana suggests that fixating on this level is like trying to quench a thirst with salt water—the satisfaction is temporary, and the craving soon returns. As the *Katha Upanishad* says, "The senses are powerful, but beyond the senses is the mind."

That brings us to the second rung, "intellectual happiness" (*mana sukha*). This state of contentment comes from engaging our minds in meaningful ways—learning, creating, problem-solving, achieving goals, and receiving praise and recognition. This type of happiness is more profound and lasting than physical happiness, as it involves the development of our cognitive abilities. As the *Amritabindu Upanishad* says, "Mind alone is the cause of bondage and liberation."

That leads us to the third rung, "emotional happiness" (*bhava sukha*). This state of bliss arises from positive thoughts and emotions and involves cultivating qualities such as love, compassion, and gratitude. This level of happiness is more enduring and deeper than mere intellectual pleasures, as it is generated from within. However, it can still be influenced by external circumstances and our reactions to them. As the *Chandogya Upanishad* says, "Where there is love, there is joy."

The fourth rung is "creative happiness" (*srijan sukha*). It results in joy from creative expression and contribution. Joy comes from being in harmony with the universe, is permanent, and has no limits at all. Often, this is described in modern psychology terminology as a state of "flow." Psychologist Mihaly Csikszentmihalyi, a pioneer in positive psychology, coined the term and studied it extensively.[177] A state of flow is a condition of deep absorption and engagement in an activity that we find challenging yet fulfilling. It is the experience of losing ourselves in the moment, where time seems to disappear and we are fully present. Flow experiences can be found in various activities, from artistic creation to athletic pursuits, and they leave us feeling energized and satisfied. In the Hindu epic Mahabharata, there is the concept of "Arjuna's eye," referring to the warrior hero who, in a state of complete focus, could see only the target and disregard everything else. This intense concentration enabled him to achieve extraordinary accuracy and precision. Across Eastern religions, flow is often equated with a state of oneness or harmony with the universe, something we now understand through modern psychology as a universal and transcendental experience. As the *Taittiriya Upanishad* says, "Creation is the expression of joy."

The fifth rung is "service" (*seva sukha*). This is the happiness that comes from selfless action, from giving back to others and making a positive impact on the world. This kind of happiness is profound and enduring, as it is rooted in our innate desire to connect and contribute.

It helps us transcend personal ego and aligns with universal dharma. As Swami Vivekananda said, "The highest service is serving humanity with humble love."

The sixth rung is "spiritual happiness" (*adhyatmik sukha*). This is how we can derive joy from spiritual practices and realizations. It's the practice of training the mind to focus and become still, allowing us to access a deeper level of awareness and inner peace. It entails practices such as meditation, prayer, and contemplation. This level of happiness is characterized by a sense of deep calm, tranquility, inner peace, and joy that arises from within. It is independent of external circumstances. It connects us to higher consciousness. As the *Taittiriya Upanishad* says, "The bliss of Brahman is supreme happiness."

The seventh and highest rung is "transcendental happiness" (*Brahmananda*). This is the state of complete union with the divine, the ultimate goal of Vedantic philosophy. It is a state of pure bliss, beyond all duality and limitation. A state of unity and oneness. It is permanent and unchanging and beyond knowing whether anything is good or bad. This experience is difficult to describe in words, as it transcends the realm of ordinary human experience. As the *Mandukya Upanishad* says, "Brahman is Bliss."

Divyanandaprana emphasizes that this ladder is not a rigid hierarchy but rather a guide for our journey toward greater happiness. We may experience different levels of happiness at different times, and we may even move up and down the ladder throughout our lives. We must acknowledge that all levels play their role in human experience and flourishing. The key is to be aware of these different levels and to strive to cultivate the higher ones, recognizing that true and lasting happiness comes from within, from connecting with our true selves and with something larger than ourselves.

NEUROSCIENCE'S SUPPORT OF THE HAPPINESS LADDER

Developments in neuroscience have revolutionized the study of brain functions, providing tangible insights into the neural mechanisms underlying happiness. Techniques such as fMRI and EEG scanning allow researchers to observe real-time brain activity, revealing how specific regions and neurotransmitters contribute to positive emotions. By mapping neural pathways and understanding the interplay of brain chemicals, neuroscience helps to demystify the biological foundations of happiness, offering a scientific framework for cultivating a more fulfilling life.

Neuroscience maps brain regions and neurochemicals linked to distinct pleasures. Physical pleasures activate the reward system (known as the nucleus accumbens) and release dopamine, a neurotransmitter associated with motivation and pleasure. This release reinforces the behavior that led to the pleasurable sensation in the first place, making us want to repeat it.

Intellectual pleasures engage higher cognitive areas such as the prefrontal cortex. When we learn, create, or solve problems, our brains release neurotransmitters such as dopamine and serotonin. In this case, dopamine may be released in anticipation of reward or satisfaction, driving curiosity and exploration. The brain seems to derive pleasure from recognizing patterns and making sense of the world. This may explain why we enjoy solving puzzles or riddles, playing chess, or learning new concepts.

Emotional pleasures involve the limbic system in areas of the brain such as the amygdala and hippocampus. Such pleasures are associated with the release of oxytocin, a hormone that promotes bonding and trust. Mirror neurons, which fire both when we perform an action and when we observe someone else performing the same action, may play a role in emotional pleasure by allowing us to empathize with others and share their feelings.

Flow states boost dopamine, norepinephrine, and endorphins, which are natural painkillers that create a sense of euphoria and well-being. Flow can strengthen neural connections, making it easier to enter flow states in the future, enhancing learning and fostering skill development.

Meditation increases gray matter and impacts neurotransmitters, including GABA (which has calming effects) and serotonin (which contributes to feelings of well-being). Meditation can decrease activity in the amygdala, the brain's fear center. This may explain why people who meditate often experience reduced anxiety and stress. The practice seems to enhance the connections between different brain regions, promoting better communication and integration of information. This may contribute to a greater sense of self-awareness and emotional regulation.

Engaging in acts of kindness and generosity can lead to a feeling of euphoria, often referred to as "the helper's high." This may be due to the release of endorphins and dopamine in the brain's reward system. Service to others often involves social interaction and connection, which can trigger the release of oxytocin, the "love hormone." Oxytocin promotes feelings of bonding, trust, and well-being.

Neuroscience also highlights the significant individual differences in how we experience pleasure. Our genes, experiences, and personalities can all influence our sensitivity to different types of pleasure. Professor Sonja Lyubomirsky's work highlights the significant role of genetics, suggesting that roughly 50 percent of self-reported happiness is heritable.[178]

This may explain why some people are more drawn to physical pleasures, while others find greater satisfaction in intellectual or emotional pursuits. Comprehending the neuroscience of pleasure is crucial for understanding addiction and other forms of dysregulated behavior. When the reward system is overstimulated, it can lead to compulsive behaviors and a decreased sensitivity to natural rewards

By combining the essences of Eastern and Western schools of thought and understanding all dimensions of the self that experience happiness, we can seek the full range of happiness and discover practical ways to increase our own well-being and the well-being of others, as we shall explore in the final part of this book.

CHAPTER FIVE

HOW MEANING-MAKING SHAPES US

> *"LIFE IS WITHOUT MEANING. YOU BRING THE MEANING TO IT. THE MEANING OF LIFE IS WHATEVER YOU ASCRIBE IT TO BE."*
> **—JOSEPH CAMPBELL**

Experience, as many great storytellers have pointed out, is not so much what happens to us as what we make of what happens to us. Therefore, two people observing the same thing can, through their differing interpretations, essentially create two distinct realities of that occurrence, even when they agree on the basic facts. In other words, they make meaning differently.

In order to understand how differences in meaning-making result in different conceptions of happiness, it is important to first understand what meaning-making is. Robert Kegan, a recently retired professor at the Harvard University Graduate School of Education, writes in *The Evolving Self* (1982) that, "It is not that a person makes meaning, as much as that activity of being a person is the activity of meaning making."[179]

"Meaning-making" is a compulsion, an imperative, and an integral part of being human, rather than something we choose to engage in. As we move through life, every new experience, every choice we make, all of our relationships are influenced by and continually reshape the way we make meaning in our lives. Meaning-making is what we do when faced with randomness, chaos, and absurdity. "We are predisposed to see order, pattern, and meaning in the world, and we find randomness, chaos, and meaninglessness unsatisfying," writes psychologist Thomas Gilovich.[180] As Kegan's assessment makes clear, it is something we all engage in every day, whether we realize it or not.

We tend to feel as though we are on a constant quest toward happiness, and that the pursuit of happiness is the guiding force behind all of our decisions and actions. However, given these insights from Kegan, it is probably more accurate to say that we are primarily motivated by the need for meaning, which in turn can contribute to a feeling of harmony in our minds, which invokes a sense of happiness. *From a neuroscientific point of view, meaning-making refers to the processes by which our brains confront and alleviate uncertainty during the course of our everyday lives.* The resulting sense of peace helps us solve our own happiness puzzle. In other words, happiness can be seen as an offshoot of meaning-making. Insofar as satisfactory meaning-making facilitates happiness, we can see how those differences in meaning-making are a major contributor to the differences we see in how people conceive of, attain, experience, and evaluate happiness. Let us now take a closer look at the roots of these differences in meaning-making across individuals, through Kegan's framework of "orders of mind."[181]

MAKING MEANING THROUGH DIFFERENT ORDERS OF MIND

Let's begin with a simple example to illustrate what an order of mind is. At night, when we look at the cosmos with the naked eye, we see lots of shining stars and the moon. But with a telescope, we can see a lot more out there. To see even further, we can use the Hubble Telescope or the Webb Telescope. By getting closer with the increasing power of observation, we can comprehend the cosmos in new ways, with new depths of meaning that are often counterintuitive. As we grow, our mind adds more frameworks to comprehend reality and reach a higher order of mind. We've already learned that it's Earth that revolves around the sun and not the other way around. We have learned that Earth is not flat, and the moon simply reflects the sun's light.

Orders of mind refer to differences in the complexity of the tool kits with which we approach meaning-making. These orders represent qualitative shifts in how we understand ourselves and our relationship to others. In earlier stages, such as the "impulsive mind" (zero-ish to six-ish), also known as the order 1 mind, the world is experienced as an extension of oneself, with limited awareness of others as separate individuals. As we develop, we progress to the "imperial mind" (six-ish to adolescence), also known as the order 2 mind, where we recognize others but primarily in terms of their usefulness to us. The "socialized mind" (adolescence to adulthood for many), also known as the order 3 mind, marks a significant shift, as individuals begin to internalize the expectations and values of their social environment, finding their identity in belonging and conforming. Finally, the "self-authoring mind" (adulthood for some), or the order 4 mind, emerges, characterized by individuals developing their own internal compass, defining their values, and taking ownership of their beliefs and actions.

The "self-transforming mind," or the order 5 mind, is relatively rare. This is the most complex stage, characterized by a profound awareness of the interconnectedness of all things and a capacity for ongoing self-reflection and growth. Individuals at this stage can hold multiple perspectives and are comfortable with ambiguity and paradox. They are driven by a desire to contribute to something larger than themselves. Self-transcendence and generativity appear to encompass most of the domains in which people strive to obtain a sense of meaning, contribute to society, leave a legacy, and transcend self-interests.

According to Kegan, "for the human, what evolving amounts to is the evolving of systems of meaning; these meaning systems shape our experience and to a great extent give rise to our behavior."[182] Even though the *activity* of meaning-making is universal across humanity, the richness and *complexity* of our meaning-making frameworks can change throughout our lives.

The majority of Kegan's stages occur during adulthood, which is one of the ways his views differ from other developmentalists who posit that development ends in early adulthood. As we grow older from childhood to adulthood, we face increasing levels of complexity with respect to existential, social, political, and many other dimensions of the human experience. The result is that the meaning we ascribe to any given object, person, or situation is subject to change, becoming more complex and nuanced, and, just as importantly, may be vastly different from the meaning other people, at different orders of mind, may ascribe to it. Unless we enhance our meaning-making framework to address the increasing complexity that confronts us, we potentially create a discord in our consciousness that can lead to unhappiness.

Until the age of sixty-two, I continued to believe, albeit with increasing levels of dissonance due to my continued exposure to wider context, that the Bhagavad Gita, the religious scripture I had admired most as I grew up, was literally uttered by Lord Krishna, the Hindu deity who came to earth in human form. After taking the course on Bhagavad Gita at Harvard with Professor Francis Clooney, I no longer believe that Krishna actually appeared on earth, although I still believe in the Gita's profound teachings, especially that of Nishkam Karma. (Kegan would point to this change in belief as evidence of a shift in the order of mind.) Krishna says in the Bhagavad (Gita 2.47), "You have a right to perform your prescribed duty, but you are not entitled to the fruits of action. Never consider yourself the cause of the results of your activities and never be attached to not doing your duty." By detaching oneself from the fruits of labor, one aims to achieve mental equanimity and spiritual growth.

Although this necessity to make meaning is a constant throughout life, the capacity with which we do it changes over time. When we're small children, for example, we might believe that Santa is a jolly fellow who slides down the chimney to reward our good behavior with toys. But by the time we're eleven or twelve, we may stop believing in him. Perhaps a classmate or older sibling presents us with information that challenges our belief that he is flesh and blood. This event forces us to ask: "Is the story my parents fed me about Santa Claus real? Does it conform with what I know about the rest of the world?" We may then think of Santa as a symbol of fun, magic, or generosity. As time goes by, we might think of him as a symbol of material excess.

HOW MEANING-MAKING CONTINUES TO EVOLVE

Over the past two thousand years, societal shifts driven by increased literacy and scientific discoveries have profoundly impacted the prevalence of these orders of mind. The worldviews of each culture and historical era have differed according to a variety of factors that influence how meaning is made, including cognitive development, our sensory capabilities, levels of education, cultural and historical contexts, and individual cognitive capacities.

Scientific discoveries have contributed to a greater emphasis on individual autonomy and self-expression, challenging traditional beliefs and encouraging individuals to question established norms and seek their own truths. The rise of literacy has also facilitated access to diverse perspectives and knowledge, fostering critical thinking and self-reflection. We live much longer now, so there are more opportunities to reach the "fourth" and "fifth" orders of mind.

However, the advent of social media has added a new layer of complexity. While it can expose individuals to diverse viewpoints and facilitate connection, it can also reinforce social pressures and create echo chambers, potentially hindering the development of self-authorship. The curated nature of online personas can blur the lines between authentic self-expression and performative conformity, potentially trapping individuals in a heightened state of socialized thinking. Furthermore, the constant connectivity and rapid-fire information consumption can make it challenging to cultivate the deep reflection necessary for self-authoring.

Understanding Kegan's frameworks, after I took his class on adult development at Harvard, a profound realization—akin to a glimpse of *satori*[183]—illuminated the human journey for me. I saw how we all had the same fundamental quest for meaning-making across millennia, yet how that quest is filtered through the unique lenses of individual experience—varying contexts, cognitive capacities, educational backgrounds, etc.—leads to different developmental orders of mind. This confluence of factors gives rise to an infinite diversity in how we apply our minds, shaping everything from the narratives we construct about our past and the way we navigate our present to the very expectations we hold for the future.

My appreciation for other people with different belief systems has increased significantly after grasping this framework. It became a very powerful tool of empathy that allowed me to understand why people believe the things they do, even if their beliefs differ from my own. That includes learning that the meaning-making worldview of someone with an order 4 or order 5 mind is not intrinsically superior to that of someone with an order 3 mind.

For instance, my mother holds it to be true that God incarnated on this earth and has indeed been the source of holy scriptures—not metaphorically or figuratively speaking, but in reality. If we are to apply Kegan's framework, then she would be characteristic of an order 3 mind. Yet, my mother is focused on giving to others. Some of my earliest memories were the times she hosted communal meals for the poor of all religions, a practice she has continued throughout her life. Recently, to celebrate her ninetieth birthday, her wish was to feed a thousand people that day. She is the very embodiment of love and compassion and is superior to me as a human being in so many ways, although I think I have evolved to an order 4 mind in Kegan's framework.

Depending on the degree of complexity with which people make meaning, many individuals are more predisposed to conjure God, for instance, as an anthropomorphic being like my mother does, while others like me (now) might prefer to conceive of God as a transcendent and impersonal force.

One of the keys to learning Kegan's framework is understanding his use of "subject" and "object." Both refer to our own traits, feelings, and behaviors. When we experience them or act on them without critical thinking, then they are subject. Subject refers to those elements of our knowing or organizing that we are identified with, tied to, fused with, or embedded in. In other words, when we are acting as subject, then we are acting as those traits and cannot distance ourselves from them in order to properly question or reflect on them. There is no detachment between these traits and our lived experience. Only when we are able to distance ourselves from them, thus achieving objectivity, do these become object.

What does this look like in practice? For order 1 minds, the entire world is subject: As newborns, we have not yet developed a distinction between the self and the other—the whole universe is the self. Later in childhood, as order 2 minds, we see other people and things as object, but we are still embedded in our impulses as subject—we do not *have* needs and wants and emotions; we *are* those things. By young adulthood, if not sooner, most of us have become order 3 minds: A lot of what was previously subject becomes object. We can step back and see that, as individuals, we are separate and can, to some extent, control our feelings and behaviors.

Most people will reach order 3, merely because of biological development and basic socialization. How many of us reach the higher levels, becoming order 4 or 5 minds? The subject-object switch that occurs in transitioning to these higher orders involves our social identities and beliefs. It is the difference between thinking, "I am a doctor" (or fireman or lawyer or teacher) and "I work as a doctor." It is the difference between "I am a Christian" or "I am a Hindu" and "I believe in Christianity" or "I believe in Hinduism." It is the difference between believing in what we are socially programmed to trust by our family and culture and subjecting these inherited ideas to critical examination to determine if they truly agree with our own individual experiences, knowledge, and meaning-making tools. Transitioning from an order 3 to an order 4 mind does not necessarily mean giving up one's beliefs. For me, I retained the same basic concept that all religions are to be respected, since each contains some essential truth. But my reasons for believing this have changed.

The fundamental principle to grasp is that happiness is not a universal constant; its source and nature are deeply intertwined with our current order of mind. What brings joy and fulfillment to an individual at one stage of development may be entirely irrelevant or even distressing to someone at another stage. For example, for some people, fully embracing their culture's collective narratives of meaning-making, as well as the corresponding social roles and identities, will be sufficient for them to be happy. Someone at the socialized mind stage might derive happiness by following along more or less with the basic social script: If they have a loving spouse, children, a steady job, and a comfortable home, they will be happy.

For a self-authoring individual, on the other hand, such a life is, on its own, not quite satisfying enough. It feels socially meaningful, but not existentially meaningful. They may find flaws or contradictions in the culturally prescribed forms of meaning-making. This is beautifully stated by Lee Kuan Yew: "For at 60, more than at 50, comes the realization of the transient nature of all earthly glories and successes, and the ephemeral quality of sensory joys and pleasures, when compared to intellectual, moral, or spiritual satisfactions."[184]

Lee is describing how the way people feel fulfilled changes with the shift in the order of their minds. For such people, happiness might be tied to personal growth, meaningful work, and living in accordance with their own values, regardless of external validation. Therefore, understanding Kegan's orders of mind is crucial for comprehending the diverse and evolving nature of human happiness, as the very definitions of a "good life" and a "meaningful life" shift along with our cognitive and emotional development.

Kegan's framework illuminates the intensely personal way in which we forge meaning, constructing our realities from the interplay of experience and evolving cognitive capacities. Yet, these individual meaning-making processes are not formed in isolation. The very fabric of our society, with its shared values, beliefs, and expectations, provides a powerful lens through which we interpret our experiences and define what constitutes "happiness." As we turn to the next chapter, we'll explore how culture acts as both a mirror and a mold—reflecting our inner narratives while also shaping them. By examining the cultural scripts that influence our ideals, desires, and definitions of success, we can begin to disentangle which parts of our pursuit of happiness are truly our own, and which have been inherited without question.

CHAPTER SIX

HOW CULTURE DEFINES HAPPINESS

> *"CULTURE MAKES PEOPLE UNDERSTAND EACH OTHER BETTER. AND IF THEY UNDERSTAND EACH OTHER BETTER IN THEIR SOUL, IT IS EASIER TO OVERCOME THE ECONOMIC AND POLITICAL BARRIERS. BUT FIRST THEY HAVE TO UNDERSTAND THAT THEIR NEIGHBOUR IS, IN THE END, JUST LIKE THEM, WITH THE SAME PROBLEMS, THE SAME QUESTIONS."*
>
> **—PAULO COELHO**

Anyone who has ever traveled abroad understands that every place has its own cultural norms. In some countries, smiling at passersby is very normal. In others, it could be considered strange, disturbing, and maybe even a bit scandalous. In certain regions, people are expected to bow, and in very specific ways, for specific occasions. Failing to do so, even if by mistake, would be considered extremely rude.

This principle holds true in different parts of the same country as well. In the United States, for example, people in big cities in the Northeast, such as New York City, mostly ignore each other on the street or during a walk in the park. However, when I was visiting Dallas and Austin, I was surprised that everyone I met while going for my walks greeted me with a genuine smile and waved hello. It is common practice in many parts of the South and the Midwest for people to greet strangers. Differences in cultural norms, however simple, can have significant impacts on happiness.

Participation in communal affairs and traditions can be paramount to happiness. Teatime is a good example. In many cultures, there are specific occasions or times of day reserved for gathering around with family, friends, or others to enjoy some tea. There are lots of ritualistic elements built into this—the way the tea is prepared, how it is served, what it is served in, what it is served with, how to drink it, etc. People find bonding, happiness, and meaning in such ritualistic practices. Similarly, every culture has its own holidays, its own assortment of spiritual and religious practices, and so on. I remember while growing up in India, we celebrated all the Hindu festivals but also Eid and Christmas—and I was always looking forward to the next holiday.

Like happiness, culture is a very broad topic. It has been defined in a multitude of ways by many different thinkers throughout history. We do not get to choose which culture or religion we are born into. As the prophet Muhammad said, "No babe is born but upon Fitra [natural way]. It is his parents who make him a Jew or a Christian or a Polytheist."

Just as none of us were born with any preprogramming on how to view the world, so too did our species emerge without much guidance on how to understand the universe; we were given the hardware necessary to find meaning, but no instruction manual for how to do so. Since then, populations of human beings in different times and places across the world have been stumbling through, doing their best to figure things out or make meaning of their existence.

HOW TEMPERAMENTS AND VOCATIONS INFLUENCE HAPPINESS

By now, it should be clear just how different we are in so many ways and how cultural differences contribute to how we each define, imagine, and experience happiness in our lives. These differences also affect the pathways by which we each try to seek out happiness within our respective societies. One of the main tracks to fulfillment is our choice of vocation and how it may stem from one's personality and temperament.

As human societies have become more complex over time, new vocational opportunities have continued to emerge, opening more possibilities for how we can fit ourselves into society. We all have our own preferences for which types of jobs we find fulfilling and enjoyable and which ones we don't. Many of us are familiar with personality tests and frameworks, such as the Myers–Briggs Type Indicator, which attempt to systematize personality differences to help people figure out which career paths will make them most happy.

We are lucky that we have the freedom to choose which types of jobs, careers, and social roles to pursue in our lives, but this has not always been the case in all times and places. Plato, in his *Republic*, imagined an ideal society in which people with certain proclivities would be essentially forced into one of three social classes that fit them best: rulers, traders, or soldiers. He emphasized the importance of matching individuals with their natural aptitudes for the good of the state. Similarly, the four Hindu Varnas—Brahmanas, Kshatriyas, Vaishyas, and Sudras—were indeed descriptions of social classes, but they were understood to correspond to the natural temperaments and proclivities of individuals. In the Bhagavad Gita, they are described as follows:

> *OF BRÂHMANAS AND KSHATRIYAS AND VAISHYAS, AS ALSO OF SUDRAS, O SCORCHER OF FOES, THE DUTIES ARE DISTRIBUTED ACCORDING TO THE GUNAS (TEMPERAMENTS) BORN OF THEIR OWN NATURE. THE CONTROL OF THE MIND AND THE SENSES, AUSTERITY, PURITY, FORBEARANCE, AND ALSO UPRIGHTNESS, KNOWLEDGE, REALIZATION, BELIEF IN A HEREAFTER—THESE ARE THE DUTIES OF THE BRÂHMANAS, BORN OF (THEIR OWN) NATURE. PROWESS, BOLDNESS, FORTITUDE, DEXTERITY, AND ALSO NOT FLYING FROM BATTLE, GENEROSITY AND SOVEREIGNTY ARE THE DUTIES OF THE KSHATRIYAS, BORN OF (THEIR OWN) NATURE. AGRICULTURE, CATTLE-REARING AND TRADE ARE THE DUTIES OF THE VAISHYAS, BORN OF (THEIR OWN) NATURE; AND ACTION CONSISTING OF SERVICE IS THE DUTY OF THE SUDRAS, BORN OF (THEIR OWN) NATURE.*

Over time, the descriptive nature of Varnas began to erode. The concept of *jati* (birth-based groups) started to intertwine with the Varna system. The transformation from a descriptive framework to a prescriptive caste system was a complex process driven by a confluence of factors. The interplay of religious ideology, political power, economic forces, and social norms contributed to the entrenchment of a rigid and discriminatory social order, which has been one of the banes of Indian society.

Recognizing the different temperaments intrinsic to our society, the Bhagavad Gita presents three diverse paths to *moksha* (liberation), or the ultimate goal of flourishing. Each path is tailored to individual temperaments. Primarily, these are Bhakti Yoga (the path of devotion), which is ideal for those with an emotional nature; Jnana Yoga (the path of knowledge), suited for those with an intellectual inclination; and Karma Yoga (the path of action), for those with an active disposition.

Bhakti Yoga, the path of devotion, embodies the essence of love. It emphasizes cultivating a loving connection with a higher power or a chosen ideal. This love is not possessive or conditional; it is a surrender of the ego to a greater force. In our daily lives, this translates to cultivating love and compassion for ourselves and others. When we approach relationships with empathy and kindness, we embody Bhakti Yoga. Just as Bhakti Yoga involves surrendering to a divine entity, it also means surrendering to love itself, allowing it to guide our actions and shape our interactions. This describes my mother's temperament.

Jnana Yoga, the path of knowledge, directly corresponds to the act of learning. It involves the relentless pursuit of truth through intellectual inquiry and self-reflection. We delve into subjects that ignite our passion, seeking to understand the world and ourselves on a deeper level. This journey of learning becomes a transformative experience, leading to self-realization and liberation from ignorance. This was the temperament of my father.

Karma Yoga, the path of selfless action, aligns beautifully with the concept of play. It emphasizes performing one's duties without attachment to the results, finding joy and fulfillment in the act itself. This mirrors the essence of play, where the process is paramount and the outcome is secondary. When we engage in activities with a playful spirit, whether it's work, hobbies, or social interactions, we embody

Karma Yoga. We act with dedication and enthusiasm, not for personal gain but for the sheer joy of participation. This transforms mundane tasks into opportunities for self-expression and connection, fostering a sense of flow and engagement. Just as a child loses themself in play, a karma-yogi becomes absorbed in their actions, transcending ego and connecting with a deeper sense of purpose. This has been the guiding principle of my life.

When we align our vocation with our inherent temperament, we create fertile ground for happiness. A person with a natural inclination toward service may find immense satisfaction in healthcare, while an analytical mind might flourish in scientific research. This alignment transcends mere job satisfaction; it fosters a sense of purpose and fulfillment.

HOW METANARRATIVES SHAPE HAPPINESS

Our upbringing and cultural context significantly shape our understanding and pursuit of happiness. The metanarrative we internalize—the overarching story we tell ourselves about the world and our place in it—profoundly influences how we define happiness, the paths we believe will lead to it, and the values we prioritize in its pursuit.

Recognizing the influence of these narratives is crucial for understanding the diverse ways humans seek fulfillment and for appreciating the validity of paths that may differ from our own. Four metanarratives of self, prevalent throughout history, offer distinct approaches to this pursuit.

THE ETHIC OF SELF-CONSTRUCTION

This Western-centric framework is rooted in ancient Greek philosophy and is prominent in modern individualistic societies such as the US. It emphasizes personal growth, self-fulfillment, and the pursuit of individual goals. Happiness is achieved through self-reflection, setting and achieving objectives, developing skills and talents, and acquiring social status through the accumulation of wealth and/or power. Ancient Greek philosophers such as Aristotle and Epictetus saw happiness as a continuous process of cultivating virtues and striving for self-improvement. Pierre Hadot highlighted the ancient schools' belief in self-formation (*paideia*) through spiritual exercises and aligning oneself with reason rather than social conventions.[185] However, the extreme individualism fostered by this ethic, exemplified by the US's high score on Hofstede's individualism scale, can create challenges for individuals seeking happiness. While self-construction works for some, it's not a universal solution, and exploring other metanarratives is crucial.

THE ETHIC OF CONNECTION

This framework prioritizes relationships, empathy, and social interactions, prominent in Eastern and collectivist cultures such as India, China, and Arab and indigenous societies. Western thinkers, including early developmental psychologists such as Piaget, have also recognized the importance of connection. This ethic encourages moving beyond individualism, instead considering our interconnectedness with others and the world. It promotes ethical decisions that assess the complex web of relationships and calls for actions promoting mutual respect and compassion.

In this ethic, happiness is sought through nurturing relationships, fostering belonging, and engaging in acts of kindness. In Indian culture, dominated by Hinduism, the interconnectedness of all beings is central, with concepts such as karma and *ahimsa* shaping ethical behavior. Hinduism emphasizes the interconnectedness of *Atman*, individual souls, with *Brahman*, the supreme deity.

This interconnectedness is found across other Eastern societies. Chinese culture, influenced by Confucianism, prioritizes social roles and relationships, with the individual self-defined within the web of social connections. Taoism, while allowing for more individualism, emphasizes harmony with nature. Arab cultures emphasize strong family and community bonds, promoting values such as hospitality and generosity. Islam provides an ethical framework emphasizing duty and connection to God and community. Indigenous cultures emphasize harmony with nature, community, and ancestors. The ethic of connection emphasizes empathy, compassion, and the well-being of all beings, promoting stewardship of the environment.

THE ETHIC OF DUTY

This framework centers on fulfilling obligations, responsibilities, and moral duties arising from various life roles toward family, community, and society. In Hinduism, dharma refers to one's duty and righteousness. The ethic of duty plays a vital role in maintaining social order and harmony. When individuals fulfill their responsibilities, it creates a sense of inner peace and fulfillment within themselves as well as stability and trust within communities. Confucianism emphasizes fulfilling social roles and responsibilities, such as filial piety and loyalty. Immanuel Kant's categorical imperative suggests that moral actions should be based on universalizable principles, demonstrating that duty is not merely about following rules but about acting according to reason.

Duties are not static; they evolve with changing circumstances and relationships. Understanding the nuances of each situation is crucial for fulfilling one's obligations effectively. For example, filial piety, while a core Confucian duty, requires adapting to the specific needs and circumstances of one's parents. This necessitates judgment and not blind adherence.

The ethic of duty complements self-construction and connection by providing a framework for considering obligations and promoting a just society.

The concept of justice is deeply intertwined with that of duty. Distributive justice, for example, is the duty of society to distribute resources fairly. Restorative justice is the duty to repair harm. Duties are often the foundation of rights. Thus, if someone has a right, someone else has a duty to respect that right.

I was taught from childhood to do my duty and leave the rest to God. That's what Karma Yoga from Hinduism is all about. The bedrock of my life, both personal and professional, has been Karma Yoga, a moral imperative instilled by my parents. I've lived by the simple truth that unwavering dedication to one's duty, executed with utmost ability, is paramount, without focusing on the reward.

My professional journey stands as a testament to the power of this principle, not that of ambition. Now, I carry the torch of Karma Yoga, sharing its transformative power and the profound wisdom behind this concept with the world. For eight years now, I have been a guest lecturer and Hindu exemplar at Scotty McLennan's class at Stanford's Graduate School of Business titled "Finding Spiritual Meaning in Business," where I talk about the concept of Karma Yoga pretty much for the whole class. This approach unburdens us from fear, guilt, and regret and aims to have equability of mind toward success or failure. The hadith of Islam says, "A believer should be duty conscious, and as far as rights are concerned he should ask of them from god—Hadith."

Marcus Aurelius writes in *Meditations*, "Just that you do the right thing. The rest doesn't matter."

THE ETHIC OF SELF-REALIZATION

This framework emphasizes realizing one's true nature, potential, and purpose. It shares similarities with self-construction but has stronger spiritual undertones. It also recognizes interconnectedness, like the ethic of connection, but it diverges from the ethic of duty. Taoism, in contrast to Confucianism's rigidity, emphasizes self-exploration, understanding one's place in life, and aligning with the natural flow.

Happiness is therefore sought through self-discovery, introspection, and aligning actions with core values. Hinduism emphasizes pursuing *Atman*, the divine essence within, with *moksha*, the goal of self-realization, through various yogas. Buddhism emphasizes self-realization as a path to liberation, with meditation and mindfulness as key practices. Mystical branches of Western religions also emphasize self-realization, with the goal of direct communion with God. The ethic of self-realization encourages a transformative journey of self-discovery, embracing individual potential while maintaining compassion for others.

These four metanarratives offer diverse pathways to happiness. Understanding these frameworks and their cultural contexts allows for a broader perspective on the human pursuit of well-being. Recognizing the validity of different approaches, rather than adhering to a single, prescribed path, may be the key to finding personal fulfillment and contributing to a more compassionate world.

EAST VERSUS WEST VERSUS BOTH

The East versus West distinction, while sometimes debated, offers valuable insights into cultural differences, particularly regarding happiness. While acknowledging the diversity within each broad category, there are recognizable differences between the categories. Joseph Henrich's concept of Western, Educated, Industrialized, Rich, and Democratic (WEIRD) societies highlights how Western research often focuses on a narrow, unrepresentative sample of humanity.[186] This underscores the importance of incorporating Eastern perspectives for a more comprehensive understanding of happiness.

The collectivism of the East and the individualism of the West are both valuable and complementary perspectives. WEIRD cultures tend to be individualistic, valuing autonomy, competition, striving, and self-expression. Happiness is often linked to personal achievement and material success. Collectivist cultures, common in Asia, Africa, the Middle East, and among indigenous peoples, prioritize relational harmony, community well-being, and contributing to others. Happiness is tied to strong family ties, social cohesion, and fulfilling social roles.

Eastern religions such as Hinduism, Buddhism, and Taoism, influential in collectivist cultures, often associate happiness with inner peace, spiritual well-being, and harmony with nature. This concept contrasts with the more individualistic relationship with God emphasized in Abrahamic religions. Eastern philosophies often promote a collective approach to happiness, in which individual well-being is linked to the well-being of all.

Many African cultures tie happiness to community bonds, while Middle Eastern cultures may emphasize family unity and religious devotion. Indigenous cultures often link happiness to harmony with nature and tradition. Even some Western cultures, such as Scandinavian countries, prioritize collective well-being through social welfare.

While Westerners may find collectivist practices unfamiliar, they represent the historical norm over millennia in most cultures. Western individualism is a relatively recent phenomenon. Therefore, Western societies can learn much from collectivist cultures, which have a longer history of emphasizing interconnectedness and community in the pursuit of happiness.

Another framework in which the cultural factors manifest is that all human endeavors can be categorized as a combination of the three ways: victory, fulfillment, and truth seeking. The LLP framework addresses these three adequately. Love makes sure that our victory-seeking behavior is directed with compassion. Learning makes sure that our truth-seeking behavior is directed toward true and not dogmatic knowledge. Love is also present in learning with the "love of truth." Play makes sure that our fulfillment is not debased. In victory, as in play, the opponent is important to enable us to play and bring out the best in us.

Culture, often invisible yet deeply influential, shapes the very contours of what we believe will make us happy. It provides the narratives, values, and expectations that influence our individual meaning-making processes. Some people choose to be happy; others choose to be disappointed and resentful, given a similar set of circumstances. By becoming aware of these cultural narratives—whether they revolve around achievement, appearance, productivity, spirituality, morality, or belonging—we reclaim the power to choose which stories we continue to live by.

Why are Danes so consistently happy? According to a landmark 2006 study by K. Christensen, A. M. Herskind, and J. W. Vaupel, published in the British Medical Journal,[187] the answer lies in their expectations. Epidemiologists from the University of Southern Denmark investigated why their citizens regularly lead Western countries in happiness and life satisfaction. Their key finding was that while Danes are highly satisfied, "their expectations are rather low," suggesting that "unrealistically high" expectations can lead to "disappointment and low life satisfaction." This outlook sharply contrasts with many other Western societies, where people are often raised to believe that a continuous state of pleasure is the ultimate goal and that they should always expect it.[188]

GLOBAL FLOURISHING STUDY

A scientific attempt of amazing scope is being made to empirically study the divergences observed for flourishing across countries and cultures. The Global Flourishing Study, with principal investigators Byron Johnson (Baylor) and Tyler VanderWeele (Harvard) and data collection by Gallup, is a longitudinal panel study of over two hundred thousand participants in twenty-two geographically and culturally diverse countries, spanning all six populated continents, with nationally representative sampling. The researchers intend to collect annual data over five years to assess numerous aspects of flourishing and their potential determinants. The study aggregates well-being across six domains of flourishing: happiness, health, meaning, character, relationships, and financial security.[189]

The first wave of data was released in February 2024, and the second wave in April 2025. A few relevant extracts from the authors' report are as follows:

> *TO PROMOTE FLOURISHING WE NEED TO UNDERSTAND ITS DETERMINANTS AND ITS DISTRIBUTION—WHO IS FLOURISHING AND WHO IS NOT? WHO NEEDS HELP, AND IN WHAT WAYS? HOW ARE THINGS CHANGING OVER TIME? WHAT WORKS TO PROMOTE FLOURISHING? WHAT IS NEARLY UNIVERSAL ... AND WHAT IS CULTURALLY SPECIFIC?*
>
> *PERHAPS ONE OF THE MOST STRIKING RESULTS OF THE STUDY IS HOW DIFFERENT COUNTRIES ARE FLOURISHING IN DIFFERENT WAYS. WHILE RICHER DEVELOPED COUNTRIES TEND TO REPORT HIGHER OVERALL LIFE EVALUATION, AND SUBJECTIVE FINANCIAL SECURITY, THE SAME IS NOT TRUE FOR OTHER ASPECTS OF FLOURISHING. GDP PER CAPITA, FOR INSTANCE, APPEARS TO BE NEGATIVELY CORRELATED WITH MEANING AND PURPOSE IN LIFE ... MANY DEVELOPED NATIONS OFTEN [REPORT] LOWER MEANING, PRO-SOCIALITY, AND RELATIONSHIP QUALITY.*[190]

Discussing more of the details is beyond the scope of this book. But the study's findings are supportive of the key messages delivered in chapters four, five, and six, attesting to the multidimensional nature of happiness, well-being, and flourishing, and highlighting the need to study the reasons for divergences.

With this awareness, we're ready to move from deconstructing happiness to actively creating it. In the next part, we'll shift from reflection to practice and explore how engaging deeply in love, learning, and play offers a powerful, grounded path to flourishing in everyday life.

PART III

PUTTING LOVE, LEARNING, AND PLAY INTO ACTION

CHAPTER SEVEN

WHAT IT MEANS TO LOVE, LEARN, AND PLAY

> *"MAN'S MATURITY: TO HAVE REGAINED THE SERIOUSNESS THAT HE HAD AS A CHILD AT PLAY."*
>
> **—FRIEDRICH NIETZSCHE**
>
> *"THE MOST SOPHISTICATED PEOPLE I KNOW—INSIDE THEY ARE ALL CHILDREN. DO YOU KNOW ANYONE WHO'S REALLY SOPHISTICATED WHO ISN'T CHILDLIKE AT HEART?"*
>
> **—PABLO PICASSO**

As we have seen earlier in this book, at the root of our existential drive lies that steady base: loving, learning, and playing. Like flowers that need air, water, and nutrients in the right proportions to blossom, we need love, learning, and play to flourish.

I have always been mesmerized by watching small children play. They never hesitate to show their emotions or affection, letting them flow freely, whether it's a loud belly laugh or a joyful hug. Children delight in giving and receiving love and are bundles of energy and curiosity, soaking up everything around them like sponges. They are wildly creative and imaginative innovators who can turn a bed sheet into a fort or a cardboard box into a grocery store, and they have no concern for outcomes, embarrassments, or failures. Kids are open-minded, nonjudgmental, and adaptable—they live completely in the moment and are completely unselfconscious.

As newborns, we emerge from the womb seeking love and attachment. Every day is a discovery, from recognizing faces to uttering first words or taking that initial step. The world is a classroom, and curiosity is the teacher. Scientific evidence from developmental psychology and neurobiology has shown that love during our first two years is essential for creating the critical neural pathways needed for normal human experiences as we grow.[191] The hugs, kisses, smiles, and tender words our parents share with us and that we instinctively seek to return at this early stage may effectively inoculate us against a host of ills later in life.

Learning, too, is hardwired into our newborn brains. While still in the womb, we learn to recognize our mother's voice and even words. As newborns, we begin learning by reaching out with our senses, to touch, taste, smell, feel, and interact with the world around us. Our very survival depends on this intense yearning to learn. Alison Gopnik, a professor of psychology and philosophy and leader in the study of children's learning, has demonstrated through multiple experiments that young children learn about the world much like scientists do. Children experiment, analyze, and form intuitive theories about what they observe around them. "Babies and young children," Gopnik writes, "are exquisitely designed by evolution to change and create, to learn and explore. Those capacities, so intrinsic to what it means to be human, appear in their purest forms in the earliest years of our lives.

Our most valuable human accomplishments are possible because we were once helpless dependent children and not in spite of it."[192]

At the same time, love is forging critical pathways in our brains, and we're absorbing information around us like mini Einsteins. As we develop language skills, we engage in pretend or dramatic play, flexing our creative muscles, dressing up as princesses and firemen, or turning the sandbox into an archaeological dig for dinosaur bones. Along the way, we learn critical emotional management skills as well, including how to regulate stress, anger, jealousy, and a range of other feelings.

Play is so critical to our development that when it, along with nurturing relationships, is missing, the resulting toxic stress can disrupt the development of executive function and the acquisition of the behavior critical to healthy social development.[193] As babies grow, play is not only a source of joy but also a means of acquiring essential life skills. Infants learn about object permanence—that objects continue to exist even when they can't be observed—through games that emphasize the visible and invisible, such as peekaboo.

It's no wonder, then, that once a child is fed, dry, and rested, they exist in a state of total well-being, doing little more than loving, learning, and playing. Think about beautiful moments from your childhood: the love of friends and family, the constant "Whys" with which you exhausted your parents to satisfy insatiable curiosity, the awe and wonder with which you tried to understand the world, and the joys of simple play.

It is to be expected that as the world becomes more and more familiar to children as they age, they will experience wonder less readily. It increasingly requires effort to see how extraordinary the earth and everything in it really is. Educators who wish to cultivate the sense of wonder therefore face the challenge, as the education philosopher Kieran Egan noted, of "defamiliarizing the familiar."[194]

Love provides the emotional foundation, learning empowers us to grow and contribute, and play infuses our lives with joy and creativity. Let's take a close look at each to try to defamiliarize the familiar, beginning with love.

WHAT IS LOVE?

> *"WHEN YOU SEEK LOVE WITH ALL YOUR HEART, YOU SHALL FIND ITS ECHO IN THE UNIVERSE."*
>
> ***—RUMI***
>
> *"IN EVERY RELIGION THERE IS LOVE, YET LOVE HAS NO RELIGION."*
>
> ***—RUMI***

Love is both obvious and deeply mysterious. As Rumi also said, "Love is an open secret, the most obvious thing in the world and the most hidden, with no answer to how it keeps its mystery."[195] Rumi was a thirteenth-century Persian poet, scholar, and Sufi mystic, whose spiritual verses transcend cultural and religious boundaries. His magnum opus, *The Masnavi*, is considered a masterpiece of mystical Islamic literature, often called the "Quran in Persian."

Scribes of all ages have marveled at how love is the tie that binds us all. "Love is the most powerful force in the universe," says the Bhagavad Gita. "It is the eternal fire that burns within the heart and connects us all." The Bible, in Matthew 22:39, famously instructs us, "You shall love your neighbor as yourself." Nobel laureate Gabriel Garcia Marquez considers love the be-all and end-all. He said, "Think of love as a state of grace, not the means to anything, but the alpha and omega. An end in itself."[196]

We often think of love in the context of romance, but that is just one manifestation. Love comes in many different, nuanced forms. The ancient Greeks, in their infinite wisdom, identified seven different kinds. *Eros* is erotic or sexual love. *Ludus* is the playful, fun-filled love of a fling or a flirtation. *Philia* is the love between friends or brotherly love. *Storge* is familial love, the unconditional, unwavering love a parent feels for a child. *Pragma* is the quiet love that is borne of devotion and commitment. It is the kind of love that a long-married couple might share. *Philautia* is the love we give ourselves that results in healthy self-esteem and self-care. Perhaps the purest, most selfless form of love is *agape*. It is a love beyond feeling or emotion, often described as universal love.

Just as the Inuit have dozens of words for snow, the Sanskrit language of ancient India possesses a rich vocabulary for love, from the divine to the deeply personal:

- Divine Love: Encompasses *bhakti* (devotion), *prema* (unconditional love), *karuna* (compassion), *maitri* (universal friendship), and *anuraga* (spiritual attachment).
- Interpersonal Love: Includes *sneha* (tender affection), *priya/vallabha* (beloved), *daya* (caring), and *vatsalya* (parental love).
- Romantic/Passionate Love: Features *kama* (sensual), *rati* (physical passion), *madana* (intoxication), *anuraga* (deep attachment), and *abhilasha* (desire).
- Family/Relational Love: Covers *mamata* (motherly), *bandhu* (familial), *sakhya* (friendship), *shraddha* (respectful), and *seva* (love through service).
- Universal/Cosmic Love: Includes *prema* (divine), *karuna* (universal compassion), *mudita* (sympathetic joy), *metta* (loving-kindness), and *advaya* (non-dual love).

- Emotional Aspects: Spans *preeti* (joy), *ishta* (cherished), *madhura* (sweet), *snigdha* (tender), and *pranaya* (trust-based).
- Devotional Love (Specific): Details *bhava* (emotional), *rasa* (essence), *anurakti* (constant attachment), *upasana* (worshipful), and *samarpana* (surrendered).

Buddhism teaches *metta* (loving-kindness), a practice of cultivating unconditional love and goodwill toward oneself and others. The Dalai Lama often speaks of love as the foundation of happiness, stating that "our prime purpose in this life is to help others, and if you can't help them, at least don't hurt them." Similarly, across cultures and eras, we can find many moving texts describing the full spectrum of love. Tyler VanderWeele, the director of the Human Flourishing Program at Harvard University, writes: "While the term 'love' means different things to different people, in much theological writing, it is understood as a desire for and/or commitment to the good of the other. That seeking of the other's good, in childhood (and arguably throughout life), is very powerful. In addition to the actions that promote the good of the beloved, that experience of love affirms the person's intrinsic value and worth. It establishes a bond. It fulfills one of the deepest human yearnings for connection with others.[197]

One of the longest-running studies in the world has proven just that. Since 1938, Harvard has been conducting its Study of Adult Development, tracking the physical and emotional well-being of more than seven hundred men who grew up in Boston in the 1930s and '40s.[198] "The seventy-five years and twenty million dollars spent on the Grant Study points … to a straightforward five-word conclusion: 'Happiness is love. Full stop,'"[199] wrote George E. Vaillant, a psychoanalyst and research psychiatrist who directed the study for thirty-five years.

The foundation of love is in the interconnectedness of everything. From the quantum entanglement of particles to the vast web of galactic clusters, interconnection is the fundamental reality. When we truly love, we transcend the illusion of separation and experience our essential unity with everyone and everything. Through loving awareness, we see ourselves in others, feel the pulse of life in all beings, recognize our shared essence, experience universal empathy, and participate in collective evolution. As French theologian Pierre Teilhard de Chardin said, "Love is the affinity which links and draws together the elements of the world. Love, in fact, is the agent of universal synthesis."[200]

Erich Fromm, in his book *The Art of Loving*, wrote of love as a spontaneous affirmation of others, as the union of the individual with others based on the preservation of the individual self.[201] The dynamic quality of love lies in this very polarity: It springs from the need to overcome separateness, but love is our universal yearning to find what we have been separated from.

As Fromm asserted, love is a state of mind and a way of being. He said: "Love is not primarily a relationship to a specific person; it is an attitude, an orientation of character which determines the relatedness of a person to the world as a whole, not toward one 'object' of love. If a person loves only one other person and is indifferent to the rest of his fellow men, his love is not love but a symbiotic attachment or an enlarged egotism."[202]

The mystics of all religious traditions have taught us that love is not to be sought; love is what we are. This is beautifully echoed by Rumi: "Your task is not to seek for love, but merely to seek and find all the barriers within yourself that you have built against it."[203] In the early fifth century, St. Augustine summarized all of human ethics in one dictum: "Love and do what you will."[204] The early Christian, Saul of Tarsus, wrote about love in a letter to his fellow Christians that is still regularly quoted today:

> *"LOVE IS PATIENT, LOVE IS KIND. IT DOES NOT ENVY, IT DOES NOT BOAST, IT IS NOT PROUD. IT DOES NOT DISHONOR OTHERS, IT IS NOT SELF-SEEKING, IT IS NOT EASILY ANGERED, IT KEEPS NO RECORD OF WRONGS. LOVE DOES NOT DELIGHT IN EVIL BUT REJOICES WITH THE TRUTH. IT ALWAYS PROTECTS, ALWAYS TRUSTS, ALWAYS HOPES, ALWAYS PERSEVERES."*[205]

The impact of love extends beyond the individual to society as a whole. Loving relationships foster cooperation and collaboration, which are essential ingredients for a thriving community. When individuals prioritize the well-being of others, they are more likely to engage in prosocial behaviors, such as volunteering and helping those in need. The social expression of love leads to justice, community health, and well-being. As Tyler VanderWeele says, "It is no wonder, then, that the experience of love appears to affect so many health and well-being outcomes. Love is not often considered in our medical and public health discussions as to what shapes health. But perhaps that should change as more and more research points to its profound importance."[206]

Hopefully, love becomes a guiding force in social policies. "Someday, after mastering the winds, the waves, the tides and gravity, we shall harness for God the energies of love, and then, for a second time in the history of the world, man will have discovered fire," said French theologian Pierre Teilhard de Chardin.[207] Mirroring this hope, Ralph Waldo Emerson said, "The power of love, as the basis of state, has never been tried."[208]

Neuroscience also sheds light on the impact of love on our well-being. Studies suggest that strong social connections and loving relationships can boost our immune system, reduce stress, and even increase our lifespan.[209] Different types of love, such as romantic love, familial love, and platonic love, activate distinct neural pathways and chemical releases. For instance, romantic love often involves the reward system, releasing dopamine and oxytocin, while familial love may rely more on vasopressin and attachment-related brain regions.

WHAT IS LEARNING?

> *"LEARNING NEVER EXHAUSTS THE MIND."*
>
> ***—LEONARDO DA VINCI***
>
> *"THE ABILITY TO OBSERVE WITHOUT EVALUATING IS THE HIGHEST FORM OF INTELLIGENCE."*
>
> ***—JIDDU KRISHNAMURTI***

The English author T. H. White summed up learning beautifully in his book *The Once and Future King*: "You may grow old and trembling in your anatomies, you may lie awake at night listening to the disorder of your veins, you may miss your only love, you may see the world around you devastated by evil lunatics, or know your honour trampled in the sewers of baser minds. There is only one thing for it then—to learn. Learn why the world wags and what wags it."[210]

Learning is the path of understanding the "how" of our environment and to keep on unfolding the mysteries of existence. It's why "know thyself," inscribed in Greek above the entrance to the Temple of Apollo at Delphi between 525 and 450 BCE, has resonated for millennia, as many have felt that this phrase sums up all philosophical commandments. An Islamic *hadith* from the prophet Muhammad proclaims, "He who knows himself knows his Lord." Similarly, in Eastern traditions, Lao-tzu said, "He who knows others is wise; he who knows himself is enlightened." The Hindu Upanishads emphasized *atmanam vidhi* (know the self), and the Buddha advised, "Be a light unto yourself." Shakespeare gives another twist to the same theme in his comedy *As You Like It*: "The fool doth think he is wise, but the wise man / knows himself to be a fool."

Imagine a world where you never stopped learning, where every day brought new insights and fresh perspectives. As Albert Einstein said, "A day without learning is a day wasted. There is so much to learn and so little time to learn it."[211] Learning is integral to what it means to be alive. It is fundamentally a process of change and growth. The beauty of life resides in the ever-unfolding quest for learning and the profound experiences we encounter along the way as a result.

In Hinduism, the concept of *jnana* (knowledge) is one of the primary paths to *moksha* (liberation). The Upanishads encourage seekers to ask profound questions about the self and the universe, emphasizing that true learning leads to the realization of one's unity with the divine.

One way to distinguish between that which is living and that which is not is the ability to learn. Inanimate objects are beholden to what is known as entropy. Following the second law of thermodynamics, these objects move irreversibly toward ever-greater disorder. Living beings, on the other hand, fight against entropy and disorder. The great physicist Erwin Schrödinger described this property of living things as "negative entropy," which is the ability to turn disorder into order.[212] Learning is a means to bring order to disorder. As John Dewey, a highly influential philosopher and educational reformer, said, "Education is not preparation for life; education is life itself."[213]

In childhood, the world is an amusement park of sensory experiences. Learning is primarily playful and experiential. Children learn through imitation, experimentation, and social interaction. Language acquisition, motor skills development, and the formation of basic social concepts are the foundational rungs of early life. Mistakes are opportunities for growth, and the joy of discovery is the primary motivator for learning. As Dewey said, "Give the pupils something to do, not something to learn; and the doing is of such a nature as to demand thinking; learning naturally results."[214]

As we transition into adolescence, formal education becomes a dominant force, introducing structured learning and abstract concepts. Adolescence features heightened abstract thinking, identity formation, and the "teen triad" of novelty-seeking, risk-taking, and peer focus, crucial for learning despite teenagers lacking full brain maturity. In adolescence, we grapple with complex ideas, develop critical thinking skills, and begin to define our interests and passions. This stage is often marked by a tension between conformity and individuality, as we strive to find our place in the world while also asserting our independence.

Adulthood sees learning branching out in multiple directions. Learning becomes more self-directed and purposeful, driven by specific goals and aspirations. We may pursue higher education or vocational training to advance our careers or explore new interests for personal enrichment. The learning ladder becomes less about climbing a predetermined path and more about forging our own way, choosing which rungs to ascend and which detours to explore.

In old age, learning may appear to plateau, but the journey is far from over. While physical and cognitive decline may present new challenges, the desire to learn and grow remains a vital part of healthy aging. Our brain has what is called neuroplasticity: the brain's ability to adapt and grow, and it's because of this neuroplasticity that one is never too old to learn or change. In fact, older adults often find joy in sharing their wisdom and experiences with younger generations.

Learning occurs in various contexts: through our jobs, families, and friendships and even through the roles life assigns us, regardless of our preferences. The lyrics of The Beatles song "The Inner Light," written by George Harrison, are taken from chapter 47 of the Chinese classic text Daodejing (or Tao Te Ching), They serve as a reminder that learning can take place anywhere, even at home:[215]

> *WITHOUT GOING OUT OF YOUR DOOR*
> *YOU CAN KNOW ALL THINGS ON EARTH*
> *WITHOUT LOOKING OUT OF YOUR WINDOW*
> *YOU COULD KNOW THE WAYS OF HEAVEN*
> *THE FARTHER ONE TRAVELS*
> *THE LESS ONE KNOWS*
> *THE LESS ONE REALLY KNOWS*
> *ARRIVE WITHOUT TRAVELING*
> *SEE ALL WITHOUT LOOKING*
> *DO ALL WITHOUT DOING*[216]

At some stage in our lives, we start to recognize the limitations to the accumulation of knowledge. Over 95 percent of the physical world is composed of a substance we know nothing about—dark matter. There is a famous saying by Socrates: "The more I know, the more I realize I know nothing." Socrates repeatedly maintained that he knew nothing. He was comparing what he knew in comparison to what he did not know.

Confucius echoed, "Real knowledge is to know the extent of one's ignorance." This is because reality has an onion-like structure. Each answer gives rise to new questions and provides opportunities for new learning. Since we can never extinguish our curiosity, as it is one of our deepest longings, it leads us to a pathway to our connection to infinity!

Stanford psychology professor and author Carol S. Dweck has pioneered the study of what she calls the growth mindset. She wrote: "Scientists are learning that people have more capacity for lifelong learning and brain development than they ever thought. Of course each person has a unique genetic endowment. People may start with different temperaments and different aptitudes, but it is clear that experience, training and personal effort take them the rest of the way."[217]

The flip side of this mindset is people creating echo chambers, surrounding themselves with news and views that reinforce what they already believe. According to neuroscientist Lisa Feldman Barrett, this reduces the metabolic cost and unpleasantness of learning something new.[218] Unfortunately, it also reduces the odds of learning something that could change a person's mind.

EXPERIENTIAL LEARNING

Learning need not be confined to classrooms or textbooks, as it occurs predominantly in modern societies. It is fascinating to know that the ancient Indian tradition recognized sixty-four *kalas*, or arts, representing a comprehensive system of learning that covers practical skills, arts, sciences, and spiritual development. They were considered essential for a well-rounded education and complete life experience. These are categorized in broad groups (the numbers in parentheses reflect the number of *kalas* in each category): fine arts and culture (nine), language and literature (four), body and movement arts (five), martial and strategic arts (five), healing arts (five), domestic and life skills (eight), science and mathematics (six), business and economics (four), social arts (five), spiritual and philosophical arts (five), entertainment and recreation (five), and advanced spiritual arts (four).[219] This emphasis on practical learning is echoed by John Dewey, who strongly believed that learning is most effective when it is rooted in real-life experiences.[220] And as Confucius said, "I hear and I forget. I see and I remember. I do and I understand."

LEARNING AND MASTERY

Another important perspective on learning comes through the lens of *Shu Ha Ri*, a Japanese concept describing different stages of mastery. *Shu* represents obeying the rules, diligently following established forms and techniques. *Ha* involves breaking the rules, experimenting and adapting the established forms to one's own needs and understanding. *Ri* signifies transcending the rules, achieving mastery to the point where one can create their own unique forms and approaches, no longer bound by tradition. This progression highlights that true learning involves not just acquiring knowledge but also internalizing it, questioning it, and, ultimately, innovating beyond it. The *Shu Ha Ri* concept is beautifully illustrated in the 1984 film *The Karate Kid.*

Shu (obey): Daniel, under Mr. Miyagi's tutelage, initially focuses on strictly adhering to the "wax on, wax off" motions, the "paint the fence," and other seemingly mundane tasks. He doesn't understand their purpose but trusts Miyagi and follows the instructions diligently. This is the *Shu* stage: mastering the fundamentals and respecting the traditional methods.

Ha (break): As Daniel progresses, he begins to understand the underlying principles behind these repetitive exercises. He starts to adapt them, incorporating them into his sparring and questioning Miyagi about their connection to karate. He's beginning to break free from simply mimicking and starts to internalize the techniques, moving into the *Ha* stage.

Ri (transcend): In the final tournament, Daniel, facing a debilitating injury, uses his crane kick, a technique he developed himself based on his understanding of balance and focus, a principle Miyagi taught him. This improvised move, born from his own interpretation and application of the fundamental principles, represents the *Ri* stage. He's transcended the traditional forms to create something new and effective, demonstrating true mastery.

The movie, therefore, provides a compelling narrative of Daniel's journey through the *Shu Ha Ri* stages, showcasing how true mastery comes from a progression of obedience, adaptation, and, ultimately, innovation.

LEARNING AND UNLEARNING

Continuous learning reflects on the perpetual human need for guidance, whether from religious prophets, philosophical thinkers, or societal norms. We tend to systematize answers into organized beliefs, such as religions, philosophies, and ideologies. These provide frameworks for understanding, moral guidance, and community. However, there is the double-edged nature of these systems: While they can provide clarity and cohesion, they can also lead to division and dogma.

That's why unlearning is a crucial aspect of life, often overlooked in our pursuit of knowledge. As William James said, "A great many people think they are thinking when they are merely rearranging their prejudices."[221] By consciously unlearning, we challenge our assumptions, expand our awareness, remove our veils of illusion, and deepen our understanding of ourselves and the world around us. It is through this continuous cycle of learning and unlearning that we evolve and reach our full potential. This has become even more important in today's world. As Alvin Toffler, a prominent American futurist and author known for works such as *Future Shock* and *The Third Wave*, said, "The illiterate of the 21st century will not be those who cannot read and write, but those who cannot learn, unlearn, and relearn."[222]

The key to unlearning is to constantly ask questions. As MIT biotechnologist Robert Langer said, "When you're a student, you're judged by how well you answer questions. But in life, you're judged by how good your questions are. You want to transition from giving good answers to asking good questions."[223] Einstein's words add to the point by saying, "The important thing is not to stop questioning. Curiosity has its own reason for existing."[224]

We learn from people, books, our own experiences, and those of others. As Niall Ferguson points out about the lessons of history, "The dead outnumber the living fourteen to one, and we ignore the accumulated experience of such a huge majority of mankind at our peril."[225] In the words of René Descartes, "The reading of all good books is like a conversation with the finest minds of past centuries."[226] That's why my emphasis is to bring you the perspectives of different continents and centuries.

Some of the most successful people in the world, such as Oprah Winfrey, Mark Cuban, Bill Gates, and Warren Buffett, credit their dedication to reading and learning to their continued success. This spirit is beautifully captured by T. S. Eliot in his series of poems, *Four Quartets*:

> *WE SHALL NOT CEASE FROM EXPLORATION*
> *AND THE END OF ALL OUR EXPLORING*
> *WILL BE TO ARRIVE WHERE WE STARTED*
> *AND KNOW THE PLACE FOR THE FIRST TIME.*[227]

Historically, learning thrived in communal settings, through storytelling, shared observations, and philosophical debates. Crucially, skills and techniques were passed down through generations. Imagine how little we knew as hunter-gatherers. Evolving in close-knit tribes, our success stemmed from collaborative problem-solving and mutual learning, often intertwined with play. We learned everything by exploring our minds and sharing our learnings with others, thus accumulating the collective body of knowledge that we possess today. As Vivekananda said, "All the knowledge that the world has ever received comes from the mind; the infinite library of knowledge is in your own mind."[228] Learning has always been the urge in each of us through which evolution carries its march forward.

Dr. Judson Brewer's research in neuroscience and education reveals that curiosity acts as a powerful catalyst for learning.[229] When we feel curious, the pleasure, reward, and memory centers of our brain light up. This stimulation primes the brain for deep learning, discovery, and even social connection. Think of it like a game of trivia or a crossword puzzle. The feeling of fun is a direct result of these neural circuits responding to information as an intrinsic reward. Whether driven by interest or a desire to fill an information gap, our brains are wired to seek out knowledge.

AI AND THE FUTURE OF LEARNING

When I want to know the answer to anything, I immediately jump on the internet and query one of the three best-known large language models (LLMs). I feel like I have access to cosmic intelligence just one click away from me. I no longer allow any curiosity to sit dormant like I did in the past. I have become even more passionate about learning, as I know that whether it is history, politics, religion, spirituality, or personal health, I will get an informed perspective from the LLMs most of the time. Sometimes, an LLM may hallucinate, so it is best to check with other LLMs. As the LLMs learn even more, they will get better at not hallucinating.

AI has the potential to revolutionize learning in profound ways. By analyzing vast amounts of data, AI can personalize learning experiences, tailoring content and pacing to individual student needs and preferences. AI-powered tutors can provide customized feedback and support, addressing specific learning gaps and helping students master concepts at their own pace. Moreover, AI can automate administrative tasks, freeing up educators to focus on what they do best: fostering critical thinking, creativity, and problem-solving skills in their students.

Looking ahead, the learning of the future will likely be far more dynamic and adaptive than what we've experienced in the past. AI will enable continuous assessment, providing real-time insights into student progress and informing instructional strategies. Learning will become more personalized, with AI curating educational resources and experiences that align with individual learning styles and interests. Furthermore, it can facilitate collaborative learning by connecting students with peers who have complementary skills and knowledge.

But we must be conscious of the dual nature of our modern era. Yes, rapid technological progress offers tools such as AI to enhance our understanding and pursuit of a meaningful life. However, AI also presents challenges that can distract or detract from this quest. I cannot overstate the importance of conscious navigation in this complex landscape. AI possesses an IQ of 200 today. However, when Steve Schwarzman visited China, Jack Ma told him that he expected AI to eventually have an IQ of 12,000. Who can predict the future impact of AI in our lives?

WHAT IS PLAY?

> *"PLAY IS OUR BRAIN'S FAVORITE WAY OF LEARNING."*
>
> ***—DIANE ACKERMAN***
>
> *"EXCHANGE YOUR CLEVERNESS FOR BEWILDERMENT."*
>
> ***—RUMI***

Most wisdom traditions emphasize love as a cornerstone of a meaningful existence. Similarly, the importance of learning is widely acknowledged. However, a crucial element seems to be missing from the dominant narratives of flourishing: The vital role of play. Pablo Neruda wrote, "A child who does not play is not a child, but the man who does not play has lost forever the child who lived in him."[230]

Think back to your earliest happy memories. What were you doing? You were likely engaged in some form of play with family or friends, or in modern times, with video games. You were full of belly laughs and pure exuberance for life. What was the purpose of the thousands of activities you made up? Why did you build forts and go on treasure hunts seeking long-lost booty hidden in our neighborhoods? Why did you run around playing tag? You didn't play to win awards or trophies. There was no agenda. You did it because it was fun, intrinsically motivating, and fulfilling. You did it to create bonds, shared memories, meaning, and so much more. You laughed and cheered and lived in those moments.

The power of imaginative play in a child's growth is well-documented. It's through these experiences that children learn to navigate social situations, understand emotions, and make sense of their world. Notably, the learning that occurs within the context of play often seems to be absorbed and integrated more readily, suggesting a unique efficiency in how the brain processes information during these engaging activities. This highlights the importance of providing ample opportunities for children to engage in imaginative play for their holistic development. Whether it be board games, crafts, puzzles, or imaginative games, a child is always learning. As Fred Rogers said, "Play is often talked about as if it was a relief from serious learning, but for children, play is really the work of childhood."[231] No wonder it's so hard for parents to wrest their children away from play.

Can you remember the last time you had so much fun you lost track of time? In our compulsively busy world, it's hard to even think about doing things that don't serve a purpose or have utility. But getting into a "flow" state doing something you love can effectively blunt feelings of anxiety, fear, and boredom.

Nietzsche believed true freedom and creativity come from a childlike spirit.[232] He saw human development in three stages. First, we're burdened by tradition like a camel is burdened by heavy loads. Then, we rebel like a lion. But the final, most important stage is the child. This represents innocence, the ability to forget the past, and the power to create new values, free from old rules. It's about playing with life, finding wonder, and affirming your own existence, rather than being bound by what others tell you is right or wrong. As Carl Jung said, "The creation of something new is not accomplished by the intellect but by the play instinct acting from inner necessity. The creative mind plays with the objects it loves."[233]

Play manifests in countless ways throughout our lives. Humor, for instance, is a sophisticated form of play, allowing us to explore ideas, challenge social norms, and connect with others through shared laughter. Art, in all its forms, is a playground for the imagination, a space where we can experiment with materials, explore emotions, and create new worlds. The artist Richard Serra said, "Play is a necessary ingredient in art because there is a kind of wonder that goes on when you play. You're directing your activity toward a conclusion that isn't prescribed by a particular method."[234]

Music, with its rhythms and melodies, invites us to move, to feel, to connect with something larger than ourselves. Confucius believed that music had the power to shape character and cultivate virtue. He emphasized that "proper" music, such as the classical *yayue*, could harmonize emotions and promote inner peace. He saw music as a reflection of the state of society.[235] Harmonious music indicated a well-ordered and virtuous society, while chaotic music reflected social disorder. "Any sublime expression of human creativity can conjure feelings of wonder and elation akin to a sacred encounter. That was my experience watching the extraordinary film *Flow*, which recently won the Academy Award for best animated feature," says Philip Goldberg.

My godson Shiv, barely two years old, and I stepped into the legendary wonderland of FAO Schwarz on Fifth Avenue in Manhattan in 2001. My mission? To find the perfect CD of music for this little bundle of joy. I decided to try *Baby Mozart*. The first notes filled the air, and within a mere fifteen seconds, something extraordinary happened. Little Shiv's feet started to shuffle, his tiny body swaying to a rhythm all his own. Soon, he was lost in the music, a blissful trance washing over his cherubic face. Around us, the bustling energy of the toy store seemed to fade away. Ten other customers, initially focused on their own pursuits, were now captivated by this impromptu performance. For a full five minutes, they stood mesmerized as they watched Shiv's innocent and joyful dance. Finally, I gently scooped him up in my arms, his little body still humming with the music. In that moment, surrounded by towering plush animals and the soft strains of Mozart, I didn't just witness the power of music—I felt it deep in my bones. It was a profound reminder that, from our earliest days, our brains are intrinsically wired to respond to the captivating language of melody and rhythm.

Dance is another form of play observed in almost all cultures. Moving our bodies to music is ubiquitous throughout human history and across the globe. So why is this ostensibly frivolous act so fundamental to being human? The answer, it seems, is in our need for social cohesion—that vital glue that keeps societies from breaking apart despite interpersonal differences. The French sociologist Émile Durkheim coined the term "collective effervescence,"[236] describing the phenomenon that emerges when people come together in some form of unifying, excitement-inducing activity such as cheering our favorite sports teams, participating in religious rituals, listening live to our favorite singers, or dancing at weddings or in clubs.

One of the ways play is institutionalized in India is the Holi festival. India erupts in a riot of revelry during Holi, where play transcends mere pastime and becomes a vibrant, societal spectacle. Imagine streets awash with the full spectrum of the rainbow, as friends and strangers alike gleefully bombard each other with colored powders and playful splashes of water. Hugs, warm and generous, are exchanged like precious gifts, and sweet treats dissolve any lingering bitterness. For a glorious, technicolor interlude, the monochrome hum of our screen-bound lives is banished, replaced by a jubilant return to the uninhibited joy of childhood. Time, that relentless taskmaster, is momentarily dethroned, allowing us to revel in the pure, unadulterated pleasure of connection, color, and mischievous celebration. Holi, a symphony of sensory delight, marks the triumphant arrival of spring, a vibrant rebirth after winter's slumber, symbolizing new beginnings.

Similarly, in many Western cultures, Halloween transforms society into a whimsical realm of costumed play. Children and adults alike engage in imaginative role-play, embodying fantastical characters. The ritual of trick-or-treating becomes a playful negotiation, a lighthearted exchange between households, fostering community interaction and a sense of shared experience. Examples of other cultures institutionalizing play are the Japanese Obon festival, the Brazilian Carnival, the Scottish Highland Games, and the Indigenous Australian corroboree games, among many others.

PLAY IN THE ANIMAL WORLD

Animals often engage in play, from the spectacular to the subtle. If you've watched a puppy frolicking in its first snowfall, that may be the only evidence you need. What about a colt running across a field in the spring? A family of otters repeatedly sledding down a muddy hillside? Birds lifting up from the water to join their first migration? Hyenas stage mock brawls, cats spin in circles chasing their tails, octopuses play push and pull with bottles, dogs bury sticks only to dig them up moments later. Even polar bears have been spotted playing with dogs, grabbing them in what looks like a hug, rolling in the snow, and letting the dogs gently nibble their lips. These glimpses into the lives of other beings offer compelling evidence that playfulness is a fundamental aspect of nature.

The universe is a cosmic playground! From swirling galaxies doing the tango to subatomic particles playing hide-and-seek, existence itself hums with a playful energy. Nature, displaying its infinite creativity through its dazzling diversity, is a master game smith; rivers giggle as they tumble over rocks, leaves whisper secrets in a rustling game of tag, and even the spider's web is a delicate game of catch. It's all a grand, joyous improvisation.

We, as part of this universe, are naturally playful beings. The concept of *leela* in Hinduism speaks to the divine play of the gods, suggesting that the entire universe is a cosmic dance of creation and destruction, driven by divine playfulness. The concept of a playful creator, suggesting a universe born not from necessity or rigid design but from sheer joy and creative impulse, resonates in many wisdoms' traditions.

THE CRUCIAL ROLE OF PLAY IN THE WORKPLACE

Alan Watts said, "This is the real secret of life, to be completely engaged with what you are doing here and now. And instead of calling it to work, calling it to play."[237] A playful work environment can boost innovation and creativity, improve morale, and foster a sense of community. When we play, we aren't locked into a rigid way of doing things. We are open to serendipity, to chance, to failure, and even to breaking rules. Sometimes, rules keep us safe. But other times, they stop us from creating, innovating, and having fun. The act of play itself may be outside of "normal" activities. But the result is that we stumble upon new behaviors, thoughts, strategies, movements, or ways of being.

In a pioneering approach to fostering innovation within a large organization, Google encouraged its employees to spend 20 percent of their work time playing with their own ideas on projects of their choosing, outside of their regular job responsibilities. The goal was to foster creativity, innovation, and employee engagement. Many successful Google products, such as Gmail, AdSense, and Google News, are said to have originated from this policy.[238] It empowered employees to drive innovation from the ground up, rather than relying solely on top-down directives.

Play offers a wealth of benefits, both biological and emotional. Biologically, it stimulates the brain, fostering the development of neural connections and enhancing cognitive function. Playful activities release endorphins, the body's natural feel-good chemicals, which combat stress and elevate mood. Play therapy is used to help children and adults process trauma, express emotions, and develop coping mechanisms.

A 2013 study examining playfulness, stress, and coping among university students found that playfulness may serve a much more extensive purpose than previously thought and that its benefits persist beyond childhood and into adulthood. Adult playfulness, according to the study, may well contribute to resilience. Playful young adults perceive lower levels of stress; they don't perceive stress as debilitating and thus attack stressors readily and directly. Data further suggests that virtually everybody possesses at least some element of playfulness and that it can be learned and enhanced.[239]

So, if play is so beneficial, why do so many of us seem to abandon it as we enter into adulthood? The answer lies in a combination of social conditioning and the acceptance of false narratives.

We are often told that play is childish, frivolous, and unproductive. We are pressured to be serious, responsible, and focused on achievement. The demands of work, family, and societal expectations can leave little room for play. Gradually, we internalize these messages, suppressing our natural inclination to play and convincing ourselves that it is no longer appropriate for us.

The impact of this decline in play in modern society is significant. We see a rise in boredom, loneliness, stress, anxiety, and even depression. A 2018 study by the health company Cigna found that young adults aged eighteen to twenty-two are the loneliest generation of Americans, more disconnected and isolated than even our nation's elderly.[240] There is a crisis—a spiritual crisis of loneliness among students in higher education.

Many people feel disconnected from themselves, from others, and from the world around them. The lack of play can stifle creativity, limit problem-solving abilities, and hinder our capacity for joy and fulfillment. We become less resilient, less adaptable, and less able to cope with the challenges of life.

THE EVOLUTION OF UNDERSTANDING PLAY

The concept of play, once largely relegated to childhood and dismissed as frivolous, is experiencing a renaissance in academic circles. One of the foundational texts in the study of play is Johan Huizinga's *Homo Ludens* (1938). Huizinga argues that play is not merely a human activity but a fundamental aspect of culture itself.[241] He explores how play permeates various aspects of human life, from ritual and law to art and language, suggesting that it is a defining characteristic of *Homo sapiens*—or rather, "Homo ludens," the playing human. Huizinga's work laid the groundwork for future explorations of the cultural significance of play. "Play is not simply the joyous rambling of children; it is central to all forms of creativity and communicates the highest ideals of communities. If we are to keep the flame of human creativity, ingenuity and culture itself alive, play is critical, as not only an activity, but as a mindset."[242]

More recently, Ian Bogost's *Play Anything* (2016) has offered a contemporary perspective on play, arguing that it is not simply about fun or enjoyment but about engaging with limitations and constraints. Bogost suggests that play is a way of operating within a structured system, finding meaning and value in the process itself. "Look at the way children play," Bogost suggested. "They have the strange ability to combine absolute concentration with free-spirited spontaneity and a palpable joy in their own actions. For them, there's no trade-off between focus and fun. Instead of looking at this childishness as undesirable, we could learn something from child's play: there's no reason why innovation and disruption should be any less stimulating for us than making sandcastles and toppling them over is for children."[243]

Stuart Brown, the founder of the National Institute for Play, says that play directly contributes to adaptation, flexibility, and social learning, which are crucial for survival.[244] A species that plays is more likely to be adaptable to changing environments, flexible in its behavior, and capable of complex social interactions. Play thus provides a safe space to practice life skills. For example, games with rules require children to control their impulses and adhere to agreed-upon guidelines. This helps them develop self-control and learn to manage their emotions in challenging situations.

The internal experience of absorption, enjoyment, and a sense of timelessness characterizes true play. We don't need external rewards to engage in it, continues Brown: "Play is a state of mind, rather than an activity. It is about learning to harness a force that has been built into us through millions of years of evolution, a force that allows us to both discover our most essential selves and enlarge our world. We are designed to find fulfillment and creative growth through play."[245]

Biopsychologist Gordon Burghardt, a professor at the University of Tennessee, summarizes play as follows: "Play is a repeated behavior that is incompletely functional in the context or at the age in which it is performed and it is initiated voluntarily when the animal (or person) is in a relaxed or low-stress setting."[246] Using Burghardt's criteria, many of our activities can be considered play—doing a crossword, chatting over dinner with friends, seeing a play, painting a watercolor, gardening, reading a novel, walking through the woods, and the thousands of other things we do for no good reason except that the activities are fun. External goals are often present in the background, but they are seldom the main reason why we engage in such play activities.

Andrew Huberman, a professor at Stanford University and founder of the acclaimed podcast *Huberman Lab*, said, "Play is an exploration of contingencies in a low stakes (keep adrenaline low) environment. Let's see what happens. Play invokes endogenous opioids. If you are in frustration and strain, a sense of play is great because in play, you have focus, and you have intention and alertness. It keeps you light enough that there's that dopamine release. As adults, we tend to be more demanding of ourselves. We don't tend to embrace as much play."[247]

Susanna Crossman beautifully summarized what play is all about: "To play is to experiment, to discover, to recover pleasure, to uncover the secret, do the possible, the impossible, to invent and make the thing that is unmakeable, to cross the bridge you couldn't cross, light wet fire, walk on water, fly. It is for an agoraphobic to sing in front of a crowd, dance, laugh and cry, paint a picture, forget worries, pain, and death, live outside of time, be in the flow, connect, disconnect, reconnect, imagine, make."[248]

For humans, play seems to lie at the core of creativity, innovation, and positive health outcomes. Scientists across disciplines have come to study and realize its importance in brain development and its role in creativity, innovation, and health in humans as well as other species. Neuroscientists are also beginning to explore the biological basis of play, examining how it affects brain function and development. This interdisciplinary approach is enriching our understanding and its significance for human well-being.

RESEARCH AND INNOVATION AS COMBINATORIAL PLAY

Research as combinatorial play is a concept introduced by Arthur Koestler, a Hungarian author and polymath. In his book *The Act of Creation*, Koestler argues that creativity arises from "bisociation," which is combining existing ideas in novel ways. This "combinatorial play" emphasizes the importance of connecting seemingly disparate concepts, rather than solely relying on originality.[249] Reinforcing Koestler's ideas, the famous economist Joseph Schumpeter said,

"The motherload of all inventions lies in recombination of existing ideas."[250] This perspective encourages interdisciplinary research and a playful mindset.

Some of the world's most brilliant thinkers and creators have talked about their work not as work, but as play. Albert Einstein described the workings of his mind as "combinatory play."[251] Isaac Newton wrote, "I do not know what I may appear to the world, but to myself, I seem to have been only like a boy playing on the seashore, and diverting myself in now and then finding a smoother pebble or a prettier shell than ordinary, whilst the great ocean of truth lay all undiscovered before me."[252]

The saying "play is the father of invention as necessity is the mother" suggests that both playfulness and necessity can be drivers of innovation and creativity. This playful exploration is crucial for navigating the complexities of modern life, ensuring that technological advancements are grounded in human values and ethical considerations.

In a 2016 TED Talk, writer Steven Johnson said, "Sometimes people invent things because they want to stay alive or feed their children or conquer the village next door. But just as often, new ideas come into the world simply because they're fun."[253] He tells the story of how modern computers evolved—essentially as the culmination of several millennia of playing with musical instruments. First came flutes, which were simple tubes punctuated with holes that could be covered with fingers to produce different sounds. Along the way, there were the inventions of organs, hammer-and-string pianos, and harpsichords, which were essentially the first typewriters. The mechanical hydraulic automated organ was invented in Baghdad over one thousand years ago. The principles behind this simple design led to the invention of today's organs, which in turn triggered the invention of a whole host of keyboard-based devices: pianos, typewriters, and eventually modern computers.

Steven Johnson's TED Talk clearly demonstrates how some of the most transformative ideas and technologies, such as the computer, didn't emerge out of necessity but instead from the strange delight of play.

Research and innovation also often involve multiple attempts, failures, and subsequent adaptations, reflecting the same iterative process seen in play. The euphoria felt upon making a significant research breakthrough is akin to the exhilaration of scoring a goal or finding a friend when you're playing tag. Experimentation allows researchers to test boundaries and hypotheses without the constraint of seeking a specific outcome. Just as children learn through tangible play, experimentation allows for tactile learning and discovery through hands-on interaction with the subject matter. In a playful setting, failure isn't feared but embraced as a stepping stone to eventual success or discovery.

A playful mindset is characterized by curiosity, openness, and a willingness to embrace the unexpected. It's about approaching life with a sense of wonder and possibility, finding joy in the process, and not being afraid to experiment and take risks. It is not about being childish but rather retaining a childlike capacity for wonder and delight. Developing this mindset requires a conscious effort to challenge the negative narratives we have internalized about play and to reclaim our natural playfulness. It's about rediscovering the joy of simple pleasures, embracing creativity, and approaching life with a sense of lightness and humor. By reintroducing play into our lives, we can unlock our full potential, enhance our well-being, and reconnect with the playful essence of our being.

Understanding what it means to love, learn, and play is just the beginning. These are not merely feel-good concepts—they are vital, dynamic forces that can transform the way we live, relate, and grow. But recognizing their value is one thing; embodying them in our daily lives is another. In the next chapter, we'll explore how to actively cultivate an LLP mindset, not as a checklist of behaviors but as a way of being—a conscious orientation to life that we can strengthen over time with intention and practice.

CHAPTER EIGHT

CULTIVATING A LOVE, LEARNING, AND PLAY MINDSET

> *"THE MIND IS EVERYTHING. WHAT YOU THINK, YOU BECOME."*
>
> **—BUDDHA**

One of my friends reviewed the draft of this book and loved the LLP framework. However, he commented that "LLP may be common to all, but is it enough for all?" He said he needs more than LLP. Some of you may have the same first reaction to the LLP framework. Cultivating an LLP mindset is not adding chores or stopping what you enjoy doing; it's about rediscovering and engaging with your three innate longings. It's like putting on new glasses that change how we experience the world. In the words of Proust, "The real voyage of discovery consists not in seeking new lands but seeing with new eyes."[254] Great painters have looked at the same trees, grass, clouds, and flowers you pass by without notice and turned them into beautiful visions. Nothing is so mundane that it cannot be a source of wonder, creativity, love, and the deep satisfaction of being alive, here and now. Albert Einstein is often quoted as saying, "There are only two ways to live your life. One is as though nothing is a miracle. The other is as though everything is a miracle."

When you live your life with the LLP mindset, you will experience the transformative power of making space for life's beautiful moments. Engaging with LLP means loving more deeply and broadly, seeing more clearly, and living more peacefully and joyfully. Any activity can incorporate LLP: Work becomes play, challenges become learning experiences, routines become expressions of love, difficulties offer growth, and simple moments enable joy. The three elements of LLP are intertwined and mutually synergistic.

To reconnect with LLP, start living consciously and heighten your awareness, as discussed in chapter three. As clinical psychologist Carla Marie Manly said, "Those who are self-aware tend to move into life's possibilities. Those who are less self-reflective often get mired in negative cycles that can lead to regret."[255]

The Dalai Lama, with his characteristic simplicity, says, "Substitute love from a verb to a noun. Rather than saying I love XYZ, say I am a loving person. I approach everyone with Loving kindness. Loving Kindness is extended to every fellow human being."[256] Substitute all three nouns—love, learning, and play—with verbs like the Dalai Lama said about love. With practice, LLP will become a way of being. You will transform into a loving, curious, and playful person. This will help you reframe daily challenges and encounters as opportunities to manifest LLP.

WEAVING LOVE INTO THE FABRIC OF YOUR LIFE

We begin by remembering that, while romantic love is significant, love goes beyond romantic notions to include the following:

- Affection: Gentle warmth and care for others
- Compassion: Empathy and a desire to alleviate suffering in oneself and others
- Kindness: Generosity, helpfulness, acceptance, and consideration
- Connection: The feeling of being seen, understood, and belonging
- Respect: Appreciating the inherent worth of every individual
- Gratitude: Being grateful for all our endowments and recognizing and valuing the love we receive

We start with self-love, embracing ourselves as we are and acknowledging imperfections. Then we expand outward, sharing love in ever-wider circles, encompassing family, friends, coworkers, communities, and eventually, all of humanity and total creation. As Mother Teresa said, "The problem with the world is that we draw the circle of our family too small."[257]

Here are a few specific actions to bring more love into your life:

- **Cultivate Gratitude:** Start and end each day by reflecting on three to five specific things you are grateful for and why. Write a gratitude journal every day.
- **The Language of Appreciation:** Tell at least one person, "I love you" or "I miss you."

- **The Power of Small Gestures:** Find small, everyday opportunities to express love—a warm hug, a supportive text, a call, an email, a note to ask how someone's doing, or a listening ear.
- **Active and Empathetic Listening:** Listen to at least one person's opinions or thoughts without assessment. As the Dalai Lama said, "Love is the absence of judgment."
- **Kindness with Awareness:** Perform at least one act of kindness daily, be it a compliment or a helping hand.
- **Cultivate Self-Love and Acceptance:** Dedicate time for self-love practices such as meditation or journaling to understand and process emotions, biases, and external pressures. Spend time in nature, engaging in creative expression. Self-love is about understanding and accepting all parts of yourself.
- **Love for the Planet:** Incorporate sustainable practices such as mindful consumption. Recycle something to show love for the planet. Choose eco-friendly products, and support businesses with sustainable practices.
- **Volunteering with Purpose:** Volunteer for an organization that resonates with your interests and concerns, transforming your altruism into deeply meaningful action.
- **Bringing Love to Difficult Interactions:** Seek to understand the other person's perspective first by doing the following:
    - Use "I" statements to express feelings without blame.
    - Focus on the issue, not the person.
    - Look for common ground.
    - Take a break if emotions become too heated.

- **Cultivate Different Needs:** Create a portfolio of friends. It should include intimate friends, real friends, deal friends, friends who share a hobby with you, or soulmates.
- **Practice Forgiveness:** Holding onto resentment blocks love. Forgiving is not necessarily for the other person's sake, but for your own peace of mind.
- **Protesting with Love—Constructive Action:** Protest for a better world because you believe in an earth where people have more love. Do so with respect and a focus on positive change, even when expressing disagreement. The power of peaceful activism and advocating for policies rooted in compassion and justice cannot be overstated.
- **Create Loving Spaces:** Cultivate environments (your home, workspace) that feel warm, welcoming, and supportive.
- **Be Open to Receiving Love:** Sometimes, we are better at giving than receiving. Be open to and appreciative of the love that comes your way.
- **The Golden Rule—Beyond Reciprocity:** Always practice the golden rule, especially when you find yourself in a heated political discussion or a personal conflict. Ask yourself how you'd want to be treated, and act accordingly. Consider the other person's unique perspective and needs, which might differ from your own. It's not just about how you want to be treated but about understanding how they might want to be treated.
- **Consider Weekly Learning Reflection:** Ask yourself a few specific questions:
    - What does love mean to me in its broadest sense?

- How do I currently experience love in my daily life?
- In what areas of my life do I feel most loved? Least loved?
- What are my biggest challenges or blocks when it comes to giving and receiving love?
- What limiting beliefs might I hold about love?
- How well do I nurture the different kinds of love in my life (romantic, familial, friendships, self-love, community)?
- What small steps could I take to cultivate more love in my life right now?

IGNITING THE FLAME OF LEARNING

Get in touch with your inner four-year-old child, the one who exhausted adults by constantly asking, "Why?" At least once or twice during the day, ask, "What can I learn?" from the people you interact with, the situations that unfold, and now from AI.

Here are a few specific actions to bring more learning into your life:

- **Cultivate Self-Awareness Through Reflection:** Regularly set aside time for reflection and introspection to become more aware. This internal dialogue that enhances your awareness serves as a foundation for personal growth.
- **Find Clarity amid Information Overload:** In the cacophony of constant notifications and distractions associated with modern life, look for the signal amid the noise, filtering the relentless stream of information to find the quiet, essential truths that guide meaningful action.
- **Take Command of Your Inner Dialogue:** Distance yourself from any negative thoughts. Tell yourself, "Let the mind

indulge in its mischief. I will not associate with this emotion. I am not my thoughts. I decide which thoughts I will attend to."

- **Harness the Power of Positive Reframing:** Replace a negative thought with a positive one. If negative thinking is disturbing you, try to focus your mind on an opposite positive concept.
- **Unlock Wisdom Through Attentive Listening:** Spend more time listening than talking.
- **Honor Others by Truly Hearing Them:** Resist the temptation to finish people's sentences, rush the conversation, or formulate your own responses while other people are talking.
- **Spark Deeper Understanding Through Inquiry:** Ask at least one open-ended question in every social interaction.
- **Expand Your Horizons Through the Written Word:** Read. For fun, for knowledge, or to escape and live vicariously through others, whether it's Wikipedia, Tom Clancy, Henry David Thoreau, Dante, opinion columns, or religious scriptures.
- **Integrate Learning into Your Daily Rhythm:** Listen to a podcast during your commute, watch a TED Talk or documentary before bed, and visit a museum on a Saturday.
- **Embrace Diverse Perspectives with an Open Mind:** Listen to people even with radically different world views without judging them. I talk to my Republican and Democrat friends with equal respect and attention.
- **Actively Pursue Skill Development:** Take a class, online or in real life, to acquire a new skill or sharpen an existing one.
- **Nurture Curiosity Through Personal Interests:** Cultivate a hobby: bird-watching, painting, growing orchids, baking,

gaming, knitting, running, tennis, golf—or anything else that works for you.

- **Challenge Your Assumptions Through Exploration:** Learn about something that contradicts your worldview or strongly held opinion.
- **Broaden Your Understanding Through Diverse Connections:** Connect with people outside your comfort zone.
- **Adapt Your Knowledge to Evolving Relationships:** Understand the changing needs of family members. Whether it's having a new baby, a child going off to college, or caring for aging parents, each shift requires a new set of knowledge and skills.
- **Sharpen Your Thinking by Recognizing Mental Traps:** Familiarize yourself with common cognitive biases such as confirmation bias, the availability heuristic, impact bias, anchoring, and many others.[258]
- **Cultivate Inner Stillness for Mental Clarity:** Find time to engage in meditation and mindfulness practices.[259]
- **Create Mental and Physical Space for Growth:** Regularly take steps to declutter your life, physically, mentally, and emotionally. I love the book *The Life-Changing Magic of Tidying Up* by Marie Kondo.
- **Engage in Collaborative Learning and Connection:** Attend conferences, workshops, speaker series, or events. Learning in groups can also be fun and a source of meaningful social connection.

- **Seek Guidance for Navigating Life's Journey:** No matter what stage of life you're in, seek help from mentors, therapists, or coaches who can offer insights, perspectives, and coping mechanisms.
- **Recognize the Emotional Dimension of Learning:** Understand the connection between emotions and learning. Emotions can impact memory retention, decision-making, and problem-solving.[260]
- **Embrace Imperfection as a Pathway to Improvement:** Welcome failure. Defeat teaches us what we need to improve to get better results the next time around. Treat obstacles and challenges as friends, not foes.
- **Grow Through Honest Self-Assessment:** Seek feedback with an open mind, in personal and professional spaces, both positive and critical (without being defensive), from peers, mentors, and even adversaries. Modern therapy has been deemed a safe space for many to have these nonjudgmental conversations that allow us to question ourselves and receive guidance along the way.
- **Harness the Power of Embodied Cognition:** Remember the "as-if effect," which suggests that acting "as if" you feel a certain way can lead to genuinely experiencing that emotion.
- **Cultivate Contentment by Defining Your Enough:** Define how much is enough for you. Otherwise, what you have will never be enough. Daniel Nettle, a British psychologist and author of the book *Happiness: The Science Behind Your Smile*, suggests that we would all probably be happier by trading income or material goods for time with people or hobbies.

- **Liberate Your Mind Through Forgiveness:** Are you holding a grudge? Let it go. Forgiveness frees you from negative thoughts and makes more room in your life for inner peace
- **Incorporate Experimentation:** Experiment with different learning practices to discover what resonates best with you and fits into your lifestyle. Not every practice will suit everyone equally.
- **Consider Weekly Learning Reflection:** Ask yourself a few specific questions:
    - What new insights did I gain this week?
    - What learning methods did I find most effective?
    - How did I step outside my intellectual comfort zone?
    - What am I curious to learn more about next week?
    - What did I unlearn this week?

RECLAIMING THE JOY OF PLAY

It's easy to forget the importance of play in our busy lives. Reclaim its joy.

In our relentless pursuit of productivity, we often neglect the simple act of losing ourselves in an activity. Rediscover the magic of "flow" by immersing yourself in passions that make time disappear, whether it's the soulful resonance of an instrument, the vibrant connection of shared laughter, the creative alchemy of cooking, or the satisfying logic of a sudoku puzzle. Embrace the uninhibited spirit of childhood. Experience play like children do: freely and focusing on the process, not the outcome. Let the sheer pleasure of the moment be your guide, and watch as play revitalizes your spirit. Enjoy fun activities simply for the joy they bring.

Here are a few specific actions to bring more play into your life:

- **Sprinkle Moments of Whimsy:** Incorporate short creative breaks in your day, such as doodling, losing yourself in the soaring melodies of your favorite music, or even daydreaming.
- **Cultivate Joy in Your Surroundings:** Create space for beauty, humor, and spontaneity in your daily life.
- **Unlock Instant Upliftment:** Want to lift your spirits? Lift the corners of your mouth. When you smile like you mean it, you can change your brain's chemistry and feel happier.
- **Move Your Body, Unleash Your Spirit:** Be it a short walk, a dance session, or a sport, ensure that there's some form of physical play in your daily routine.
- **Connect and Thrive Through Shared Fun:** Make time for social activities, be it a chat with a colleague, a call with a friend, or a family game night.
- **Inject Laughter into Your Day:** Laugh out loud at least once a day. Watch a funny video on YouTube, go to a stand-up comedy show, check out your favorite late-night talk show host's monologue, take in old slapstick movie clips, or just view animal antics.
- **Break Free from the Mundane:** Once a week, set aside a few hours to do something that takes you out of your routine.
- **Nourish Your Soul Through the Arts:** Engage in arts-related activities, including making visual art, performing, going to a museum or gallery, reading great literature, or going to a concert or play.

- **Recharge and Reconnect with Nature's Playground:** Immerse yourself in nature. Spending two hours a week in nature, either in short or concentrated visits, whether it's in an urban park, secluded forest, or anything in between, is the threshold for reaping real benefits.[261]
- **Gift Yourself Moments of Escape and Delight:** At least once a year, allow yourself a concentrated dose of fun and novelty, whether that's a staycation to putter in the garden, a yoga retreat, or an exotic trip. A single four-night vacation, whether in your backyard or at a luxury resort, has big, immediate, and positive effects on mitigating stress, strain, and enhancing well-being. Those benefits can last thirty to forty-five days post-vacation.[262]
- **Tap into Pure Joy with Furry and Little Friends:** Play with animals and children. Few activities have the power to connect us more viscerally to the magic and joy of play.
- **Reclaim Presence in a Connected World:** Designate phone-free zones, such as the dinner table. You may be surprised at how much time this frees up.
- **Embrace Silliness:** Let go of the need to be serious all the time, and embrace moments of lightheartedness and silliness.
- **Revisit Childhood Joys:** Think back to what you loved doing as a child, and try reincorporating some of those activities into your life.
- **Play with Ideas:** If you are intellectually inclined, get engaged with intellectual pursuits—brainstorming, creative problem-solving, and exploring new concepts with an open and curious mind.

- **Mindful Play:** Bring mindfulness to playful activities, fully engaging in the sensory experience without judgment.
- **Consider Weekly Learning Reflection:** Ask yourself a few specific questions:
    - This week, in what ways did I experience joy and spontaneity?
    - What activities made me lose track of time?
    - Did I allow myself to be silly or uninhibited?
    - How did play impact my mood and energy levels?
    - What small steps can I take next week to incorporate more types of play?

LOVE, LEARNING, AND PLAY REFLECTION

At the end of each week, reflect on your LLP activities. Adjust and adapt based on what feels fulfilling and what areas might need more attention. When the epiphany of the LLP mindset dawned on me, I realized that I should have played more in my adult life. Engaging deeply with an LLP mindset will help you

- develop a deeper understanding of yourself and your mind,
- cultivate positive emotions and manage negative ones,
- build strong and meaningful relationships,
- find meaning and purpose in life, and
- promote overall well-being and happiness.

This chapter has laid out the road map for developing an LLP mindset, detailing the key shifts in perspectives and behaviors that pave the way for a more flourishing existence. The individuals profiled in the following chapter provide compelling case studies of this mindset in action. Their lives, while diverse in circumstance and expression, share a common thread: a deep engagement with love, learning, and play that fuels their well-being and allows them to thrive.

CHAPTER NINE

PEOPLE WHO LOVE, LEARN, AND PLAY

> *"IMAGINE ALL THE PEOPLE LIVING FOR TODAY."*
> **—JOHN LENNON AND YOKO ONO**

Having explored the principles and practices of cultivating an LLP mindset in the preceding chapter, the question naturally arises: How does this translate into lived experience? This chapter showcases individuals who have deeply embodied this mindset in diverse and remarkable ways. Their stories serve not only as powerful illustrations of the LLP framework in action but also as testaments to its universal accessibility. These are individuals who, through conscious choices and a commitment to authenticity, demonstrate that the path to flourishing—to a life rich in connection, growth, and joy—is open to us all. Here are a few examples.

Lord Krishna, a central figure in Hinduism, embodies eternal love, divine playfulness, and profound wisdom. His many antics as a child, such as stealing butter, are interpreted as symbolic expressions of his love for the *gopis* (damsels), representing a divine reciprocation of their devotion. His enchanting flute music and the *ras lila* dance symbolize the soul's yearning for union with the divine, illustrating the transformative power of love. Even in his role as Arjuna's charioteer during the Mahabharata, Krishna maintains a sense of playful wit, using his strategic thinking to guide the Pandavas while simultaneously serving as a moral compass through his teachings in the Bhagavad Gita. His actions and counsel provide ethical models for Hindus as an embodiment of LLP. If you want to learn more, I like the book *Kṛṣṇa, the Supreme Personality of Godhead* by A. C. Bhaktivedanta Swami Prabhupada.[263]

Fred Rogers was more than just a children's television host; he was a champion for children's emotional well-being and a pioneer in educational programming. His show, *Mister Rogers' Neighborhood*, wasn't just entertainment. It was a carefully crafted tool for teaching children about their feelings, the world, and how to navigate the challenges of growing up. Rogers' love for children was genuine and palpable. He saw them as individuals with unique thoughts, feelings, and potential.

Perhaps more famously than anyone else, Rogers understood the importance of play in a child's development. He incorporated imaginative techniques, puppets, and music into his show, creating a safe and engaging space for kids to explore their emotions and learn about the world. He recognized that learning could be joyful and fun, not just a chore.

Rogers was ahead of his time in recognizing the importance of emotional intelligence. He addressed topics such as anger, fear, sadness, and jealousy with honesty and empathy, helping children understand and manage their feelings. He taught them that it's OK to have big feelings and that they are loved unconditionally.

He viewed his work as a "ministry of love," not just a job. He saw it as his calling to nurture and support children, providing them with a sense of security and belonging, and he believed that every child deserves to be seen, heard, and valued. Rogers' legacy extends far beyond his television show. He inspired generations of children to be kind, compassionate, and empathetic while also teaching them the importance of self-acceptance and the power of love. His message is as relevant today as it was decades ago, reminding us that we all have the potential to make a difference in the lives of others.

Rabindranath Tagore was the first non-European to win a Nobel Prize. A Renaissance Man if there ever was one, he was a poet, author, playwright, composer, philosopher, painter, innovative educator, social reformer, and champion of Indian independence. He embodied the essence of LLP throughout his life. Tagore's life was a celebration of love in its many forms—romantic, familial, universal, and spiritual. He was deeply moved by the suffering of others and used his voice to advocate for social justice, education, and freedom. In his works, such as *Gitanjali,* which won him the Nobel Prize for Literature, Tagore expresses a profound love for the divine, often addressing God as a beloved friend.

Tagore was a perpetual learner, driven by an insatiable curiosity about the world. From a young age, he rejected formal schooling, finding it rigid and stifling, and instead pursued knowledge through self-directed exploration. He immersed himself in literature, philosophy, science, and the arts, drawing inspiration from both Eastern and Western traditions. His travels across the world exposed him to diverse cultures and ideas, which he synthesized into his own unique worldview.

He established Shantiniketan, an experimental school that later became Visva-Bharati University.[264] At Santiniketan, Tagore created an educational environment where students could learn through direct experience, surrounded by nature and encouraged to question and explore.

Tagore's musical legacy, particularly through his style dubbed "Rabindra Sangeet,"[265] is deeply ingrained in Bengali culture worldwide. His poetry seamlessly integrates with his melodies, creating a holistic artistic experience. Sangeet is not simply music but a distinct genre. It's characterized by a fusion of Indian classical music (Hindustani and Carnatic), Bengali folk traditions, and Western musical influences.

Richard Feynman was a truly unique figure in the world of physics. He was a brilliant mind, captivating teacher, playful problem-solver, and passionate advocate for understanding the world around us. His passion for physics was infectious. He saw the universe as a giant puzzle to be solved, and he approached it with a sense of wonder and excitement. This love for his subject fueled his relentless curiosity and his desire to share his knowledge with others.

He was a master communicator. He had a knack for breaking down complex concepts into simple, understandable terms, often using analogies, stories, and humor to engage his audience. He believed that anyone could understand physics if it was explained in the right way, and he made it his mission to make science accessible and exciting.

This led him to develop a learning technique that is still widely used today.[266] It involves explaining a concept in simple terms, identifying gaps in your understanding, and then going back to the source material to fill those gaps. This process of simplification and clarification is a powerful way to deepen your understanding of any subject.

Feynman approached problem-solving with a sense of playfulness. He wasn't afraid to try new things, experiment, and think outside the box. He saw challenges as opportunities for creativity and innovation. He was a talented drummer, a skilled artist, and a keen observer of human nature.

He was also known for his quirky personality and unconventional ways, as he was a free spirit who didn't conform to traditional expectations. His playful and irreverent approach to life made him a beloved figure in the scientific community and beyond. His legacy is a reminder that learning can be joyful, engaging, and deeply meaningful.

Mahatma Gandhi's love for humanity, particularly for the marginalized and oppressed, fueled his lifelong dedication to social justice and nonviolent resistance. Gandhi's commitment to learning was equally profound. He was a voracious reader, constantly seeking knowledge and understanding from diverse sources, including religious texts, philosophical works, and the experiences of ordinary people.

His experiments with truth were lived experiences, a playful testing of his beliefs and principles in the crucible of existence. He treated his life as a laboratory, constantly experimenting with different approaches to nonviolence, self-discipline, and social change. The Dandi March of 1930, while a powerful act of civil disobedience, also had an element of playful defiance.[267] It was a symbolic gesture and a theatrical performance that captured the imagination of the world while exposing the absurdity of the salt laws imposed by the British on Indian citizens. Even his fasts, though undertaken in moments of great seriousness and often at great personal risk, can be seen as a form of playful engagement with the human spirit. They were a way of testing the limits of nonviolence, of appealing to the conscience of his opponents, and of mobilizing public opinion.

Albert Einstein was deeply concerned about social justice and peace. He actively campaigned for disarmament and spoke out against racism and discrimination. His love for humanity extended beyond abstract ideals; he genuinely cared about the well-being of others and believed in the inherent dignity of all people.

His passion for understanding the universe was a driving force in his life. He wasn't just interested in accumulating facts. Instead, he wanted to unravel the mysteries of the cosmos and share his knowledge with the world. This love for learning fueled his relentless pursuit of scientific breakthroughs. Einstein possessed an insatiable curiosity that led him to question everything. He challenged existing theories and wasn't afraid to explore new ideas. This intellectual curiosity was the engine of his scientific discoveries. He was a lifelong learner, constantly seeking new knowledge and expanding his understanding of the world. He read widely, engaged in intellectual discussions, and remained open to new perspectives throughout his life.

Einstein often used thought experiments, playful scenarios, and imaginative visualizations to explore complex scientific concepts. This playful approach to thinking allowed him to break free from conventional assumptions and develop groundbreaking theories. He found solace and joy in music, particularly playing the violin. Music was a form of play for him—a way to relax, recharge, and express his creativity. It was a counterpoint to the intensity of his scientific work.

He was also known for his wit and sense of humor. He didn't take himself too seriously and often used humor to connect with others and to make light of difficult situations.

Einstein approached science with a sense of wonder and curiosity, engaged with the world with compassion and empathy, and lived his life with a sense of joy and playfulness. His life serves as a powerful example of how the LLP philosophy can lead to both personal fulfillment and significant contributions to the world.

Jony Ive, Apple's design chief officer until 2019, told the *Financial Times* upon his departure from the company about how **Steve Jobs** created products with love in mind. "There was an employee meeting a number of years ago and Steve [Jobs] was talking. He [said] that one of the fundamental motivations was that when you make something with love and with care, even though you probably will never meet the people that you're making it for, and you'll never shake their hand, by making something with care, you are expressing your gratitude to humanity, to the species."[268] Jony so identified with that motivation that he named his new independent design company LoveFrom. Learning and play are the obvious other ingredients for a successful designer.

The producer, writer, and author **Shonda Rhimes** has created thousands of hours of some of the most-watched television in the world and generated millions, if not billions, of dollars in revenue.[269] The leader of Shondaland, an American production company, credits play with saving her career. In her 2016 TED Talk, "My Year of Saying Yes to Everything," Rhimes said that the simple act of playing with her children during a period of career burnout was the fuel that reignited her love for work and life itself. Regularly playing with her three kids for just fifteen minutes at a time connected her deeply to love and joy. "Work doesn't work without play," she said. "It takes a little time, but after a few months, one day the floodgates open and there's a rush. I said yes to play, and somehow, I still run my world. The more I play, the happier I am."[270]

Rhimes also focuses her "yes principle" on love. The Shondaland website regularly runs blog posts about how characters in her shows, such as Bridgerton, "say yes to love," but also highlights stories of real-life, non-famous people who have put love and play at the center of their lives.

Self-made billionaire **Jack Ma**, cofounder and former executive chairman of Alibaba Group, has expressed the importance of love and learning in a number of speeches and keynote addresses around the world. "I think both EQ and IQ are necessary to succeed in business.

But there is another important Q. LQ. The Q of love. Without LQ, even though you are very rich, you won't win respect," he said.[271]

Ma was trained as a high school teacher. Although he failed his exams numerous times and finished at the bottom of his class, he says he never stopped learning. After his retirement from Alibaba in 2018, Ma began focusing on philanthropy, particularly education reform to help children meet the demands of a global, digital future.

These stories demonstrate that flourishing is not a one-size-fits-all concept, but rather a journey of authentic self-expression that can be pursued and achieved by anyone, regardless of their background or circumstances. These examples demonstrate that the principles outlined in chapter eight are not abstract ideals but practical pathways to a richer, more meaningful existence, accessible to anyone willing to embrace them.

CHAPTER TEN

BRINGING THE LOVE, LEARN, AND PLAY MINDSET TO WORK

> *"BEING THE RICHEST MAN IN THE CEMETERY DOESN'T MATTER TO ME. GOING TO BED AT NIGHT SAYING WE'VE DONE SOMETHING WONDERFUL, THAT'S WHAT MATTERS TO ME."*
> **—STEVE JOBS**

We can engage in LLP in all our activities. Even work.

It's not a stretch to see the importance of learning in relation to work of all kinds. But what about love? It might seem uncomfortable to talk about love in this context. After all, it's emotional, soft, and personal. Not all of us have jobs we love, and we may not feel a great deal of control or agency over our workday. But even for those of us lucky enough to have jobs we love, knowing how to manifest love in the workplace may not be obvious.

Play, too, might seem like a frivolous pursuit when there are clients to tend to, deadlines to meet, and bills to pay. But there are more opportunities in the workplace and in the context of business than you may think to manifest LLP. After all, service is love, and innovation is learning and play, as is progress in science and technology.

Most Americans work a little more than eight hours a day, five days a week. New research shows that job quality is closely related to quality of life. Thus, a terrible job may even harm our health.[272] Unfortunately, less than half of Americans have a high degree of satisfaction with their jobs. There is broad agreement, however, on what matters most when it comes to job quality: enjoying the work and having a sense of purpose.[273]

The modern workplace, often perceived as a site of stress and competition, can be reimagined as a dynamic gymnasium for flourishing, a space where loving, learning, and playing are not only possible but essential. This shift in perspective reframes work from a mere transactional exchange to fertile ground for human flourishing. Just like physical exercises build muscle memory, the LLP gym at work cultivates a form of cognitive and emotional muscle memory. Repetitive physical actions create neurological pathways, making those actions automatic. When a team consistently practices open communication and mutual support, these behaviors become responses. This reduces stress, enhances team cohesion, and allows for more efficient problem-solving.

A workplace that cultivates a sense of belonging and psychological safety allows individuals to express their authentic selves and build meaningful relationships. When colleagues feel supported and valued, they are more likely to take risks, share ideas, and contribute their best work. This translates to mentoring relationships, team-building exercises, and a culture that prioritizes respectful communication and emotional intelligence.

Given that most Americans are employed in service industries,[274] let's use a hospital janitorial job as an example to show how the LLP framework works.

In a fascinating study, Amy Wrzesniewski, a professor at the Wharton School, University of Pennsylvania, showed how twenty-eight members of a hospital cleaning staff experienced and constructed the meaning of their work very differently from one another, despite being tasked with the same responsibilities. The workers who did the minimum number of necessary tasks and connected as little as possible with others, not surprisingly, had low levels of job satisfaction. Those who tailored tasks, stepped outside the parameters of their job description to perform additional tasks, and engaged frequently with coworkers, patients, and visitors liked their jobs. They viewed their work as highly skilled, believing their efforts made the hospital as a whole function more smoothly, and viewed their cleaning as vital to patient healing.[275]

Many of the cleaners in the satisfied group, reported Wrzesniewski, went out of their way to learn as much as possible about the patients whose rooms they cleaned, down to which chemicals were likely to irritate them less.[276] They engaged with patients and colleagues, bringing warmth and connection to their tasks. By infusing their work with personal care and a sense of purpose, they transformed their job's meaning.

BRINGING THE SPIRIT OF LOVE TO WORK

It's as natural to bring love to a job caring for people in a hospital as it is to a job in banking, sales, or manufacturing, whether you're at the bottom of the totem pole or in the executive suite. That's because every job gives us an opportunity to express the most fundamental aspect of love: caring for others. We can express love for the work itself, for coworkers, for customers, and for the communities in which we do business. We can create products with love and that our customers will love. And we can offer the highest, most caring levels of customer service.

In 2005, Steve Jobs gave the commencement speech to Stanford's graduating class. In it, he delivered a powerful message about love and work—or rather, the love of one's work. He described being very publicly fired from Apple, the company he'd founded. "I'd been rejected, but I was still in love."[277] The only thing that kept him going as he started over was that he loved what he did. "You've got to find what you love. That's as true for your work as it is for your lovers. Your work is going to fill a large part of your life, and the only way to be truly satisfied is to do what you believe is great work. And the only way to do great work is to love what you do."[278]

But how do we actualize love at work if we don't love the work we do or if our employer or our workplace is not particularly loving? In short, as Mahatma Gandhi said, "We need to be the change we want to see," which actualizes love at an individual level. It can be as simple as loving the people around us or offering coworkers and customers alike warm smiles, a sympathetic ear, or supportive compliments, day in and day out. If you don't love every—or any—aspect of your job, you can still love the purpose or mission behind it.

All work has a higher purpose. If you're a hospital janitor, it's love for creating an environment that allows people to heal. If you're a banker, it's the love of safeguarding and growing someone's life savings so they can support a family or become a philanthropist. We can always love the higher purpose, other people, and making other people's lives better through our work. To paraphrase Kant, we express love when we treat coworkers, employees, customers, and the communities our work serves as ends in themselves, rather than as means to our ends.

WHY LEARNING AT WORK IS PARAMOUNT

Learning has been a key component in the workplace as long as there have been workplaces. There is no doubt that it's a practical necessity, but the benefits reach much deeper. Employees who spent time learning at work were less likely to feel stressed and more likely to feel productive, successful, confident, happy, and ready to take on additional responsibility, according to a recent survey by the popular networking platform LinkedIn.[279] When asked about what made them happy and want to work harder and what inspired them, employees reported that they're most inspired by the work itself and the chance to grow.

Why do people leave jobs? Because they can't grow and develop. Among those who answered the survey by LinkedIn, a significant number spent five hours or more a week learning. They're reading, taking classes, and watching courses online to enhance skills. Not surprisingly, the heavy learners outperform their peers.[280] Learning something new is also an effective strategy to cope with stress at work. Recent research suggests that on-the-job learning is even better at reducing stress than relaxing.[281] In short, if you want to enjoy your job, spend more time learning.

One of the top concerns among CEOs is the skills gaps in their workforces. Historically, organizations tended to lay off employees when their skills became obsolete, then hire for new skills to meet new demands. However, with tight labor markets, business leaders are beginning to recognize that retraining existing people for new roles is more expedient and less expensive than competing for scarce talent. AT&T, for example, recently retrained 180,000 employees as part of its Future Ready program.[282]

But what if you don't work somewhere that values and rewards learning? Again, be the change you want to see. Operate at an individual level. Don't wait for the opportunity to arise; create it for yourself. If time and resources are in short supply, shore up your weaknesses rather than building on your strengths. Take advantage of organic learning from the work itself, from peers, from bosses, and from mentors. Think in terms of both hard skills, such as marketing, sales, and video production, and soft skills that help you learn how to better communicate, collaborate, persuade, and innovate. These are people-oriented skills that strengthen emotional intelligence, which will be increasingly important as artificial intelligence and machine learning technologies play bigger roles in the workplace.

The rapid pace of technological advancement and the ever-evolving nature of industries demand even greater emphasis on continuous learning and adaptation. This can manifest in workshops, online courses, mentorship programs, and a culture that celebrates both successes and failures as learning opportunities.

WHY PLAY AT WORK IS VITAL

"Playing" in this context signifies creativity, innovation, and a sense of joy in one's work. Reframing the way we think about our jobs, whatever they may be, is one way to bring play to the workplace. Peter Gray, a research professor in psychology at Boston College, play expert, and author, writes on *Psychology Today*, "You can work for a valued end while still focusing on and enjoying the process. To the degree that you focus on the process, your work is play."[283]

Job crafting, a recent social science theory, offers additional strategies for customizing or redesigning work. It allows us to do this in three ways. First, we can choose how we do our jobs, crafting the physical way we go about our work and actively shaping the scope and number of tasks we take on. Second, we can choose who we interact with and how frequently we interact, as well as shape the quality and nature of those interactions. Do we take the time to get to know our coworkers or clients? Do we socialize with them, forming meaningful connections? Third, we can choose our cognitive framing, just as Peter Gray did, meaning we can decide how we define ourselves in relation to our work and whether we focus on the end goal, or, in Dr. Gray's case, the process. Job crafting is a method for finding openings or opportunities for play as well as love and learning.

Bringing a playful attitude or mindset to work can help relieve stress, encourage teamwork and cooperation, boost creativity and innovation, and help find new ways to solve problems. Use play to open the door to creativity, and let go of assumptions or predetermined outcomes. Play allows us to accommodate unrelated ideas, which can help us find new ways to relate to coworkers and clients. When we play, we also open ourselves up to the element of chance because then we explore things we otherwise wouldn't have, and that can help open up other avenues to sell, solve a problem, or develop a new product.

The LLP mindset is key to being more effective and enjoying your work. Hitendra Wadhwa, adjunct professor at Columbia Business School, focuses on one's "inner core" as a way to drive exemplary leadership in his book, *Inner Mastery, Outer Impact*. "Your inner core is that space within you from where your best self arises, where your highest potential resides," he writes. "When you're at your core, you're beyond ego, beyond attachment, insecurities—and you get your life's most beautiful work done."[284] Hitendra talks about five energies in our inner core, three of them translate to Loving, Learning, and Playing.

Bringing the LLP mindset into work environments not only enhances individual fulfillment but also transforms the culture of organizations—inviting more creativity, connection, and resilience into the professional sphere. And yet, the power of LLP doesn't stop at the office door. Perhaps nowhere is its impact more profound—or more urgently needed—than in how we raise the next generation. In the next chapter, we will explore how cultivating love, learning, and play in parenting can shape children's development and help them grow into thriving, conscious individuals.

CHAPTER ELEVEN

BRINGING THE LOVE, LEARN, AND PLAY MINDSET TO PARENTING

> *"CHILDREN HAVE NEVER BEEN VERY GOOD AT LISTENING TO THEIR ELDERS, BUT THEY HAVE NEVER FAILED TO IMITATE THEM."*
>
> ***—JAMES BALDWIN***
>
> *"YOUR CHILDREN ARE NOT YOUR CHILDREN. THEY ARE THE SONS AND DAUGHTERS OF LIFE'S LONGING FOR ITSELF. THEY COME THROUGH YOU BUT NOT FROM YOU. AND THOUGH THEY ARE WITH YOU YET THEY BELONG NOT TO YOU."*
>
> ***—KAHLIL GIBRAN, LEBANESE-AMERICAN POET***

Bringing the LLP mindset to parenting requires a conscious shift in perspective. It's about recognizing that parenting is a continuous process of learning and adaptation and that children are our greatest teachers. By embracing this mindset, we can create a nurturing environment where kids thrive, not just as students or performers, but as whole, happy, caring, and well-adjusted individuals. And one of the most important things we can do is to get out of the way so they can do what comes naturally.

FOUNDATIONS OF LOVE

The loving bond between parent and child is the strongest in nature. We wouldn't be able to perpetuate the species if we weren't wired to love and care for our kids and if they weren't wired to deeply bond with us in return. But even for people who are not biological parents or parents at all, babies trigger potent emotions. Their cuteness, delightful baby smell, and even their laughter activate the reward centers in the brain, whether you're male or female, parent or non-parent.[285] Some scientists have labeled the sudden rush of emotion, caring, and love we feel toward babies as *kama muta*, a Sanskrit phrase that describes the feeling of our hearts going out to another.[286]

While I never got married, I do have ten godchildren. The mutual love between my godchildren and me is nothing less than what they have with their biological parents. When I was working for Reliance Industries in Mumbai, I lived with the Ambani family in their eighteen-story palatial residence. Founder Dhirubhai Ambani's elder son, Mukesh Ambani, went to business school with me at Stanford. When Mukesh's son Akash, one of my godchildren, was interviewed for admission to nursery school, he was asked several questions, which he answered correctly. But when it came to his father's name, he said, "My father's name is Akhil uncle." His mother responded, "Your father's name is Mukesh Ambani." He said, "No, it's Akhil uncle." After many attempts, he relented to say, "OK, it's Mukesh Akhil uncle." This is because I spent more time with him in the first five years of his life than his dad did, as Mukesh was burning the midnight oil seven days a week. I have several stories like these with almost all of my godchildren, in which their bond with me was as strong as with their fathers.

Loving parenting builds a foundation of emotional security, allowing children to develop resilience and self-confidence. A recent Harvard study concluded that kids who felt well-loved by their parents were physically and emotionally healthier in their later years. Parenting styles matter too when it comes to physical and emotional well-being, but according to research and what most of us know deep in our hearts, nothing is nearly as important as love.[287]

Discussing the research on *Psychology Today*, Harvard professor Tyler VanderWeele, one of the study's authors, wrote:

> *I BELIEVE THE RESULTS POINT TO THE CENTRALITY OF LOVE WITHIN PARENTING. WE CALL THIS "RELATIONSHIP SATISFACTION" IN THE PAPER BECAUSE THE QUESTIONS THAT ARE ASKED CONCERN SATISFACTION WITH DIFFERENT ASPECTS OF THE PARENT-CHILD RELATIONSHIP, BUT THOSE ASPECTS REALLY ARE ABOUT LOVE, ABOUT THE PARENT DESIRING AND SEEKING THE GOOD OF THE CHILD. THAT LOVE PROFOUNDLY SHAPES CHILDHOOD OUTCOMES LATER IN LIFE. I THINK WE PERHAPS NEED TO RE-INTRODUCE THE NOTION OF LOVE BACK INTO PUBLIC HEALTH DISCOURSE. IT IS CLEARLY IMPORTANT.*[288]

We might argue that all parenting is one big act of love. We love our children when we work because we are earning the money that allows us to house, feed, clothe, and educate them. Love is even more powerful when it's given with no strings attached. That means loving a child exactly as they are, not as we would like them to be. Fred Rogers said it best: "I don't think anyone can grow unless he's loved exactly as he is now, appreciated for what he is rather than what he will be."[289]

Parents often overestimate what makes a child feel loved. It can be as simple as telling them you love them and why. Say "I love you" often, and explain what innate qualities you value and admire about them, whether it's their helpfulness, kindness, silly sense of humor, or whatever else is unique about them. Give them your time and uninterrupted attention. Take a walk in the park, read, or cook together. Put down your phone, turn off the television, and be fully present. Ask open-ended questions about their day and how they're feeling, and listen to what they have to say without judgment. Resist the urge to interrupt, jump in, or offer advice.

You can also create a family culture rooted in love and establish traditions such as eating meals together. My own large extended family, with members aged two to ninety-two, is scattered over several continents. We don't get to see each other often enough, so we've started a tradition of weekly Zoom calls. We share news, tell stories, and laugh. The children show us their artwork and sing songs. They tell us how they loved, learned, and played in the previous week. We record these calls, preserving precious family memories for generations to come.

Lead by example by speaking and acting with kindness, compassion, and forgiveness. Let your children see you prioritize love, caring, and empathy in all aspects and spheres of life. At the most basic level, it is the love between parents that has a powerful effect on a child's current daily life and their later life. Children who believe their parents love each other stay in school longer and marry later.[290]

Talk openly about love—for each other, your extended family, your friends, your community, and humanity as a whole—and help children understand that it grows outward, like the roots of a tree spreading far and wide. Use love as a bridge to connect your child to the community beyond your home. Children intuitively know that we're all interconnected. They're naturally giving, kind, and loving. Amplify these qualities by regularly providing opportunities for them to share and give. It can be as simple as encouraging them to collect books for a nursing home, organize their old clothes and toys for donation, or participate in a food drive. Ask them to imagine what it must be like for a senior to be lonely or for people to lack the essentials they need every day.

When Fred Rogers was a child and would see something scary in the news, his mother would say to him, "Look for the helpers. You will always find people who are helping."[291] Teach children to look for evidence of love in the world, and they will find it everywhere.

In my family, one of the most loving acts I remember was when my mother prepared my favorite foods for my tenth birthday, and we then shared that food with the poor who hung around the respective places of their faith: a Hindu temple, a Sikh Gurdwara, a mosque, and a church. As I filled bowls that day, I didn't see Hindus, Muslims, or Christians—only grateful human beings. It's a lesson in love and embracing diversity that has stayed with me to this day and continues to influence how I live my life. In fact, the seed for my book *Bridges Across Humanity* was sown on that day.

When love is given back by children, it can be especially powerful. Ruby Kate Chitsey, a then ten-year-old girl from Arkansas, was moved by the impoverished residents in the nursing home where her mother worked. She was heartbroken to see seniors living without simple things such as comfortable pillows or well-fitting shoes. She started asking them for wish lists of three things they'd love to have. Sometimes, it was a book or a favorite candy bar or a piece of fruit. Her generosity inspired dozens of other kids to make wishes come true in their communities. Through the charity she founded, Three Wishes for Ruby's Residents, she and these other kid activists have improved the lives of more than 1.5 million elders.[292] Not every act of love ripples so widely, but every act ripples beyond our individual actions.

FOUNDATIONS OF LEARNING

Children come into the world with a voracious curiosity and keen powers of inquiry. Indeed, they learn by asking questions, experimenting, collaborating, and creating. When left to their own devices, they do so without regard for results, blissfully unconcerned about whether things are correct or even possible.

Kids who believe they can develop and improve their intellectual abilities over time outlearn their peers. They're also less afraid to try learning new things than children who believe that their intelligence is fixed. It can be as simple as telling children that their brain's capacity to learn is malleable. When they buy into that concept, they're more likely to view failure as an opportunity to learn more rather than a reason to give up.[293] When children adopt this mindset, they're more likely to explore, experiment, and discover.

Making sure our kids know how to learn, rather than just telling them what to learn, is more important than ever. Modes of education have remained relatively static over time compared to the workplace, which has seen rapid shifts thanks to technology and globalization. Of children who entered primary school in 2017, 65 percent will end up working in jobs that don't yet exist.[294] In a world where Google knows mostly everything, content is less important than asking questions, understanding concepts and ideas, and knowing how to integrate and synthesize them. And, as the world shrinks, our kids need to know how other people around the world think, too. Andreas Schleicher, an education researcher and statistician, writes:

> *TOMORROW'S SCHOOLS NEED TO HELP STUDENTS THINK FOR THEMSELVES AND JOIN OTHERS IN WORK AND CITIZENSHIP. THEY NEED TO HELP STUDENTS DEVELOP A STRONG SENSE OF RIGHT AND WRONG AND SENSITIVITY TO THE CLAIMS THAT OTHERS MAKE. AT WORK, AT HOME AND IN THE COMMUNITY, PEOPLE WILL NEED A DEEP UNDERSTANDING OF HOW OTHERS THINK, WHETHER AS SCIENTISTS OR ARTISTS, AND HOW OTHERS LIVE, IN DIFFERENT CULTURES AND TRADITIONS.*[295]

If you want to raise a learner, be a learner. Model the behavior you want to see. We know kids don't always do what we say, but they do as we do. Read to them and with them often. Embrace their innate curiosity and encourage questions, no matter how many they ask. Repeat to them that there are no silly or stupid questions. If an older child's sense of inquiry has already started to wane, make it a habit to ask them to pose questions regularly and ask them questions in return. Family meals are an excellent opportunity to build a tradition of questioning, beginning with everyone at the table saying "Tell me about your day" and "In what ways did you learn, love, and play today?"

Expose your children to new ideas, cultures, foods, and people by turning family outings into learning field trips. Visit zoos, museums, libraries, farms, concerts, or other cultural activities. Learning isn't just about books and numbers and facts; it happens in the classroom of life, too, through new experiences that invite hands-on interaction, engaging all five senses and the imagination. Students exposed to a single museum trip, for example, demonstrated stronger critical thinking skills, higher levels of social tolerance, and greater historical empathy and developed a taste for art museums and cultural institutions.[296]

When it comes to school, emphasize subject mastery rather than simply preparing for tests and striving for good grades. Instead of talking about winning, coming in first, or comparing a child to their peers, encourage them to focus squarely on learning as a process of inquiry. That's not to say grades don't matter; they serve practical purposes out in the world. But praising or rewarding children for grades and performance rather than mastery does them a disservice. Rather than building confidence, it may actually discourage them from tackling difficult subjects and risking failure.

When talking about college, discuss *why* before *where*. Frame the discussion around what the child might want to study, and how those studies might lead to the lifestyle the child might want to lead. Striving for years to get into a great school is fine, but remind your child that it's a means to an end, not an end in itself.

When a child is involved in sports, music, dance, or other competitive or performance pursuits, use the LLP mindset to help them experience the activity in a healthier and more positive way. Remind a child who is performing that what they're really doing is sharing love. Preparing for a performance inculcates discipline and personal growth. Performing is an act of giving, a gift of joy to those who are watching. Similarly, team sports are an opportunity to learn how to work in collaboration with others and to entertain spectators. Winning is important, but it's not the whole story.

Bring the element of play into learning new things by emphasizing that experimentation and failure are part of learning. Take the pressure off by focusing on the process rather than the outcome. Let your child lose, and encourage and even celebrate their efforts to take risks and innovate. Allow them to create with abandon, color outside the lines, and make a mess. In the process, your child will become a more confident learner and creator and enjoy the process of acquiring new skills.

Passion for learning transforms everyday experiences into opportunities for growth and discovery. It's about creating a learning-rich environment where children are encouraged to ask questions, experiment, and develop their own unique talents and interests. It's about recognizing that learning is a lifelong journey, and that parents are facilitators, not just instructors.

FOUNDATIONS OF PLAY

"When I was a child, I played too much," said no adult ever. Just as we can't love too much or learn too much, no child—or adult—can play too much. Yet many of us are shortchanging our children when it comes to play. Kids' schedules are packed with school and extracurriculars at earlier ages than ever before, and parents are busier too. A study by pediatricians concluded:

> *AN INCREASING SOCIETAL FOCUS ON ACADEMIC READINESS (PROMULGATED BY THE NO CHILD LEFT BEHIND ACT OF 2001) HAS LED TO A FOCUS ON STRUCTURED ACTIVITIES THAT ARE DESIGNED TO PROMOTE ACADEMIC RESULTS AS EARLY AS PRESCHOOL, WITH A CORRESPONDING DECREASE IN PLAYFUL LEARNING. SOCIAL SKILLS, WHICH ARE PART OF PLAYFUL LEARNING, ENABLE CHILDREN TO LISTEN TO DIRECTIONS, PAY ATTENTION, SOLVE DISPUTES WITH WORDS, AND FOCUS ON TASKS WITHOUT CONSTANT SUPERVISION.*[297]

Play is so fundamental to a child's well-being that the United Nations declared play a basic human right of every child.[298] "The very existence of youth is due in part to the necessity for play; the animal does not play because he is young, he has a period of youth because he must play," said Karl Groos, the early twentieth-century German philosopher and psychologist.

Beyond the fun and enjoyment—which are worthy enough ends in themselves—play has serious benefits for all aspects of development and health. Age-appropriate play with parents and peers enhances children's brain structure and function and nurtures meaningful social interactions and connections. Just think about how kids instantly assemble themselves into groups or teams to create games. Recall those moments on the playground figuring out with friends who would lead and who would follow and other rules of the game. Just watch a group of three-year-olds deciding who's going to be the mom and who's going to be the baby while playing make-believe.[299]

Play also involves experimenting, trying new things, adapting, discovering, and testing boundaries. In sum, exactly the sorts of skills children need to live in a world changing so fast that much of what they learn today will be obsolete tomorrow—a world that will demand innovation rather than imitation and creativity rather than conformity. Of course, physical play also has obvious benefits for physical health. Children from preschool through adolescence need at least one hour a day of aerobic and muscle-strengthening activity, such as running, jumping, and climbing.[300]

Perhaps the biggest challenge, aside from our busy school and work schedules, is the ubiquity of screens. School-age children are sedentary for about eight hours a day, and most are engaging in excessive screen time, on average, just under five hours.[301] Screen time only increases with age, most notably during preadolescence. According to Common Sense Media, the average daily screen time among thirteen- to eighteen-year-olds is nearly seven hours.[302] You should construct places where kids can play, away from this incredibly addictive technologically attached phase that we are creating.

Although a child might describe much of that screen time as fun, it's no substitute for physical play. "We have shifted our culture from one that is engaged in a healthy, interactive, imaginative way to one that is inwardly facing, sedentary, and expecting things to be fed to us," says Dr. Michael Rich, director of the Center of Media and Child Health and adolescent medicine physician at Boston Children's Hospital, in a report on how outdoor play develops a child's mind, body, and spirit.[303] Some of the benefits of replacing screen time with green time include more attentiveness and preparedness at school; reduction in ADHD symptoms; less nearsightedness, reducing the need for glasses; less vitamin D deficiency; and lower stress levels.[304]

What happens when children don't get enough time for unstructured play? According to Stuart Brown, founder of the National Institute for Play, "whenever the unique, intrinsic motivation of the child is not honored and the child is lock-stepped into a performance to please the adult ambition model, something very precious and authentic for that child's future is lost … or at least needs to be recovered later. A child's intrinsic motivation is driven by play, which really begins to shape who and what they are. Thus, when play is not given a fair shake, the individual loses something very important."[305]

Clearly, prioritizing play is an imperative. Children don't need much from us, except time. Creating that time and space for play does not mean nonstop activity. It does not entail expense. Simply give children the time and safe spaces to engage their senses, to explore new experiences, and to laugh. The criteria are simple:

- Playing is fun. Children must find it enjoyable, for its own sake, not in order to please the adults around them.
- Play is intrinsically motivated. Children engage in play without an expected outcome, goal, or utility.
- Play is about the process, not the end result. There are no expectations.
- Play is voluntary, freely chosen by the child.
- Play is not literal. It's imaginative, creative, and make-believe. The floor can be an ocean of lava, and a cardboard box can be a fort, grocery store, or animal hospital. There is no right or wrong.

Proactively schedule time for play, allowing children of all ages as much time as possible for self-directed, screen-free, unstructured play. Resist the temptation to fill every moment with activity. Allow children open-ended time to explore by poking around the muck in a pond looking for tadpoles or making something—anything—with crayons, paper, and scissors. In a child's hands, a stick becomes a magic wand, a blanket a cape. Embrace empty time and reframe it as a catalyst for fun and creativity.

For babies, play means simple interaction with a caregiver smiling and cooing, crawling, exploring, and cause and effect games such as peekaboo. For toddlers, it means interacting with peers, movement, music, and make-believe. Play with toys throughout childhood, and especially in infancy, is not educational at all but rather facilitates warm, supportive interactions and relationships, according to pediatricians.[306] When choosing childcare and preschool, choose environments that favor unstructured play over didactic activities and instruction.

As children grow, they'll engage in rough-and-tumble play, increasingly independent outdoor play, and more complex pretend and social play. As they enter adolescence, play may become oriented around competitive games, sports, or socializing. Whatever their age, allow children the freedom to take the lead in choosing their play activities, as long as they are safe, active, and screen-free, so they can develop and follow their curiosity. No one style of play fits all.

No matter what your child's age, spend a little time playing together as a family. Most kids love it when adults join in on the fun and games. It can be a meaningful way to create strong bonds. When we take time for our children, they feel valued and important. And for the grown-ups, playing with children can reconnect us with our fondest childhood memories and our own desires for fun, wonder, and joy.

The surest way to ensure our children's lifelong engagement with play is to reconnect with our own longings for play and lead by example. We can show our children through our own attitudes and behaviors that taking time for fun, pleasure, enjoyment, and experimentation as well as participating in artistic activities, embracing diversity, and taking calculated risks through play are acceptable and desirable. We can demonstrate through our own actions that play is a way to take a break from stress, from accomplishment, from doing—and just be. Play, like love and learning, is about being present. And like love and learning, opportunities for play are everywhere.

Parenting through the lens of love, learning, and play is not about being perfect—it's about being present, intentional, and open to growing alongside our children. By modeling the LLP mindset, we give young people the tools to navigate life with resilience, curiosity, and compassion. And in doing so, we're not only nurturing their flourishing—we're reinforcing our own. As we conclude this journey, we will turn inward once more to reflect on how all the insights explored throughout this book can come together in your personal path toward a more flourishing, conscious life.

CHAPTER TWELVE

BRINGING LOVE, LEARN, AND PLAY INTO OUR BROKEN WORLD

BY RICHARD PARKER, SENIOR FELLOW AND LECTURER, SHORENSTEIN CENTER, HARVARD KENNEDY SCHOOL

> *"NOTHING THAT IS WORTH DOING CAN BE ACHIEVED IN OUR LIFETIME; THEREFORE WE MUST BE SAVED BY HOPE. NOTHING WHICH IS TRUE OR BEAUTIFUL OR GOOD MAKES COMPLETE SENSE IN ANY IMMEDIATE CONTEXT OF HISTORY; THEREFORE WE MUST BE SAVED BY FAITH. NOTHING WE DO, HOWEVER VIRTUOUS, CAN BE ACCOMPLISHED ALONE; THEREFORE WE MUST BE SAVED BY LOVE."*

These words are theologian Reinhold Niebuhr's—a teacher of great importance to me and to the LLP framework—who can help us explore the role of happiness in the world we face beyond our family and our work. I'll call this "our public life," though for reasons I'll explain later, Niebuhr called it "our broken world." In chapters ten and eleven, Akhil focused on how an LLP mindset can help create a fulfilling family life and a fulfilling work life. Here in chapter twelve, I want to share the ways it can shape that world we all must inhabit—by truly letting our happiness flow into the vast matrix of other lives around us.

In chapter four, Akhil outlined the complex structures embedded in the concept of "self." Akhil then introduced you to a powerful synthesis of ancient Vedantic teaching and modern psychology to describe "the six rungs of the ladder to happiness." I want to revisit that ladder here by drawing on Reinhold Niebuhr and explain the fifth rung on that ladder, the rung of "service to others," the *seva sukha* in Vedic terms, and its place in LLP.

We arrive at that fifth rung after climbing four earlier rungs—the immediately personal experiences of fulfillment: first, sensory fulfillment, then intellectual fulfillment, then emotional fulfillment, and finally, creative fulfillment. What these four rungs share is the way in which they are "inward-turned" on our personal selves as autonomous beings. The fifth rung, gently but insistently, seeks to turn us "outward" and initiates us into the meaning of that "outwardness" and, most importantly, what a life lived in service in and to that world looks like.

"This is the happiness," Akhil said in chapter four about this "outward-facing" fifth rung, "that comes from *selfless action, from giving back to others and making a positive impact on the world.* This kind of happiness is *profound and enduring*, as it is rooted in our innate desire to connect and contribute. It helps us transcend personal ego and aligns with universal dharma. As Swami Vivekananda said, 'The highest service is serving humanity with humble love.'" In a quote widely attributed to Rabindranath Tagore, he echoes the same sentiment: "I slept and dreamt that life was joy. I awoke and saw that life was service. I acted and behold, service was joy."

What makes this fifth rung so distinct from the first four, is that it calls on us to recognize the significance of self beyond what we so often naturally think of as "ourselves." Ultimately, it asks us to come to terms with several enduring challenges that the world presents.

First and most fundamentally, in Niebuhr's terms, we will come to see *how* "the world" exists beyond our individual consciousness as "selves" alone. Second, we will learn why and how we should embrace this larger world as a "historically describable" existence—one that existed before and will exist after our own unique lives are complete.

Third, we will come to see that, in this historically based world, other human selves—indeed, a vast multitude of selves whom we will never know personally—exist simultaneously with us. What's more, like us, they consciously live their own lives as individuals within human communities that range from neighborhoods to villages to towns to cities to nation-states.

Fourth, like us, we'll come to understand why those human selves and their communities contain both a harmony of longings and desires and a conflicting disharmony of egoistic impulses and fears.

Finally, we will see how we are born into, grow up, and incorporate what we imagine as uniquely "ourselves," a shared web of inherited beliefs about who "I," "we," and "they" are. In chapter six, Akhil called that web simply "cultures"—it has other names, but the web is anything but simple.

As Akhil explained earlier, our complex "cultural" web of inherited beliefs both manifests in and acts on us in quite different ways, forms, and layers. As children, we experience commonality: We learn to speak our culture's language, to see our locale as "home," and to adopt its types of dress, food, and living arrangements as "normal."

"Culture" also contains—and this is fundamental to having a "self"—what our communities consider normal, allowable, and impermissible behaviors and relations, including a working knowledge of the rule-setting hierarchical social structure that governs us in that community. Without those essential cultural commonalities, the idea of "self" becomes almost unimaginable.

At this fifth rung, however, we are invited to do something more than "inhabit" this common "culture" we've inherited. Here, we learn as adults why, in order to find true happiness, we must engage with that community through "selfless action"—action that lets us "give back to others" in ways that will let us make "a positive impact on the world." We are, in short, invited by our quest for happiness to see that it depends on an embrace—ultimately, a loving embrace—of what lies beyond our imaginatively individual existence as just one of nature's billions of beings.

But what does Reinhold Niebuhr specifically contribute here? How does this twentieth-century Christian theologian inform this rung of our LLP ladder to happiness in the twenty-first century? And from what insights and teachings—since Niebuhr was a close and ecumenical reader of many religious traditions—did he draw lessons relevant to LLP?

I'll say more about who Niebuhr was shortly, but here, I'll concentrate on his importance to LLP and particularly to the fifth rung of service.

For me, his relevance announces itself in the title of his first and perhaps most enduring work: *Moral Man and Immoral Society.*

Published in 1932 amid the ruined landscape of the Great Depression, *Moral Man and Immoral Society* was not a work of abstract theology but of applied social ethics. It begins by recognizing the industrial-scale violence of the recently ended First World War as well as the devastation the Depression has inflicted on millions. Looking around him, Niebuhr sees threats to democracy in many places and warns that murderous men—he names Stalin, Hitler, and Mussolini—are the rising political powers of the age, and that their power poses the foreseeable risk of a second world war, one that democracy might well not survive.

This now-century-old historical context in which Niebuhr was writing may at first seem almost irrelevant to our search for happiness—but it isn't, because it contextualizes what Niebuhr identifies as the key challenge we face in living as democratic citizens in such a world. Today, we sadly face a world afflicted by too many of the same dangers—of innovative ways of "othering," of violence, of greed, of vengeance, and of cruelty—dangers that threaten not just our democratic institutions but the very social fabric we need for human flourishing.

Niebuhr's book—which he pointedly subtitled *A Study in Ethics and Power*—was a stark challenge to those readers who might have wanted to look away from the dark realities of his times (or, today, from ours) or who naively might try to claim that the abstractly good intentions of well-meaning people could somehow disperse the gathering storm.

The reason for readers to look away, he argued, rested on a universal dichotomy.

A gulf, he wrote, *always* exists between us as individuals and the societies we collectively inhabit. Niebuhr absolutely believed (as I do) that as individuals, we can and should seek to live happy and productive lives, lives aligned with the values we hold most deeply. He was not, in other words, a cynic, a stoic, or a cold-eyed "realist" who simply accepted the collective "power" in the large institutions of our "public life"—and those who control them—as inevitably ruinous to our individual virtue or ethics. His was a call to infuse our lives with courage as we live and share our happiness with the world.

But he insists that we first recognize a stark caveat: *that societies cannot do or be what individuals can*—and that only by understanding that dialectic tension between self and society can we, in LLP terms, *truly* master the fifth rung of the ladder and move on to our own true happiness.

"Societies," Niebuhr explained, meaning nations but also their underlying cultures and subcultures, always contain a competing welter of individual egos, experiences, and circumstances, each feeding their own appetites and aspirations. For thousands of years, those nations (in earlier times, as kingdoms or empires) have come into being—and sustained their existence—by exacting compromises that are never perfectly stable, internally or externally, and never perfectly or even nearly just.

Within a given nation, those struggles can be channeled and disciplined by various forms of what amounts to "hard" and "soft" coercion. It can sometimes be violent and imposed from above. Sometimes, it is orderly, exercised through the application of law. Sometimes, it is almost invisibly used because we've internalized its rules and roles so completely that we, the individuals who are citizens of those nations and members of their various subgroupings, act more or less cooperatively, believing that "nature" or "culture" or "custom" simply expect them.

But there is always the latent fact of conflict within those nations.

Between nations, the risk of conflict—of many kinds and degrees—is even greater, because the kinship ties and traditions that temper individual behaviors within families and the ties of mutual acquaintance that are at play in the workplace or neighborhood are absent. Niebuhr explicitly warned his readers, with fascism and communism on the rise in the early 1930s—and with World War I vivid in memory—that other nations are literally "the others" and that fear of "the other" is alive and well.

He reminds us that in Greek, the word *xenia*—the root of our word *xenophobia*, which names our fear of the other—originally meant the opposite of fearful to the Greeks 2,500 years ago. Xenia instructed the Greeks to welcome the stranger and emphasized generosity, hospitality, and respect for unfamiliar "others" in place of fear. In fact, for those ancient Greeks, xenia described a formalized practice to be followed with specific rules and obligations for both the guest and the host, because strangers were meant to be seen as envoys of the gods. The same thought is present in the Hindu culture with the famous aphorism *Atithi Devo Bhava*—the guest is god.

In the modern world, however, Niebuhr says we cannot know with any assuredness, given their "otherness," whether today's foreigner will honor the same code of constraints. And of course, he adds, in the minds of those others, *we* are "the other" to *them*, our existence arousing the same fears and concerns.

The great risk we face in LLP terms is that, after climbing the first four rungs of our ladder to happiness, when brought face-to-face with "the other," we may try to somehow reduce, ignore, or skip past the challenge of that fifth rung.

For example, in personal terms, we may think we can fulfill our need for "outward turning" through small acts of charity—by giving, say, to a homeless person on the street. Or, we may try to count elementary acts of citizenship, such as casting our votes, then otherwise ignore the nation's messy social and political struggles. In both cases, the mistake is to think we are left free to turn back to what seems more immediately "personal."

Both LLP and Niebuhr recognize that such gestures, isolated from our quest for our own happiness, cannot meet our truly deep need to make "a positive impact on the world," one that is "profound and enduring."

But how *can* we have a positive impact that is profound and enduring?

For Niebuhr, there is, above all, a core three-layered composite of understandings he believes we must internalize if we are to climb the fifth rung toward true happiness. Let me explain that by quoting Niebuhr's most succinct summary of that trio, a summary that I placed for you as the epigraph that begins this chapter.

The first layer of Niebuhr's triad invites us to embrace the role of "hope": "Nothing that is worth doing can be achieved in our lifetime; therefore we must be saved by hope."[307]

Don't misunderstand Niebuhr here. He isn't saying that individual actions to "give back" aren't meaningful or can't be individually successful in our lifetimes. We *can* act—and be successful in giving back. What he wants us to see instead is that as we perform such acts, we must understand—and accept—why the sum of our acts will, in our own lifetimes, not produce a world of happiness for all that we seek for ourselves. What Niebuhr insists you must see is that the world's brokenness remains.

That's why, he explains, we must nonetheless learn to give back—because it is an expression of our own true happiness—while reluctantly accepting that the conflicts inherent to societies will undercut the consequential sum of those acts. But by maintaining hope, we teach ourselves (and others) the saving grace of humility—a humility that balances the joy of service with its many disappointments and recognizes the limits of our own individual powers without surrendering to power.

True humility, for Niebuhr, is thus not an expression of weakness but rather of great strength—the strength that LLP can help bring forth. "Hope" is, in other words, the posture we show others of our own unbending courage set against the setbacks that societies inescapably inflict.

The second of the three layers is the role "faith" plays in underpinning that posture of courageous humility and spirit of "hope": "Nothing which is true or beautiful or good makes complete sense in any immediate context of history; therefore we must be saved by faith."[308]

Niebuhr chooses to name the concepts of Truth, Beauty, and Goodness to us here as interlocking facets of the goals of human consciousness that structure our eternal search for life's underlying meaning. He's referring, as he explains, to the modern belief in the interconnection of truth, beauty, and goodness as the objective of our most basic human faculties.

As the power of religion receded in the West, enlightenment and early modern European thinkers searched in classical philosophy for ways to describe those human faculties as innate and independent of the divine. "Truth" had long been tied by the classical Western philosophers conceptually to the human capacity for logic as formal reasoning—but by the early nineteenth century, the idea of science, itself profoundly "logical," was replacing traditional logic as a *telos* as knowledge of the material, empirical world and its own physical rules grew exponentially.

"Beauty," meanwhile, defined a *telos* of the senses, an innate appreciation for an order that was neither formally "logical" nor scientifically "empirical" but whose power, most often experienced in works of painting, sculpture, and music or the contemplation of nature around us, seemed, to modern thinkers, undeniably profound.

Of our three goals, the "Good" was considered the ultimate objective of ethics—our attempt to use reason to guide both our own and others' actions and words. This effort sought to bring justice to our social and political lives by limiting the constant deference societies show to power and the powerful.

What Niebuhr is inviting us to realize is that these faculties, however conceptually powerful in naming fundamental human drives and their goals—which we find in all societies—nonetheless remain as goals that will be ever-elusive in terms of their achievement in the immediate context of not just our own lives but of human history. Only by "faith"—the irrational commitment that underpins "hope" by giving it constancy—can we move forward in what is, from history's evidence, "a broken world."

Finally for Niebuhr comes "love," the most profound and most essential of the gifts we can accept through faith and hope—and the true binding link between him and LLP: "Nothing we do, however virtuous, can be accomplished alone; therefore we must be saved by love."[309]

Here, Niebuhr is sharing his Christian understanding of *agape*, the selfless love that God has for mankind and which humans are called upon to share with others—especially "others" through our own form of xenia. Agape is not *eros*, denoting sexual attraction, nor is it *philia*, the Greek word for deeply affectionate friendship. Agape is rather the way we live our happiness, in LLP terms, into the world.

So how do we do that? How do we take what we've learned from the first four rungs of the ladder to happiness—which introduced us to fulfillment in sensory, intellectual, emotional, and creative terms—"outward" into the world so that we can give back in the most profound and enduring ways?

The lessons I invite you to take from Niebuhr through LLP are these:

1. Recognize that, in order to truly "give back," you and I are individual selves in a world of others who are equally individual selves.
2. Embrace what you've learned here about the creation of happiness in your own life, and face that world of those others in ways that clearly bear witness to your happiness.
3. Watch for the telltale signs of the others searching for their own happiness—and encourage that search through words and actions you take in your encounters.
4. Do the above by first manifesting your humility in voice and gesture and the posture in which you listen. Recognize that such humility by itself is an invitation for others to respond—and that your expressed humility is not just about showing an aspect of your character alone but an invitation to a deeper and more human conversation and connection.
5. Look for opportunities to join others in common work that itself "gives back" in "profound and enduring" ways. That work can take many forms, but the test for you is whether you can bring your happiness to this work, willingly and lovingly.
6. As you grow comfortable in this "common work," let the realization emerge that what you are actually engaged in is "common play." Cultivate that playfulness—and celebrate it in others. There will come a lightness that sustains when you do—the sign that you are truly giving back in a way that is profound and enduring.

7. *Most importantly, do not pull back in fear when you encounter the fear of others.* That fear can appear—often suddenly—as anger, withdrawal, or even outright rejection of you and your ideas about how best to give back. This is what makes the fifth rung so different from the "inward-looking" first four rungs. You are now encountering "the other" in what Niebuhr wants you to understand as an inevitability; respond, he says, not out of your own fear but with both your humility and your courage.

Niebuhr's teachings have influenced a strikingly wide range of men and women who've shaped our public life, an influence that endures. Since 2000, political figures, from John McCain on the right to Barack Obama on the left, have fulsomely recounted Niebuhr's influence on their thoughts, while political intellectuals, from David Brooks to E. J. Dionne, invoke him regularly when assessing American foreign policy. Moreover, scores of conferences, papers, books, and broadcasts have taken up the questions Niebuhrian thought continues to raise about how a powerful nation, flawed by its very nature, should act in a world corrupted by fears of "the other," foreign and domestic.

Martin Luther King Jr. began reading Niebuhr as a young seminarian, wrote several papers on Niebuhr, and personally wrote to Niebuhr for advice on key points in his doctoral dissertation. At the height of the civil rights movement, King singled out Niebuhr and Gandhi as the two greatest influences in the struggle for civil rights—and King personally invited Niebuhr to march with him across the Edmund Pettus Bridge in Selma, Alabama. Inscribing a copy of his reflections on the Montgomery bus boycott to Niebuhr, King praised him as a theologian of "great prophetic vision" with an "unswerving devotion to the ideals of freedom and justice."[310]

Niebuhr's own career as a very public theologian in many ways embodied the tension his inescapable dichotomy between the self and society creates for leaders and their advisors in our public life. His implacable opposition to fascism and communism endured, but by the 1950s, at the height of the Cold War, this opposition was joined by his growing concern about what he called "the irony of American history." Armed with nuclear weapons and quick to intervene in the affairs of other nations, America nonetheless insisted on the selfless virtues—often, the unalloyed virtues—of its actions. For a time in the late 1940s, Niebuhr had been sought out by senior government officials for advice on the nation's emergent Cold War policies, because many of those officials were privately aware that America's actions were never perfectly virtuous and, in some cases, were proving malignantly destructive of the values America professed to protect and extend.

Having left his advisory role, he nonetheless remained in frequent contact with many senior public officials and influential public figures—but now critiqued publicly the ways the state's overreaching in the name of virtue had left the country entangled in the impossibility of achieving what it said it wanted most. It was an act of calculated balance on Niebuhr's part—the recognition of inescapable limits joined with the determination to sustain hope, faith, and the love that is agape, which still motivated him.

For LLP, acquiring that Niebuhrian balance is key to ascending rung five of the ladder to happiness and, ultimately, reaching the final sixth rung. Equipped with the personal motivation to seek positive impact on the world, we can recognize Niebuhr's essential dichotomy as a limit to worldly perfectibility—but not of imperfect improvement—and now explore how giving and seeking love both humbly and courageously will bring true fulfillment to our lives.

CONCLUSION

YOUR PATH TO FLOURISHING

> *"FOLLOW YOUR BLISS. THE BLISS IS THE MESSAGE OF GOD TO YOURSELF. THAT'S WHERE YOUR LIFE IS."*
> **—JOSEPH CAMPBELL**

"Live long and prosper."

Popularized in Western culture as the Vulcan salute in *Star Trek*, this saying is, in fact, an ancient blessing often delivered by Indian elders to anyone who touches their feet as a mark of respect. Sometimes, I feel my success in life has to do with those blessings I received from my parents as I touched their feet every day until I went to college!

While modern science has indeed enhanced human longevity, prosperity is not an issue for many people today. Instead, now more than ever, we yearn to live wholesome, fulfilled lives and make a difference in the world around us. We yearn to flourish. But what does it mean to truly flourish? And how does one accomplish this goal?

To answer these questions, we must acknowledge the fundamental yearnings that shape the human experience. Our minds relentlessly seek understanding and coherence in the world around us, driven by an innate curiosity to unravel its mysteries. Our hearts yearn for solace and meaning in the face of mortality and the vastness of existence, seeking to transcend the fear of insignificance. Our societies necessitate structure and shared values to harmonize individual liberties and foster collective well-being. Yet, our very intellect, while a powerful tool, is susceptible to cognitive illusions and inherent biases, demanding constant vigilance and critical self-reflection. Deep within, our hearts also crave connection and belonging, a desire often nurtured by the communal bonds found in religion. Finally, the need for a dependable ethical framework is woven into the fabric of our social interactions, guiding our choices and shaping our shared future. To flourish is to engage with these core human demands with intention and grace.

From Socrates's focus on self-knowledge to Aristotle's emphasis on rational excellence, ancient Greek philosophers explored diverse paths to human flourishing. Stoicism highlights the power of internal control amid external chaos while contrasting hedonistic and ascetic approaches to desire. Utilitarianism values actions that bring the greatest good to the greatest number. Religious and spiritual traditions offer further frameworks: Judaism's adherence to law, Islam's submission to Allah, Christianity's seeking grace, Buddhism's Eightfold Path, Confucianism's emphasis on social harmony, virtue, and fulfilling one's role in society, and Hinduism's pursuit of realization of our divine nature by piercing through the veil of maya.

We can see that the concept of happiness/flourishing has been central to human thought across continents, centuries, and traditions. However, I was struck by the absence of a singular, universally applicable formula, in spite of believing that human nature is the same for all of us. Varied ideas have come and gone in waves. Some have been tsunamis full of sound and fury, others gentle swells, but ultimately, they have all ebbed, giving way to new philosophies. Each proposed path, though partially valid, proved inadequate in capturing the full scope of human experience. True fulfillment demands a holistic perspective, one that acknowledges the nuances of individual lives, as discussed in chapters four, five, and six. Here is a summary of the issues with a few of the most famous happiness prescriptions.

Hedonism: In its simplest form, hedonism can be understood as the pursuit of immediate gratification and sensory pleasures. It is the most superficial form of life satisfaction and, therefore, the easiest. There are plenty of options that provide cheap dopamine shots. Pleasure is what's marketed to us. However, these kinds of pleasures are contingent, short-lived, and often lead to long-term dissatisfaction. Excessive indulgence can lead to addiction and harmful behaviors.

Eudaemonia: Aristotle introduced the concept of *eudaemonia*, often translated as flourishing or well-being. Aristotle argues that human happiness lies in fulfilling our unique function, which he identifies as rational activity. However, human beings are incredibly diverse, with varying talents, inclinations, temperaments, interests, and life circumstances, as discussed in chapters four to six. What constitutes excellence in one context might be irrelevant or even detrimental in another.

Ataraxia: *Ataraxia* emphasizes the importance of finding inner peace and tranquility. However, seeking complete tranquility risks diminishing life's richness. Emphasizing ataraxia as the ultimate goal may lead to a lack of motivation, drive, and ambition. The downside is that little social good would happen if each of us lived within our privileges without stepping outside the zone to accept, fight for, and welcome change. Slavery would still exist. Apartheid South Africa would still be here. Modern society has made the choice in favor of romanticism, and there are few takers of ataraxia.

Transformation of Desires: According to many wisdom traditions, prominently Buddhism, desires/cravings are the root cause of suffering. However, attempting to eradicate all desires is impractical and potentially harmful. Some scholars argue that the Buddha's teachings on desire were more nuanced than a simple condemnation of all forms of wanting. They suggest that the focus was on unwholesome desires, those driven by greed, attachment, and ignorance, rather than on desire itself. Tantra, a discipline of Hindu thought, distinguishes between desires that arise from a sense of lack, deficiency, or ego and desires that arise from the authentic self or the divine essence within. The former are indeed seen as sources of suffering. They are the *tanha* or craving described in traditional Buddhism. However, tantra also recognizes the existence of desires that stem from the *spanda*, from the very core of our being. These are expressions of our true nature, our inherent creativity, and our longing for connection with the divine. The key is discerning between authentic and socially constructed ones. To crave is to want something that doesn't satisfy us or nourish us.

Positive Psychology: While positive psychology has made significant contributions to the study of well-being, it has been criticized for its individualistic focus and its tendency to overlook the role of social and structural factors in shaping happiness. It can also lead to a "tyranny of positivity," in which individuals feel pressure to be happy all the time, even in the face of adversity.

Beyond Selfishness: This is a key prescription of many wisdom traditions. As Shantideva said, "All joy in this world comes from wanting others to be happy, and all suffering in this world comes from wanting only oneself to be happy."[311] However, we are not ants. While altruism is crucial, it must be balanced with self-care. Rabbi

Hillel expressed the balance between self and others in his famous three questions: "If I am not for myself, who will be for me? And if I am not for others, what am I? And if not now, when?"[312]

One of the most powerful Eastern metaphors that corroborates what Hillel said is the ancient Chinese concept of yin and yang. Yin and yang represent opposing yet complementary forces, constantly interacting and seeking equilibrium. The yin and yang of human flourishing are interdependence and agency. In the words of Buddhist monk Dekila Chungyalpa, "Embracing interdependence as the central organizing principle is to dissolve that boundary between ourselves and 'the other' and to expand the circle of community so that there is no 'other' left; there is only us made whole."[313]

Yin encourages us to embrace our receptive nature, fostering empathy, compassion, and deep connection with others. This involves active listening, emotional vulnerability, and the ability to nurture relationships. It highlights the importance of rest, reflection, and introspection, allowing us to replenish our inner resources and cultivate inner peace.

Yang fuels our drive, ambition, and ability to take action. It empowers us to pursue our goals, assert our needs, and make a positive impact on the world. It encourages us to embrace our autonomy, cultivate self-reliance, and develop our unique talents and abilities.

The modern tendency to overemphasize agency has led to a societal imbalance. We see this in the rise of individualistic lifestyles. Digital platforms offer a sense of connection yet often foster superficial interactions. This creates a situation where the yang aspect of life, individualization, is overemphasized, and the yin aspect, connection to others, is undernourished.

With deep respect for these diverse traditions and philosophies, I humbly propose that the LLP framework I stumbled upon offers a more universally resonant approach—not because it negates their wisdom but because it distills it into a language that speaks directly to the human heart, across cultures and contexts. Its strength lies not in dogma but in its simplicity and accessibility. The "happiness guru" Arthur C. Brooks said, "If the secret to pure happiness existed, we all would have found it by now."[314]

Unlike many external prescriptions for happiness, this framework seeks to facilitate an inward journey, empowering each individual to cultivate a flourishing life from the wellspring of their own innate wisdom.

PASCAL'S WAGER APPLIED TO THE LOVE, LEARN, AND PLAY FRAMEWORK

But what if I'm wrong and the LLP mindset is not a good way to increase human happiness? How can we even address this question? Blaise Pascal, the seventeenth-century mathematician, formulated a wager to address the question of God's existence as a bet on a coin toss. What Pascal's Wager shows is that whether it comes up heads or tails doesn't matter. Even if you don't believe that God exists, if you live in accordance with God's golden rules, such as treating others kindly, you and the world will benefit. So, if you win, you gain it all. If you lose, you lose nothing. Also, you must wager. It's not optional.

Applying Pascal's wager to the premise of this book, that to flourish is to love, learn, and play, we see four different outcomes to the bet:

To Flourish is to Love, Learn, and Play			
You live as if it is true		You live as if it is false	
If it is true, you experience true flourishing.	If it is false, you may have spent unnecessary effort, but you likely still learned, loved, and played—which is still intrinsically good in any wisdom tradition.	If it is true, you miss out on potential flourishing.	If it is false, you may avoid the full "effort," but you also miss out on the "intrinsic efforts."

In other words, you have nothing to lose and everything to gain. In the most optimal outcome, you experience flourishing. If you don't embrace love, or learning, or play, you'll save yourself the energy and efforts it takes to pursue those actions, but you'll miss out on the potential for flourishing. Applying Pascal's wager to the LLP hypothesis suggests that it's a rational approach to live as if it's true. Even if it's not the only path to flourishing, it's a path that likely leads to a more fulfilling life. When you engage in LLP, you don't need to choose between happiness and meaning. You will cultivate both. Ultimately, to truly flourish is to reclaim our inherent authenticity—to learn with open curiosity, to love with genuine connection, and to play with unburdened joy.

LOVE, LEARN, AND PLAY AS THE FOUNDATIONAL TRIFECTA

Wisdom often finds its richest expression in triads. The power of three strikes a vital balance—offering enough simplicity for clarity, enough pattern for recognition, and enough completeness for a deep sense of wholeness. Triads distill ideas more digestible, memorable, and impactful for the human mind. As we draw the final threads of this exploration, it becomes clear that the seemingly simple triad of love, learn, and play isn't just one perspective among many; rather, it serves as the very foundation upon which numerous other frameworks for a flourishing life are built. These three longings are deeply ingrained in human nature and are observable across cultures and throughout development. They form the bedrock upon which more complex motivations and experiences are built. Let us trace how the wisdom embedded in other insightful trifectas ultimately finds its home within the embracing arms of the LLP triad.

COHERENCE, PURPOSE, MATTERING

When we love, we feel connected to something larger than ourselves, bringing order to our inner world. The journey of learning often ignites our sense of purpose, revealing our passions and how we can contribute. Feeling valued and significant (mattering) is nurtured by the connection of love, and competence is gained through learning. Play is fundamentally about exploring possibilities, testing boundaries, and experimenting without the pressure of serious consequences. This playful exploration helps us make sense of the world in a dynamic and experiential way. This contributes to a feeling that the world is understandable and coherent.[315]

AGENCY, MEANING, CONNECTION

Richard Rowe's model suggests that well-being stems from a sense of agency, deep meaning in one's pursuits, and connection to others.[316] The realm of play is where agency thrives, where we experiment, explore our capabilities, and feel a sense of control over our actions. Learning is intrinsically linked to the discovery of meaning, as we seek to understand the world and our place within it. And love, in its purest form, is the wellspring of connection, binding us to others and fostering a sense of belonging.

HOPE, FREEDOM, FLOW

Hope drives vision, freedom enables autonomy, and flow represents deep engagement—together, they describe an optimal psychological state.[317] The embrace of love provides the essential bedrock of hope, offering the security and support that allow us to look toward the future with optimism. Play, in its unburdened nature, embodies freedom, a space for exploration and uninhibited expression. And the deep engagement of learning, particularly when driven by curiosity and intrinsic motivation, can lead to the state of flow, that immersive and joyful experience where we are fully present and engaged.

PURPOSE, COMMUNITY, WELLNESS

The Stanford Distinguished Careers Institute centers on purpose as a life compass, community as a source of belonging, and wellness as the baseline for sustainable engagement.[318] This trifecta is particularly powerful for navigating midlife and transitions. The pursuit of learning often clarifies our purpose, guiding our actions and giving us a sense of direction. Love naturally cultivates community, fostering the vital bonds of belonging and mutual support that underpin our well-being. Play, in its various manifestations and with its inherent capacity for joy and stress reduction, significantly contributes to our overall wellness, nurturing both mind and body.

AWARENESS, TRANSFORMATION, INTENT

Rooted in spiritual wisdom, this trio guides personal evolution.[319] Awareness fosters clarity, transformation is the process of change, and intent is the conscious force behind action. It's a path to mastery of self and life. The diligent practice of learning expands our awareness, deepening our understanding of ourselves and the world around us. The profound connections forged through love often catalyze significant personal transformation, shifting our perspectives, values, behaviors, and priorities. And when we approach play with mindfulness, it can help us clarify our intent, allowing us to act with greater authenticity and purpose.

READ, PRAY, SING

A sacred trifecta of practices: reading for wisdom, praying for communion, and singing for devotion. This blend of the intellectual, spiritual, and expressive nurtures a full-spectrum relationship with the divine. This triad is most notably associated with Donald S. Whitney, a pastor and author known for his work on spiritual disciplines.

***

In our search for wisdom from centuries and continents, we have attempted to marry ancient wisdom with modern science. The enduring wisdom of our ancestors stems from their ability to see beyond the biases of their time, accessing profound truths through a deep inner listening cultivated by quieting the noise of the world. Modern science contributes uniquely through its systematic observation and technological advancements, improving our physical well-being and expanding our knowledge of the universe. Combining the inner clarity of ancient wisdom with the practical power of modern science offers a potent path toward a more complete and enhanced human flourishing, embracing happiness and meaning.

WHY NOW? THE KAIROS MOMENT

We stand at a precipice, a unique juncture in human history where the confluence of unprecedented forces necessitates and enables a fundamental restructuring of human consciousness. The exponential surge of knowledge, the intricate web of interconnectedness, a growing disillusionment with established belief systems, and an unprecedented level of education among the masses have created fertile ground for a profound shift in how we perceive ourselves, our world, our purpose, and our potential. The time for a conscious evolution of our inner landscape is not the distant future; it is now.

The sheer volume of knowledge we collectively possess is expanding at an astonishing rate. The doubling of knowledge—once taking centuries—now occurs in mere months. As Buckminster Fuller observed, "Humanity is acquiring all the right technology for all the wrong reasons."[320] This explosion of information, readily accessible through the internet's intricate network, envisioned by Tim Berners-Lee as a "collaborative medium ... a place where we can meet and share our thinking,"[321] offers an unparalleled opportunity for collective learning and understanding. Yet, without a corresponding evolution in our capacity to process, synthesize, and apply this knowledge with wisdom and ethical considerations, we risk being overwhelmed by its sheer magnitude.

Simultaneously, the hyper-connectivity fostered by the internet has woven a tapestry of human interaction unlike any seen before. Marshall McLuhan's concept of the "global village" has become a tangible reality, breaking down geographical barriers and fostering a sense of shared humanity. However, this hyper-connectivity, while offering unprecedented opportunities, also presents significant perils in the form of artificial intelligence and pervasive social media. The rapid advancement of AI, while holding immense promise for solving complex problems, also carries the risk of eroding human skills, exacerbating inequalities, and even challenging our very sense of agency. The algorithms that increasingly shape our information landscape and automate tasks can, if unchecked, lead to societal fragmentation, job displacement, and a dependence that diminishes our innate capacities to learn, love, and play authentically.

Similarly, the ubiquitous nature of social media, initially envisioned as a tool for connection, has also revealed a darker side. The curated realities, the constant comparison, and the potential for manipulation and misinformation can foster anxiety, erode self-esteem, and distort our understanding of ourselves and others. The very interconnectedness that holds such promise can become a breeding ground for division and the erosion of genuine human connection if not navigated with awareness and critical thinking. As Pierre Teilhard de Chardin eloquently stated, "The future of the world, the future of your children, depends on the enlargement of consciousness and the deepening of compassion."[322] This interconnectedness demands a consciousness capable of empathy, collaboration, and a recognition of our shared destiny.

Adding impetus to this potential transformation is a growing disappointment with traditional and even modern religious frameworks. For many, these systems no longer provide satisfactory answers to existential questions or effective guidance in navigating the complexities of the modern world. As Friedrich Nietzsche famously declared, "God is dead," which highlights a shift away from reliance on external authorities for meaning-making. This void, however, need not be a source of despair but rather an invitation to cultivate inner sources of meaning and purpose, grounded in reason, ethics, and a deeper understanding of ourselves and the universe.

Furthermore, the level of education in the masses has reached unprecedented heights. Access to information and diverse perspectives empowers individuals to critically examine established norms and question inherited beliefs. This intellectual awakening fosters a "clear break from the shackles of formal authority," as these shackles are increasingly recognized as being maintained "only due to our own ignorance," as suggested by thinkers such as Socrates, who emphasized the importance of self-examination. An educated populace is better equipped to engage in nuanced thinking, challenge dogma, and contribute to a more informed and equitable society.

The remarkable increase in human life expectancy also plays a crucial role. More individuals are now living long enough to attain what might be termed "higher-order minds"—minds capable of greater reflection, wisdom, and a broader perspective on the human condition. As Simone de Beauvoir noted, "The body of an aged person is not just the wreck of what it was, it's also the instrument of a memory."[323] This accumulated experience, coupled with extended lifespans, offers a greater potential for collective wisdom and a more mature understanding of life's complexities.

Advances in neuroscience are providing profound insights into the very fabric of consciousness. We are beginning to unravel the neural correlates of thought, emotion, and self-awareness. This scientific exploration, as championed by figures such as V. S. Ramachandran, who seeks to understand the "ghost in the machine," offers the potential to not only treat neurological disorders but also to understand and potentially enhance human cognitive and emotional capacities. This deeper understanding of the brain can inform strategies for cultivating greater self-awareness, emotional regulation, and cognitive flexibility—key components of a restructured consciousness.

Consequently, this generation of human beings has access to a highly informed meaning-making system. We can draw upon scientific understanding, philosophical inquiry, diverse cultural perspectives, and personal experience to construct a more robust and adaptable framework for understanding our existence. This is a departure from relying solely on inherited narratives and allows for a more personalized and evidence-based approach to finding meaning and purpose, echoing Viktor Frankl's emphasis on the human drive for meaning even in the face of suffering.

Ultimately, human consciousness has reached its most evolved state ever in terms of its potential. We possess the tools, the knowledge, and the interconnectedness to transcend outdated modes of thinking and being. As Carl Sagan urged, "Our species needs, and deserves, a citizenry with minds wide open and a sense of wonder."[324] The challenges we face—climate change, social inequality, technological disruption—demand a level of critical thinking, empathy, and collaborative action that can only arise from a more evolved and integrated consciousness.

Now is the *kairos* moment, the opportune time to consciously and deliberately restructure human consciousness. It is a call to move beyond reactive patterns and embrace a more proactive, mindful, and interconnected way of being. By leveraging our collective knowledge, embracing our interconnectedness, fostering critical thinking, and cultivating inner wisdom, we can navigate the complexities of the twenty-first century and create a future where human potential is not only realized but also guided by compassion, understanding, and a shared vision for a thriving planet. The evolution of consciousness is not a passive process; it is an active and urgent imperative for our time. I believe this can be accomplished very simply by consciously adopting an LLP mindset!

If you told me twenty years ago that I would one day write a book about human flourishing, I might not have believed you. I wanted to be India's best chemical engineer when I graduated from Indian Institute of Technology, Delhi, in 1973. But as the ancient myths taught us, we must be willing to let go of the life we planned to have for the life that is waiting for us.

I invite you to not only embrace this timeless yet timely wisdom but to also reach out to others who may benefit. Life offers limited time to embrace authenticity, build meaningful connections, and create joyful experiences. Start today.

I want to leave you with a final but very insightful comment my dad made in conversation with my mom. My mother, concerned by my divergence from certain traditional religious observances, shared her worries with my father. His response, however, offered a different lens through which to view a meaningful life. He inquired if I had strayed from what was right or neglected my responsibilities because he wanted to provide proper guidance. My mother's reply was telling: "He really helps many people," she said. "And he doesn't tell me, but they tell me." Her measure of a good person lay in selfless action and the positive impact on others. My father, with quiet wisdom, then reassured her, "If you are sure and you're satisfied that he is doing everything right, don't worry, as he does not have to find God. God will find him."

Translating my father's wisdom into our present context, I believe that whatever path you choose, if you navigate it with an LLP mindset—a spirit of love, a thirst for learning, and an embrace of play—then that which we might call the divine or its secular equivalent, flourishing, will inevitably find you.

ACKNOWLEDGMENTS

First of all, I want to acknowledge the debt to my parents who brought us up with what I now recognize as an LLP mindset. They exemplified this mindset in their lives. I am grateful to all my sisters and their children who are very loving and caring toward me, which helped me remain anchored in the values inculcated by my parents. I also have the greatest fortune of having over ten godchildren who give me emotional richness with their unconditional love. Akash Ambani and Shiv Chadha are the two standouts, although I love all my godchildren equally. A special gratitude to Aashi Mittal, daughter of my nephew, as I got this epiphany of the LLP framework while playing with her when she was nine months old.

My upbringing would not have translated into this book but for the fellowship I received at Harvard's Advanced Leadership Initiative, which afforded me the opportunity to take more than thirty classes, letting me soak in the intellectual diversity and depth of Harvard and connecting the dots for me through interdisciplinary exposure.

Next in line is Donald Frederick, who transitioned from Harvard's Human Flourishing Program to be my first colleague at my foundation, Universal Enlightenment and Flourishing, with whom I brainstormed the original framework for this book, and who conducted initial research for this book. Kelly Reardon continued research for over a year after Donald, and I remain grateful for the many insights that she brought to the book.

Thanks to Tony James, who, in spite of his hectic schedule, took the time to read the draft and offer critical and constructive suggestions. Thanks also to Sara Al-Zubi, who reviewed the draft and made a lot of suggestions based on her experience as a teaching fellow for Harvard's class on happiness taught by Professor Susan Rinard. Thanks to Richard Parker, who was my professor at the Harvard Kennedy School teaching a course titled "Leadership: From Lincoln to Obama," for writing chapter twelve, which adds to the academic rigor of the book, and for critiquing the last version of the book. I owe many insights incorporated in this book to his course and Barbara Kellerman's course on leadership literacy. Thanks to Manny Singh and Hau H. Lee, who made profuse comments on the first draft of the book. Finally, thanks to the editor, who so enthusiastically endorsed this publication and made very useful suggestions to make the book more reader-friendly.

ENDNOTES

1 The Vedas, Upanishads, and Vedanta are deeply interconnected pillars of Hindu philosophy. The Vedas are the oldest scriptures, containing hymns, rituals, and early philosophical concepts. The Upanishads form the concluding sections (the anta or end) of the Vedas and delve into deeper philosophical and spiritual inquiries about the nature of reality, the self (Atman), and the ultimate reality (Brahman). Vedanta literally means "the end of the Vedas" and refers to the philosophical systems that developed from and interpret the teachings of the Upanishads.

2 Jeremy Bentham, *An Introduction to the Principles of Morals and Legislation* (n.p., 1789).

3 His Holiness the Dalai Lama and Howard C. Cutler, *The Art of Happiness: A Handbook for Living* (Riverhead Books, 1998).

4 "Global Self-Improvement Market 2024–2033," Custom Market Insights,accessed January 7, 2025, https://www.custommarketinsights.com/report/self-improvement-market/.

5 Isaac Asimov and Jason A. Shulman, *Isaac Asimov's Book of Science and Nature Quotations* (Weidenfeld & Nicolson, 1988), 281.

6 John F. Helliwell et al., *World Happiness Report 2025* (University of Oxford: Wellbeing Research Centre, last modified March 13, 2025), https://worldhappiness.report/ed/2025/.

7 Nicole Brown Chau, "2025 World Happiness Report Shows U.S. in Lowest-Ever Spot on List," *CBS News*, last modified March 20, 2025, https://www.cbsnews.com/news/2025-world-happiness-report-us-lowest-ranking/.

8 Centers for Disease Control and Prevention, "Suicide Mortality in the United States, 2002–2022," National Center for Health Statistics, September 26, 2023, retrieved from https://www.cdc.gov/nchs/products/databriefs/db509.htm.

9 David G. Myers, *The American Paradox: Spiritual Hunger in an Age of Plenty* (Yale University Press, 2000).

10 Shanthie Mariet D'Souza, "Mumbai Terrorist Attacks of 2008," *Britannica*, last modified May 21, 2025, https://www.britannica.com/event/Mumbai-terrorist-attacks-of-2008.

11 David Brooks, "The Moral Bucket List," *The New York Times*, April 11, 2015, https://www.nytimes.com/2015/04/12/opinion/sunday/david-brooks-the-moral-bucket-list.html.

12 Frederick Buechner, *Wishful Thinking: A Seeker's ABC* (Harper & Row, 1973).

13 Joseph A. Schumpeter, *The Theory of Economic Development: An Inquiry into Profits, Capital, Credit, Interest, and the Business Cycle* (Harvard University Press, 1911).

14 Derek Bok, "The Official Pursuit of Happiness," Project Syndicate, January 4, 2011, https://www.project-syndicate.org/commentary/the-official-pursuit-of-happiness.

15 Leo Rosten, *Passions & Prejudices* (McGraw-Hill, 1978).

16 Roy F. Baumeister et al, "Some key differences between a happy life and a meaningful life," *The Journal of Positive Psychology* 8, no. 6 (2013): 505–16.

17 Ephrat Livni, "A Nobel Prize-Winning Psychologist Says Most People Don't Really Want to Be Happy," Quartz, December 21, 2018, https://qz.com/1503207/a-nobel-prize-winning-psychologist-defines-happiness-versus-satisfaction.

18 Mark Wallace, "Work and Happiness in Sigmund Freud's Civilization and Its Discontents and in Thomas Carlyle," The Victorian Sage, August 30, 2021, https://thevictoriansage.wordpress.com/2021/08/30/work-and-happiness-in-sigmunds-freud-civilization-and-its-discontents-and-in-thomas-carlyle/.

19 Andrew Weil, "Video: Happiness vs. Contentment," Dr Weil, accessed September 11, 2024, 1 min., 17 sec. https://www.drweil.com/videos-features/videos/happiness-vs-contentment/.

20 David Robertson, *Fifth Business* (Macmillan of Canada, 1970).

21 Viktor E. Frankl, *Man's Search for Meaning* (Beacon Press, 1959).

22 Alexander Pope, "An Essay on Man," *Four Epistles* (1734).

23 The word "meditation" itself comes from the Latin meditari, which means "to think or reflect upon, consider, design, purpose, or intend." And this is all about the surface of the human mind. Sadhana is the Sanskrit word used for millennia in India, and later Tibet/Mongolia, to denote specific practices one does on a regular basis to evolve one's mindstream toward enlightenment. This removes mental afflictions (laxity, over-excitation, grasping or aversion) and reveals our true identity, below all the layers of its impermanent ego-elements. (Rami Dhanoa, *Medium*)

24 Daniel Gilbert, "The Surprising Science of Happiness," TED Talk February 2004, 20.51 minutes.

25 Ilya Prigogine, *The End of Certainty: Time's Arrow and the Laws of Nature* (The Free Press, 1997), 217.

26 John Marks Templeton, *Wisdom from World Religions* (Templeton Foundation Press, 2002).

27 Rudyard Kipling, "The Ballad of East and West." *Barrack-Room Ballads and Other Verses* (Methuen and Co., 1892).

28 Robert Nozick, *Anarchy, State, and Utopia* (Basic Books, 1974).

29 Ibid.

30 Joseph A. Campbell, *Joseph Campbell Companion: Reflections on the Art of Living* (HarperCollins, 1991).

31 Kenta Minamitani, "Social Media Addiction and Mental Health: The Growing Concern for Youth Well-Being," Stanford Law School, May 20, 2024, https://law.stanford.edu/2024/05/20/social-media-addiction-and-mental-health-the-growing-concern-for-youth-well-being/.

32 Robert Biswas-Diener and Ed Diener, "Making the Best of a Bad Situation: Satisfaction in the Slums of Calcutta." *Social Indicators Research* 55, no. 3 (2001): 329–52. http://www.jstor.org/stable/27526958.

33 Ed Diener, "Subjective Well-Being," *Psychological Bulletin* 95, no. 3 (1984): 542–75.

34 John Maynard Keynes, "Economic Possibilities for our Grandchildren," 1930.

35 Jean Baudrillard, *Social Futures* (Pluto Press, 1981).

36 *Albert Camus, Le Mythe de Sisyphe (*Éditions Gallimard, 1942).

37 Harvard University, "Healthy Minds Survey," 2025, https://www.harvard.edu/wellbeing/healthyminds/.

38 Laurie Santos, "The Science of Well-Being: My Journey to Help Students Thrive." *Yale Alumni Magazine*, Fall 2018.

39 Jim Carrey, interview by Oprah Winfrey, *The Oprah Winfrey Show*, 1997.

40 Rebecca Leung, "Carrey: 'Life Is Too Beautiful,'" CBS News, November 18, 2004, https://www.cbsnews.com/news/carrey-life-is-too-beautiful/.

41 Jim Carrey, "Jim Carrey at MIU: Commencement Address at the 2014 Graduation (EN, FR, ES, RU, GR,...)," Maharishi International University, May 30, 2014, 26 min., 8 sec., https://www.youtube.com/watch?v=V80-gPkpH6M.

42 Devdutt Pattanaik, "Dharma Hormones: What is the path to happiness?" *The Economic Times*, last modified February 21, 2020, https://economictimes.indiatimes.com/news/politics-and-nation/dharma-hormones-what-is-the-path-to-happiness/articleshow/74248836.cms?from=mdr.

43 Paramahansa Yogananda, *Autobiography of a Yogi* (The Philosophical Library: New York, 1946).

44 Thich Nhat Hanh, *Being Peace* (Parallax Press, 1987).

45 Václav Havel, "The Responsibility of Intellectuals," address delivered at Independence Hall, Philadelphia, July 4, 1994.

46 Joan Didion, "On Keeping a Notebook," *Slouching Towards* (Bethlehem, 1968).

47 World Bank Group, "Lifting 800 Million People Out of Poverty – New Report Looks at Lessons from China's Experience," April 1, 2022, https://www.worldbank.org/en/news/press-release/2022/04/01/lifting-800-million-people-out-of-poverty-new-report-looks-at-lessons-from-china-s-experience.

48 Evelyn Cheng, "China calls for curbs on 'excessive' income and for the wealthy to give back more to society," CNBC, August 18, 2021, https://www.cnbc.com/2021/08/18/chinas-xi-emphasizes-common-prosperity-at-finance-economy-meeting.html.

49 Ajay Chaudry et al. "Poverty in the United States: 50-Year Trends and Safety Net Impacts," U.S. Dept. of Health & Human Services, March 2016.

50 Oxfam International, "World's top 1% own more wealth than 95% of humanity," September 23, 2024, https://www.oxfam.org/en/press-releases/worlds-top-1-own-more-wealth-95-humanity-shadow-global-oligarchy-hangs-over-un.

51 Josh Bivens et al., "CEO Pay Declined in 2023," Economic Policy Institute, September 19, 2024, https://www.epi.org/publication/ceo-pay-in-2023/.

52 History Matters, "'One Third of a Nation': FDR's Second Inaugural Address, delivered January 20, 1937, https://historymatters.gmu.edu/d/5105/.

53 Federal Reserve Bank of St. Louis, "Table Data - Real Gross Domestic Product," n.d., https://fred.stlouisfed.org/data/GDPCA.

54 Federal Reserve Bank of St. Louis, "Table Data."

55 Tanya de Sousa and Meghan Henry, "The 2024 Annual Homelessness Assessment Report (AHAR) to Congress," The U.S. Department of Housing and Human Development, https://www.huduser.gov/portal/sites/default/files/pdf/2024-AHAR-Part-1.pdf.

56 John Maynard Keynes, "The End of Laissez-Faire," in *Essays in Persuasion* (Macmillan, 1931).

57 Nick Hanauer, "The Pitchforks Are Coming... For Us Plutocrats." *POLITICO Magazine*, July/August 2014,

https://www.politico.com/magazine/story/2014/06/the-pitchforks-are-coming-for-us-plutocrats-108014/.

58 Robert Wright, *The Evolution of God* (Little, Brown and Company, 2009).

59 Geert Hofstede, *Culture's Consequences: Comparing Values, Behaviors, Institutions, and Organizations Across Nations* (SAGE Publications, 2003).

60 Jonathan Sacks, *Morality: Restoring the Common Good in Divided Times* (Hodder & Stoughton, 2020).

61 David Brooks, *The Second Mountain: The Quest for a Moral Life* (Random House, 2019).

62 Robin Wall Kimmerer, *Braiding Sweetgrass: Indigenous Wisdom, Scientific Knowledge, and the Teachings of Plants* (Milkweed Editions, 2013).

63 Desmond Tutu, *No Future Without Forgiveness* (Ebury Publishing, 2012).

64 Thich Nhat Hanh, *Peace Is Every Step: The Path of Mindfulness in Everyday Life* (Bantam Books, 1992).

65 Bill Clinton, *Back to Work: Why We Need a Smart Government for a Strong Economy* (Knopf, 2011).

66 Albert Einstein, "Why Socialism?" *Monthly Review*, May 1949.

67 Martin A. Nowak and Roger Highfield, *SuperCooperators: Altruism, Evolution, and Why We Need Each Other to Succeed* (Free Press, 2011).

68 Nowak and Highfield, *SuperCooperators.*

69 Joseph Henrich, *The Secret of Our Success: How Culture Is Driving Human Evolution, Domesticating Our Species, and Making Us Smarter* (Princeton University Press, 2015).

70 Adam Smith, *An Inquiry into the Nature and Causes of the Wealth of Nations* (W. Strahan and T. Cadell, 1776).

71 Bruce C. Greenwald and Joseph E. Stiglitz, "Externalities in Economies with Imperfect Information and Incomplete Markets," *The Quarterly Journal of Economics* 101, no. 2 (1986): 229–64.

72 Isaac Newton, Letter to Robert Hooke, February 5, 1675/76.

73 Juliet B. Schor, *The Overspent American: Why We Want What We Don't Need* (Harper Perennial, 1998).

74 Dallin H. Oaks, "Good, Better, Best." Ensign or Liahona, November 2007.

75 Arthur C. Brooks, *Gross National Happiness: Why Happiness Matters for America—and How We Can Get More of It* (Basic Books, 2008).

76 Jeremy Lent, *The Web of Meaning: Integrating Science and Traditional Wisdom to Find Our Place in the Universe* (New Society Publishers, 2021).

77 Adam Smith, *The Theory of Moral Sentiments* (A. Millar, 1759).

78 Elisabet Sahtouris, *EarthDance: Living Systems in Evolution* (iUniverse, 2000).

79 Milton Friedman, "The Social Responsibility of Business Is to Increase Its Profits," *The New York Times*, September 13, 1970.

80 Business Roundtable, "Business Roundtable Statement on the Purpose of a Corporation," https://www.businessroundtable.org/purposeanniversary.

81 Tata Group, Our Founder, https://www.tata.com/about-us/tata-group-our-heritage.

82 Brand Finance, "Global 500 2025," https://brandirectory.com/global.

83 Robert F. Kennedy, "Remarks at the University of Kansas," University of Kansas, March 18, 1968.

84 Philip Brickman and Donald T. Campbell, "Hedonic Relativism and Planning the Good Society," in *Adaptation-Level Theory: A Symposium*, ed. M. H. Appley (Academic Press, 1971), 287–305.

85 Daniel T. Gilbert, *Stumbling on Happiness* (Knopf, 2006).

86 Roberto M. Unger, *The Self Awakened: Pragmatism Unbound* (Harvard University Press, 2007).

87 Albert Einstein, "Religion and Science," *The New York Times*, November 9, 1930.

88 Steven Pinker, *The Better Angels of Our Nature: Why Violence Has Declined* (Viking, 2011).

89 Arthur C. Brooks, "Three Myths and Four Truths About How to Get Happier," *The Atlantic*, September 12, 2023.

90 Katie Canales and Aaron Mok, "China's 'Social Credit' System Ranks Citizens and Punishes Them with Throttled Internet Speeds and Flight Bans if the Communist Party Deems Them Untrustworthy," Business Insider, November 28, 2022, https://www.businessinsider.com/china-social-credit-system-punishments-and-rewards-explained-2018-4.

91 Jordan Moreau, "'Matrix' Co-Creator Lilly Wachowski Slams Ivanka Trump, Elon Musk for Using Her Movie Reference," *Variety*, May 17, 2020, https://variety.com/2020/film/news/matrix-lilly-wachowski-ivanka-trump-elon-musk-red-pill-tweet-1234608887/.

92 Elisa Leonelli, "Keanu Reeves Explains 'The Matrix' Trilogy," Golden Globes, December 27, 2021, https://goldenglobes.com/articles/keanu-reeves-explains-matrix-trilogy/.

93 Leonelli, "Keanu Reeves Explains."

94 Leonelli, "Keanu Reeves Explains."

95 Leonelli, "Keanu Reeves Explains."

96 Leonelli, "Keanu Reeves Explains."

97 Yuval Noah Harari, *Homo Deus: A Brief History of Tomorrow* (Harper, 2017).

98 Vance Packard, *The Hidden Persuaders* (David McKay, 1957).

99 The term "continuous partial attention" was coined by Linda Stone in 1998.

100 Aldous Huxley, *The Doors of Perception* (Harper & Brothers, 1954).

101 Jack Kornfield, *Buddha's Little Instruction Book* (Bantam Books, 1994).

102 Thich Nhat Hanh, *Your True Home: The Everyday Wisdom of Thich Nhat Hanh* (Shambhala, 2011).

103 John J. Wiens, "How Many Species Are There on Earth? Progress and Problems," *PLOS Biology* 21, no. 11 (2023): e3002388, https://doi.org/10.1371/journal.pbio.3002388.

104 Yuval Noah Harari, *Sapiens: A Brief History of Humankind* (Harper, 2014).

105 Edward O. Wilson, *Consilience: The Unity of Knowledge* (Knopf, 1998).

106 Edward O. Wilson, *The Meaning of Human Existence* (Liveright Publishing Corporation, 2014).

107 Warren Buffett, *The Essays of Warren Buffett: Lessons for Corporate America*, edited by Lawrence A. Cunningham (The Cunningham Group & Carolina Academic Press, 2015).

108 Vipassana is the Pali word most famously used by the Buddha to denote "seeing reality clearly." Its etymology means "special" or "distinct" (vi), and "seeing" (pasyanti). To practice this kind of mediation is to see things as they occur, not as we project them to be based on past experience. (Rami Dhanoa, *Medium*)

109 Carl Sagan, *Cosmos* (Random House, 1980).

110 "Nikola Tesla Quotes," Goodreads, accessed April 19, 2025, from https://www.goodreads.com/quotes/8657030.

111 A. G. Krishna Warrier (trans.), "Sixty Upanishads of the Veda," in *Maha Upanishad* (Motilal Banarsidass), vol. 1, p. 799 (Original work published ca. eighth century BCE).

112 Mark Epstein, *Thoughts Without a Thinker: Psychotherapy from a Buddhist Perspective* (W. W. Norton & Company, 1995).

113 Neil deGrasse Tyson, "Standing Up in the Milky Way," *Cosmos: A Spacetime Odyssey*, directed by Brannon Braga, Ann Druyan, Bill Pope, and Andre Bormanis (Fox/National Geographic Channel, 2014).

114 A. C. Bhaktivedanta Swami Prabhupada (trans.), *Bhagavad-gītā As It Is*, 2nd ed. (The Bhaktivedanta Book Trust, 1983) (Original work published ca. fifth century BCE).

115 Department for Digital, Culture, Media and Sport, "A Connected Society: A Strategy for Tackling Loneliness – Laying the Foundations for Change," HM Government, October 14, 2018.

116 "Japan appoints 'minister of loneliness' to battle pandemic side effects." TRT World, Feb. 13 2021, www.trtworld.com/asia/japan-appoints-minister-of-loneliness-to-battle-pandemic-side-effects-44145.

117 Maria Popova, "The Art of Living: The Great Humanistic Philosopher Erich Fromm on Having vs. Being and How to Set Ourselves Free from the Chains of Our Culture," The Marginalian, https://www.themarginalian.org/2016/03/23/erich-fromm-the-art-of-living/.

118 CS Lewis, *Mere Christianity* (Geoffrey Bles, 1952).

119 Thomas Merton, *A Thomas Merton Reader,* ed. Thomas P. McDonnell (Image Books, 1971).

120 Arthur Schopenhauer, *On the Basis of Morality*, trans. E. F. J. Payne (1840; repr., Dover Publications, 2009).

121 Albert Einstein, *The New Quotable Einstein*, ed. Alice Calaprice (Princeton University Press, 2005).

122 Albert Einstein, *Mein Weltbild [My Worldview]*, in *Ideas and Opinions*, ed. C. Seelig (Crown Publishers, 1931), 40–41.

123 Mother Teresa, *A Gift for God: Prayers and Meditations* (Harper & Row, 1989).

124 Henri J.M. Nouwen, *The Wounded Healer: Ministry in Contemporary Society* (Doubleday, 1972).

125 Ibid.

126 His Holiness the Dalai Lama, *Ethics for the New Millennium* (Riverhead Books, 1999).

127 Embrace Global, "Our Impact," https://embraceglobal.org/impact.

128 Stanford Graduate School of Business titled "Hard Lesson: Learning to Embrace Personal Growth," October 13, 2023.

129 Ursula M. Niebuhr, "The Serenity Prayer," *The Prayers of Reinhold Niebuhr* (Charles Scribner's Sons, 1968).

130 Thich Nhat Hanh, *No Mud, No Lotus: The Art of Transforming Suffering* (Parallax Press, December 2, 2014).

131 Glenn R. Fox, et al. "Neural correlates of gratitude," *Frontiers in Psychology*, vol. 6, 2015, p. 1491.

132 Georg Simmel, "The Sociology of Sociability," *American Journal of Sociology* 55, no. 3 (1949): 254–61.

133 Laurie Santos, "How Leaders Find Happiness — And Teach It," *Harvard Catalyst*, July 18, 2024, catalyst.harvard.edu/news/article/how-leaders-find-happiness-and-teach-it/.

134 Carl Jung, "Aion: Researches into the Phenomenology of the Self," *Collected Works of C.G. Jung*, vol. 9, part II, p. 70-71.

135 Neil Postman, *Amusing Ourselves to Death: Public Discourse in the Age of Show Business* (Penguin Books, 1985), 4.

136 Gary Zukav, *The Seat of the Soul.* (Simon & Schuster, 1989).

137 Bronnie Ware, *The Top Five Regrets of the Dying: A Life Transformed by the Dearly Departing* (Hay House, 2012).

138 Eckhart Tolle, *The Power of Now: A Guide to Spiritual Enlightenment* (New World Library, 1999).

139 Lao-tzu, *Tao Te Ching: A New English Version*, trans. S. Mitchell (Harper Perennial, 2006) (Original work published ca. sixth century BCE).

140 Carl G. Jung, *Psychology and Alchemy,* trans. R. F. C. Hull, vol. 12, 2nd ed., in *The Collected Works of C. G. Jung* (Princeton University Press, 1968).

141 Herman Hesse, *Siddhartha*, trans. H. Rosner (S. Fischer Verlag, 1922; repr., New Directions Publishing, 1951).

142 Edwin F. Bryant, *The Yoga Sutras of Patañjali: A New Edition, Translation, and Commentary* (North Point Press, 2009).

143 Linda Stone, "Our Powerful Attention," March 19, 2014, https://lindastone.net/2014/03/19/our-powerful-attention/.

144 Thich Nhat Hanh, *Peace Is Every Step: The Path of Mindfulness in Everyday Life* (Bantam Books, 1992).

145 Shunryu Suzuki, *Zen Mind, Beginner's Mind* (Weatherhill, 1970).

146 Erich Fromm, *The Art of Loving* (Harper Perennial, 1956).

147 Blaise Pascal, *Pensées*, trans. A. J. Krailsheimer (Penguin Classics, 1995).

148 Michael A. Singer, *The Untethered Soul: The Journey Beyond Yourself* (New Harbinger Publications, 2007).

149 Joseph Campbell, *The Hero with a Thousand Faces*, 3rd ed. (Princeton University Press, 2008).

150 William Blake, "Auguries of Innocence," in *Poems,* ed. D. G. Rossetti (Publisher, 1863).

151 Albert Einstein, "Old Man's Advice to Youth: 'Never Lose a Holy Curiosity.'" *LIFE Magazine*, May 2, 1955, 64.

152 Manly P. Hall, *The Secret Teachings of All Ages* (Philosophical Research Society, 1928).

153 Rachel Carson, *The Sea Around Us* (Oxford University Press, 1951).

154 Roy T. Bennett, *The Light in the Heart: Inspirational Thoughts for Living Your Best Life*, 2020.

155 Jiddu Krishnamurti, *The First and Last Freedom* (Harper & Row, 2002).

156 David Abram, *The Spell of the Sensuous* (Vintage, 1997).

157 John Milton, *Paradise Lost*, Book I, lines 254-255, first published 1667, edited by Merritt Y. Hughes (Hackett Publishing, 2003).

158 "Antahkarana," Wikipedia, accessed April 19, 2025, https://en.wikipedia.org/wiki/Antahkarana.

159 Joseph B. Soloveitchik, *The Lonely Man of Faith* (Doubleday, 1992).

160 Sam Harris, *Free Will* (Free Press, 2012).

161 Joe Dispenza, *Breaking the Habit of Being Yourself: How to Lose Your Mind and Create a New One* (Hay House, 2012).

162 James Allen, *As a Man Thinketh*. (James Allen, 1903).

163 Deepak Chopra and Rudolph E. Tanzi, *Super Genes: Unlock the Astonishing Power of Your DNA for Optimum Health and Well-Being* (Harmony Books, 2015).

164 Daniel Kahneman, *Thinking, Fast and Slow* (Farrar, Straus and Giroux, 2011).

165 Richard Wiseman, *The As If Principle: The Radically New Approach to Changing Your Life* (Simon & Schuster, 2014).

166 Laurie Santos, "The Science of Well-Being," Coursera, Yale University, 2018.

167 Michael Alan Singer, *The Untethered Soul: The Journey Beyond Yourself* (New Harbinger Publications, 2007).

168 Eckhart Tolle, *The Power of Now* (Namaste Publishing, 1997).

169 Isabelle Lina de Laia Almeida et al., "Social Isolation and Its Impact on Child and Adolescent Development: A Systematic Review," (2021).

170 Immanuel Kant, *Critique of Pure Reason* (1781).

171 Eliot Deutsch, *Advaita Vedanta: A Philosophical Reconstruction* (University of Hawaii Press, 1973).

172 Antoine de Saint-Exupéry, *Wind, Sand and Stars,* trans. L. Galantière (Reynal & Hitchcock, 1939).

173 Patanjali, *The Yoga Sutras of Patanjali* (1990).

174 Pierre Teilhard de Chardin, *The Phenomenon of Man* (1955).

175 George Eman Vaillant, *Spiritual Evolution: A Scientific Defense of Faith* (Broadway Books, 2008), 203.

176 Pravrajika Divyanandaprana, *Science of Happiness* (Ramakrishna Sarada Mission, 2020).

177 Mihaly Csikszentmihalyi, *Flow: The Psychology of Optimal Experience* (Harper & Row, 1990).

178 Sonia Lyubomirsky et al., "Pursuing Happiness: The Architecture of Sustainable Change," *Review of General Psychology* 9, no. 2 (2005): 111–31.

179 Robert Kegan, *Evolving Self: Problem and Process in Human Development* (Harvard University Press, 1982).

180 Thomas Gilovich, *How We Know What Isn't So: The Fallibility of Human Reason in Everyday Life* (Free Press, 1991).

181 Kegan, *The Evolving Self.*

182 Kegan, *The Evolving Self.*

183 *Satori* is a Japanese Buddhist term, particularly in Zen, referring to a sudden, intuitive experience of awakening or enlightenment where one "sees into their true nature," transcending ordinary conceptual thought.

184 Kuan Yew Lee, "Speech by Prime Minister Lee Kuan Yew at His 60th Birthday Dinner Held at the Mandarin Hotel," National Archives of Singapore, September 16, 1983.

185 Pierra Hadot, *Philosophy as a Way of Life: Spiritual Exercises from Socrates to Foucault*, ed. A. I. Davidson, trans. M. Chase (Blackwell Publishing, 1995).

186 Joseph Henrich et al., "The Weirdest People in the World?" *Behavioral and Brain Sciences* 33, no. 2–3 (2010): 61–83.

187 Kaare Christensen, Anne Maria Herskind, and James W Vaupel, "Why Danes Are Smug: Comparative Study of Life Satisfaction in the European Union," British Medical Journal 333, no. 7582 (December 21, 2006): 1289–91, https://doi.org/10.1136/bmj.39028.665602.55.

188 Christensen et al, "Why Danes Are Smug."

189 Tyler J. VanderWeele et al., "The Global Flourishing Study: Study Profile and Initial Results on Flourishing," *Nature Mental Health* https://doi.org/10.1038/s44220-025-00423-5.

190 Ibid.

191 Jack P. Shonkoff and Deborah A. Phillips, eds., *From Neurons to Neighborhoods: The Science of Early Child Development.* (National Academy Press, 2000).

192 Alison Gopnik, "Physics for Babies," *Scientific American*, July 2010, https://brianesty.com/bodywork/PDF/How%20Babies%20Think.pdf.

193 Michael Yogman et al., "The Power of Play: A Pediatric Role in Enhancing Development in Young Children," *PEDIATRICS* 142, no. 3 (2018): e20182058, https://doi.org/10.1542/peds.2018-2058.

194 Kieran Egan, eds., *Wonder-Full Education: The Centrality of Wonder in Teaching and Learning Across the Curriculum* (Routledge, 2014).

195 Rumi, *Rumi: The Book of Love: Poems of Ecstasy and Longing*, trans. Coleman Barks.

196 Gabriel García Márquez, *Love in the Time of Cholera*, trans. E. Grossman (Knopf, 1985).

197 Tyler J. VanderWeele, "Parenting Practices Have a Profound Influence on the Lives of Children," *Psychology Today*, June 28, 2019.

198 Harvard University, "Harvard Study of Adult Development," Harvard Second Generation Study," https://www.adultdevelopmentstudy.org/.

199 Scott Stossel, "What Makes Us Happy, Revisited," *The Atlantic*, May 2013, https://www.theatlantic.com/magazine/archive/2013/05/thanks-mom/309287/.

200 Pierre Teilhard de Chardin, *Activation of Energy*, trans. R. Hague (Harcourt Brace Jovanovich, 1971).

201 Erich Fromm, *The Art of Loving* (Harper & Row, 1956).

202 Ibid.

203 Rumi, *Rumi: The Book of Love.*

204 St. Aurelius Augustine, *Sermon on 1 John 4:4–12*, Christian History Institute.

205 The Holy Bible, 1 Corinthians 13:4–7 (New International Version)

206 Tyler J. VanderWeele, "How Parental Love Impacts Flourishing Later in Life," *Psychology Today*, June 28, 2019.

207 Pierre Teilhard de Chardin, *Toward the Future*, trans. R. Hague (Harcourt Brace Jovanovich, 1975).

208 Ralph Waldo Emerson, "Politics," in *Essays: Second Series* (1844).

209 Julianne Holt-Lunstad et al., "Social Relationships and Mortality Risk: A Meta-Analytic Review," *PLOS Medicine* 7, no. 7 (2010): e1000316.

210 T. H. White, *The Once and Future King* (Collins, 1958).

211 Albert Einstein, *The Ultimate Quotable Einstein*, ed. A. Calaprice (Princeton University Press, 2010).

212 Erwin Schrödinger, *What Is Life? The Physical Aspect of the Living Cell* (Cambridge University Press, 1944).

213 John Dewey, *My Pedagogic Creed* (School Journal, 1897).

214 John Dewey, *Democracy and Education: An Introduction to the Philosophy of Education* (Macmillan, 1916).

215 Lao-tzu, *Tao Te Ching: A New English Version*, trans. Ursula K. Le Guin (Shambhala, 1988).

216 Lao-tzu, *Tao Te Ching*, trans. S. Mitchell (Harper Perennial Modern Classics, 1995).

217 Carol S. Dweck, *Mindset: The New Psychology of Success* (Ballantine Books, 2016).

218 Lisa Feldman Barrett, *Seven and a Half Lessons About the Brain* (Houghton Mifflin Harcourt, 2020).

219 "Kalā," Wikipedia, accessed February 10, 2025, https://en.wikipedia.org/wiki/Kal%C4%81.

220 John Dewey, *Experience and Education* (Kappa Delta Pi, 1938).

221 William James, *Pragmatism* (Dover Publications, 1995).

222 Alvin Toffler and Heidi Toffler, *Revolutionary Wealth: How It Will Be Created and How It Will Change Our Lives* (2006).

223 Julia Brodsky, "Why Questioning Is the Ultimate Learning Skill," *Forbes*, December 29, 2021, https://www.forbes.com/sites/juliabrodsky/2021/12/29/why-questioning-is-the-ultimate-learning-skill/.

224 "Old Man's Advice to Youth: 'Never Lose a Holy Curiosity.'" *LIFE Magazine*, May 2, 1955, p. 64.

225 Niall Ferguson, *Civilization: The West and the Rest* (Penguin Press, 2011).

226 René Descartes, *Discourse on the Method and Related Writings*, trans. D. Clarke (Penguin Classics 1999).

227 T. S. Eliot, *Four Quartets* (Harcourt, Brace and Company, 1943).

228 Swami Vivekananda, *The Complete Works of Swami Vivekananda*, vol. 1 (Advaita Ashrama).

229 Judson Brewer, *Curiosity: Our Superpower for Just About Everything.* Psychology Today, September 24, 2019.

230 Pablo Neruda, *Memoirs*, trans. H. Shuchman (Farrar, Straus and Giroux, 1977).

231 Fred Rogers, *You Are Special: Words of Wisdom for All Ages from a Beloved Neighbor* (Penguin Books, 1994).

232 Friedrich Nietzsche, *Thus Spoke Zarathustra*, trans. A. Del Caro (Cambridge University Press, 2006).

233 Carl G. Jung, *Psychological Types* (1921).

234 Harvard Business Review, "Life's Work: Richard Serra," March 1, 2010, https://hbr.org/2010/03/lifes-work-richard-serra.

235 Confucius, *The Analects of Confucius*, translated by Arthur Waley (George Allen & Unwin, 1938).

236 Émile Durkheim, *The Elementary Forms of Religious Life*, trans. K. E. Fields (Free Press, 1995).

237 Alan Watts, "Work and Play" [Lecture transcript]. The Library of Consciousness, 1972.

238 David Gurteen, "The Google 20% Free Time Policy," Conversational Leadership, https://conversational-leadership.net/google-free-time-policy/.

239 Cale Magnuson, and Lynn Barnett, "The Playful Advantage: How Playfulness Enhances Coping with Stress", *Leisure Sciences* 35, no. 2 (2013): 129—44.

240 Cigna, "Cigna U.S. Loneliness Index: Survey of 20,000 Americans Examining Behaviors Driving Loneliness in the United States," May 2018.

241 Johan Huizinga, *Homo Ludens: A Study of the Play-Element in Culture*, trans. R. F. C. Hull (Random House, 1938; repr., Beacon Press, 1950).

242 Thomas S. Henricks, "Play Studies, A Brief History," *American Journal of Play*, 12, no. 12 (2020): 117–55.

243 Ian Bogost, *Play Anything: The Pleasure of Limits, The Uses of Boredom, and the Secret of Games* (Basic Books, 2016).

244 Christopher Vaughan and Stuart Brown, *Play: How It Shapes the Brain, Opens the Imagination, and Invigorates the Soul* (Avery, 2009).

245 "Play: The Basics," National Institute for Play, accessed June 9, 2025, https://nifplay.org/what-is-play/the-basics/.

246 Gordon M. Burghardt, "The Comparative Reach of Play and Brain," *American Journal of Play* 2, no. 3, (2010): 338–356.

247 Andrew Huberman, "Using Play to Rewire & Improve Your Brain," February 7, 2022.

248 Susanna Crossman, "Play Is Cathartic, Allowing People to Sit with Their Shadows," October 1, 2019.

249 Arthur Koestler, *The Act of Creation* (Hutchinson, 1964).

250 Joseph A. Schumpeter, *The Theory of Economic Development: An Inquiry into Profits, Capital, Credit, Interest, and the Business Cycle*, trans. R. Opie (Harvard University Press, 1934).

251 Abby M. Steketee and Samantha M. Harden, "Einstein's Combinatory Play: A Promising Practice for Creativity and Well-Being Among Public Health Professionals," *Public Health in Practice* 8 (2024): 100546.

252 John Conduitt, Keynes Ms. 130.6, King's College Library, Cambridge.

253 Steven Johnson, "The Playful Wonderland Behind Great Inventions," TED Talk, https://www.ted.com/talks/steven_johnson_the_playful_wonderland_behind_great_inventions/transcript.

254 Marcel Proust, *Remembrance of Things Past*, trans. C. K. Scott Moncrieff and T. Kilmartin (Random House, 1934).

255 Carla Marie Manly, *Joy from Fear: Create the Life of Your Dreams by Making Fear Your Friend.* (Familius, 2019).

256 Widely attributed to Dalai Lama.

257 Widely attributed to Mother Teresa.

258 Kendra Cherry, "How Cognitive Biases Influence the Way You Think and Act," Verywell Mind, last modified May 7, 2024, https://www.verywellmind.com/what-is-a-cognitive-bias-2794963.

259 "Meditation: A Simple, Fast Way to Reduce Stress," Mayo Clinic, https://www.mayoclinic.org/tests-procedures/meditation/in-depth/meditation/art-20045858.

260 Nina Hood, "The Brain, Emotions, and Learning," The Education Hub, May 24, 2019, https://theeducationhub.org.nz/the-brain-emotions-and-learning/.

261 Mathew P. White et al., "Spending at Least 120 Minutes a Week in Nature Is Associated with Good Health and Wellbeing," *Scientific Reports* 9, no. 1 (2019): 7730.

262 Cornelia Blank et al., "Short Vacation Improves Stress-Level and Well-Being in German-Speaking Middle-Managers—A Randomized Controlled Trial," *International Journal of Environmental Research and Public Health* 15, no. 1 (2018): 130.

263 A.C. Bhaktivedanta Swami Prabhupada, *Kṛṣṇa, the Supreme Personality of Godhead* (The Bhaktivedanta Book Trust, 1970).

264 Rabindranath Tagore, Towards Universal Man (Rupa Publications India, 2003).

265 Tagore, R. (2011). *Songs of Rabindranath Tagore* (A. Bose, Trans.). Rupa Publications.

266 Richard P. Feynman, *The Pleasure of Finding Things Out: The Best Short Works of Richard P. Feynman*, ed. J. Robbins (Perseus Books, 1998).

267 Mahatma K. Gandhi, *The Story of My Experiments with Truth*, trans. M. Desai (Dover Publications, 2001).

268 Tim Bradshaw, "Jony Ive on Leaving Apple, in His Own Words," *Financial Times*, June 27, 2019, https://www.ft.com/content/0b20032e-98cf-11e9-8cfb-30c211dcd229.

269 Marisa Dellatto, "Here Are the 15 Richest Women Celebrities in America," *Forbes*, June 1, 2023, https://www.forbes.com/sites/marisadellatto/2023/06/01/here-are-the-15-richest-women-celebrities-in-america/Forbes.

270 Shonda Rhimes, "My Year of Saying Yes to Everything," TED Talk, https://www.ted.com/talks/shonda_rhimes_my_year_of_saying_yes_to_every thing?language=en#t-1100994.

271 Jack Ma, "Alibaba Founder Jack Ma Delivers Keynote Speech at China Conference," South China Morning Post, December 3, 2016, https://www.youtube.com/watch?v=X6RR22KZTzs.

272 Tarani Chandola and Nan Zhang, "Re-Employment, Job Quality, Health and Allostatic Load Biomarkers: Prospective Evidence from the UK Household Longitudinal Study," *International Journal of Epidemiology* 47, no. 1 (2018): 47–57.

273 Jonathan Rothwell and Steve Crabtree, "How COVID-19 Affected the Quality of Work," Gallup, Inc., accessed April 1, 2025.

274 Drew DeSilver, "10 Facts About American Workers," Pew Research Center, August 29, 2019, https://www.pewresearch.org/short-reads/2019/08/29/facts-about-american-workers/.

275 Amy Wrzesniewski and Jane E. Dutton, "Crafting a Job: Revisioning Employees as Active Crafters of Their Work," *Academy of Management Review* 26, no. 2 (2001): 179–201, https://doi.org/10.5465/amr.2001.4378011.

276 David Zax, "Want to Be Happier at Work? Learn How from These 'Job Crafters,'" *Fast Company*, June 3, 2013, https://www.fastcompany.com/3011081/want-to-be-happier-at-work-learn-how-from-these-job-crafters.

277 Steve Jobs, "Steve Jobs' 2005 Stanford Commencement Address," Stanford University, March 8, 2008, https://www.youtube.com/watch?v=UF8uR6Z6KLc.

278 Jobs, "Steve Job's 2005."

279 LinkedIn Learning, "4th Annual 2020 Workplace Learning Report," 2020, https://learning.linkedin.com/content/dam/me/learning/resources/pdfs/LinkedIn-Learning-2020-Workplace-Learning-Report.pdf.

280 LinkedIn Learning, "4th Annual."

281 "Chen Zhang, et al. "Buffering the stress of daily hassles: The moderating role of daily learning and relaxation," *Journal of Applied Psychology*, 2021.

282 William R. Kerr et al., "AT&T, Retraining, and the Workforce of Tomorrow" (Harvard Business School Case No. 820-017). *Harvard Business School*, July 2019.

283 Peter Gray, *Play Makes Us Human IV: When Work Is Play*, Psychology Today, June 25, 2009.

284 Hitendra Wadhwa, *Inner Mastery, Outer Impact: How Your Five Core Energies Hold the Key to Success* (Balance, 2022).

285 Kamilla Knutsen Steinnes et al., "Too Cute for Words: Cuteness Evokes the Heartwarming Emotion of Kama Muta," *Frontiers in Psychology* 10 (2019), https://doi.org/10.3389/fpsyg.2019.00387.

286 Melanie L. Glocker et al., "Baby Schema Modulates the Brain Reward System in Nulliparous Women," *Proceedings of the National Academy of Sciences* 106, no. 22 (2009): 9115–119, https://doi.org/10.1073/pnas.0811620106.

287 Ying Chen et al., "Positive Parenting Improves Multiple Aspects of Health and Well-being in Young Adulthood," *Nature Human Behaviour* 3, no. 7 (2019): 684–91, https://doi.org/10.1038/s41562-019-0602-x.

288 Alison Escalante, "In Parenting, Love Wins," *Psychology Today*, May 7, 2019.

289 WQED, *Creative Person,* "Fred Rogers" [Television broadcast], CBC Television, 1967.

290 University of Michigan, "Love Matters: How Parents' Love Shapes Children's Lives," ScienceDaily, February 12, 2020, https://www.sciencedaily.com/releases/2020/02/200212150134.htm.

291 Fred Rogers, *Pittsburgh Magazine*, 1986, quoted in various later works and documentaries, including *Won't You Be My Neighbor?* (2018).

292 "Who We Are: Meet the Team," Three Wishes for Ruby's Residents," https://3wishesproject.org/who-we-are/.

293 Andreas Schleicher, "The State of Education Globally – Insights from PISA 2018," *Teacher Magazine*, June 15, 2020.

294 World Economic Forum, "Realizing Human Potential in the Fourth Industrial Revolution: An Agenda for Leaders to Shape the Future of Education, Gender and Work," January 2017, https://www3.weforum.org/docs/WEF_EGW_Whitepaper.pdf.

295 Andreas Schleicher, "Educating Students for Their Future, Not Our Past," *Teacher Magazine*, November 12, 2018.

296 Brian Kisida, "Art Makes You Smart," *The New York Times*, November 23, 2013.

297 Yogman, "The Power of Play."

298 Convention on the Rights of the Child, Article 31, United Nations, September 2, 1990.

299 Yogman, "The Power of Play."

300 "Child Activity: An Overview," Physical Activity Basics, January 8, 2024, https://www.cdc.gov/physical-activity-basics/guidelines/children.html?CDC_AAref_Val=https://www.cdc.gov/physicalactivity/basics/children/index.htm.

301 Tracie A. Barnett et al., "Sedentary Behaviors in Today's Youth: Approaches to the Prevention and Management of Childhood Obesity: A Scientific Statement from the American Heart Association," *Circulation* 138, no. 11 (2018), https://doi.org/10.1161/cir.0000000000000591.

302 "The Common Sense Census: Media Use by Tweens and Teens, 2019," Common Sense Media, October 28, 2019, https://www.commonsensemedia.org/research/the-common-sense-census-media-use-by-tweens-and-teens-2019.

303 Michael Rich, "Developing Mind, Body and Spirit Through Outdoor Play," *Whole Child*, 2010.

304 National Wildlife Federation et al., "Unstructured Outdoor Play Is Critical to Children's Health and Development," *National Wildlife Federation*, 2010, https://www.BeOutThere.org.

305 Stuart Brown and Christopher Vaughan, *Play: How it Shapes the Brain, Opens the Imagination, and Invigorates the Soul* (Avery, 2009).

306 Aleeya Healey and Alan Mendelsohn, "Selecting Appropriate Toys for Young Children in the Digital Era," *PEDIATRICS* 143, no. 1 (2018): e20183348.

307 Reinhold Niebuhr, *The Irony of American History* (Charles Scribner's Sons, 1952).

308 Ibid.

309 Ibid.

310 Martin Luther King, Jr, inscription to Reinhold Niebuhr, November 1958. As referenced in the Martin Luther King, Jr. Research and Education Institute at Stanford University.

311 Shantideva, *A Guide to the Bodhisattva's Way of Life*, trans. V. Wallace and B. Wallace (Snow Lion Publications, 1997).

312 Jacob Neusner, trans., *The Mishnah: A New Translation* (Yale University Press, 1988), 675.

313 Dekila Chungyalpa, "At the Center of All Things is Interdependence," Humans and Nature, May 17, 2021, https://humansandnature.org/at-the-center-of-all-things-is-interdependence/.

314 Arthur C. Brooks, "Three Myths and Four Truths About How to Get Happier," *The Atlantic*, September 12, 2023.

315 Frank Martela and Michael Steger, "The Three Meanings of Meaning in Life: Distinguishing Coherence, Purpose, and Significance," *The Journal of Positive Psychology* 11, no. 5 (2016): 1–15.

316 Richard Rowe, "The Strengths of the Poor: What Can We Learn from the Poor about Psychological Well-being?" (unpublished manuscript or presentation), Harvard University, 2016.

317 Csikszentmihalyi, *Flow.*

318 "Stanford Distinguished Careers Institute," Stanford University, https://dci.stanford.edu.

319 Don Miguel Ruiz, *The Four Agreements: A Practical Guide to Personal Freedom* (Amber-Allen Publishing, 1997); Carlos Castaneda, *The Power of Silence: Further Lessons of Don Juan* (Simon and Schuster, 1987); Don Miguel Ruiz Jr., *The Five Levels of Attachment: Toltec Wisdom for the Modern World* (Hierophant Publishing, 2013).

320 Fuller, R. Buckminster, *Critical Path* (St. Martin's Press, 1981).

321 Tim Berners-Lee, *Weaving the Web: The Original Design and Ultimate Destiny of the World Wide Web* (Harper Business, 2000).

322 Pierre Teilhard de Chardin, *The Future of Man* (Harper & Row, 1955).

323 Simone de Beauvoir, *The Coming of Age* (G.P. Putnam's Sons, 1972).

324 Carl Sagan and Ann Druyan, *The Demon-Haunted World: Science as a Candle in the Dark.* (Ballantine Books, 1995).